Third Girl From the Left

Third Girl from the Left

A Memoir

Christine Barker

DELPHINIUM BOOKS

Third Girl from the Left

Library of Congress Cataloguing-in-Publication Data is available
on request.
ISBN 978-1-953002-22-8
23 24 25 26 27 LBC 5 4 3 2 1

First Edition

Jacket and interior design by Colin Dockrill

for my family

Prologue

Eight times a week as the house lights go out, the stage manager calls, "Places!" and we run from the theater's wings in single lines, holding hands through space so thick, I can't see in front of me. A tiny white signal, the orchestra conductor's baton, floats at a distant point like a speck of phosphorus on a midnight sea. Those of us in the front line use it or the red exit signs at the back of the house to navigate our way. Each of us has a spot, a nearly invisible, small mark on the stage floor, and once we find it, we drop hands and freeze—feet together, arms at our sides. Sometimes I think I might burst with the pressure and terrible aloneness, my feet pressed to my mark, my hands so cold I can't feel them.

For a few partial seconds we stand in the dark at what feels like the edge of the world as it comes alive with the breathing of 1,472 theatergoers, the rhythm of their anticipation lapping toward us in oncoming waves. People come to Broadway ready to engage, hoping the music and story will give them what their hearts are reaching for. What they don't know is that our hearts are reaching, too, and the wall that separates us is only imaginary from their side. For us, this story and this moment with them is in real time.

Thankfully, it's less than a minute before the downbeat starts, and then there is no more thinking or holding back, only the relief of sudden light and music, a warmth and a sound we have absorbed so thoroughly, they've become our sun and our air.

With the music in us, our job is to translate it with every spinning step or hurtling leap, so someone sitting in the orchestra or balcony can feel its power, too. We on the stage are attuned to the audience, the subtle differences between those attending a matinee or an evening show, a Saturday or a Tuesday night. We listen for what stirs their sensibilities: a single, quick intake of breath; the rustle of embarrassment; or a hush so desperate, it beats with an almost audible pulse. From the deep privacy of their seats, the audience engages unselfconsciously, as if we are figments inside their heads singing in a language akin to prayer. Some people go to church to experience grace; others go to the theater.

An Outbreak of Fear
—
Fall–Early Winter 1984

Backstage at the Shubert Theatre in New York City, all of us have our own approximately three by four by six–foot cubicle, drawn with invisible lines and delineating our personal space—much like a spot in a pew, somehow private even during a crowded holiday service. We each have a mirror framed in lights and a chair that tucks under our small wooden make-up tables. In dressing room number five, the dressing room I share with two other girls, a small electric heater is chained and padlocked to each of our tables to keep our feet warm. The only other heat source on the floor is a single radiator sitting outside our dressing room beneath a window leaking with the cold wind blowing through Shubert Alley.

In *A Chorus Line*, we never infringe on one another's space, even so much as to reach across and borrow a Kleenex. Likewise, onstage, we each have marks that we hold to while dancing. The Shubert stage is painted on its lip with numbers: center stage is zero, then going both right and left from the center, numbers are listed in sequence, zero to eight or nine. The wings, running the depths of stage right and left, are defined by several tall black flats that serve as different entrances and exits, as well as visual clues to our positions going from downstage to up.

In our dancers' minds, the stage is a three-dimensional

grid, and we always know exactly where we are on that grid. When we rehearse, we practice keeping our bodies moving rapidly in tempo, kicking our legs, reversing position, flinging our arms, all within inches of one another. When the entire cast is onstage at the same time, only a thin pane of air rests between one dancer's hip and another's shoulder, or one's leg and another's arm. We are so close we can smell each other, but we never, ever touch; never does a foot get in another's way or an arm recklessly land on someone else's face. We are skilled technicians who move in time to the music, controlling our bodies' movements within millimeters, our senses keen as echolocators, except that we don't use sound to tell us what is what; we use our own highly developed perception of space and our acute kinesthetic intelligence.

Still, we are human, and a show is a live thing, so every performance has a certain organic quality that can produce disaster as easily as poetry. The director, choreographer, stage managers, and dance captains all hope for a level of predictable perfection. And we performers, who do the show eight times a week, try to get as close to that ideal every time, even as doing the same thing day after day cultivates the right conditions for mental boredom—and mistakes.

What keeps us focused is the fluid and unpredictable dynamic between audience and dancer. Plus, our training teaches us to bring something new to the demands of the play, to create fresh internal stakes that personalize and heighten our needs as characters. But the truth is that much of the time, doing eight shows a week is no more than a brute feat of discipline; to manage it, you put aside everything that weighs on you and do your job, because the show must, and will, always go on.

But in the late fall of 1984, it was as if a winged jinx,

a dragonfly-sized sprite, flew through Shubert Alley, slipping through the window grates and under the doors to our dressing rooms, spreading mischief. Theaters are superstitious places, and while preshow nerves are the norm, this jinx was of another magnitude entirely. The cast experienced a collective outbreak of paralyzing stage fright, a contagion that spread from performer to performer. It wore on us, eroded our confidence, brought Buddha, Jesus, a Jewish prayer shawl, and other talismans into the wings, plus new rubber soles on all our shoes, and nervous impatience from the dance captain and stage manager. Most shows never run long enough to develop such tricky, intangible breakdowns, but in the early winter of 1984, the loss of our mettle, individually and collectively, was a very real phenomenon on Broadway.

"Mo-Mo Mouth," the dreaded affliction of a momentary stutter or dropping of lines, had become more commonplace. The biggest fear was that it would occur during a song, particularly a patter song, when there is no way to catch up to an entire orchestra that has raced ahead. Neither is there a way to protect the sweet and gentle actor who holds your hand and sings the song with you, which is what happened one night when I tripped over a rattle of eighth-note syllables that are supposed to roll like castanets, that *had rolled* like castanets easily and consistently for (literally) hundreds of shows. But on this one night, I choked with a gulp that lasted the length of a millisecond. I may as well have stepped on a live electrical wire for the hot volt of lightning streaking through my brain. Outside, all was noise and blackness. Inside was a searing burn, lasting for eternity. A chattering clenched my jaw until the actor who held my hand and sang our song with me reached out with his

5

other hand, the one secretly made of wood, and rested it heavily on my shoulder, improvising so I could come back to him. He was rooted firmly to the ground, enabling me to lean in and right myself, as well as shrug and make my character silly with the singed tip of my tongue, even as I searched for additional certainty, looking for the red exit sign at the back of the house, the exit sign that we'd been taught to play to or spot when turning because that bright light is the sole lifeline from our side of the stage, a world swollen with darkness.

When it was all over and I was back in the dressing room smearing Albolene cream over my face, lifting away the rouge, eyeliner, and exhausted humiliation, other cast members came by to pat my shoulder. Some had also had such moments in the recent streak of mishaps large and small; one dancer had come onstage wearing her leotard inside out, her name tags sticking out of the exposed seams during the opening number; another had missed his entrance and arrived onstage through a portal on the wrong side. We all hoped that my error marked the end of this streak, even as we were intimately acquainted with the god of fear and knew that all our ritualized supplications could never really placate him.

Fear didn't just make you small; it latched on to any vulnerability and magnified it, especially because we had so little time to recover. We finished with one show and did another the next night, going to that same spot again, the one where we got fried, facing the site of our ruinous shame with vigilance and balls of steel. Most times we could get past it by the time a few shows had gone by, but we *remembered*, and everybody else in the cast did, too.

Soon after the night I dropped words from my song, someone fell in the opening dance sequence—a double pirouette into arabesque, then *splat*, and a collective gasp from the audience. The next night, the same dancer wobbled grotesquely through her turn. Then the several of us who followed her a few bars of music later ran to the same mark on the stage, setting our turns in a space alive with the whiff of her burnt air. Instinctively, we executed single pirouettes, altering the choreography. That was how we survived, and how we protected ourselves for the remainder of the week, until the dance captain came around at half hour and berated us, then had us practicing in the warm-up area before each show. The pressure tightened.

In a bit more than a week, thankfully, gratefully, the double pirouettes were restored to their original splendor, all of us once again as faithful to the choreography as mechanical tops on Christmas morning. Still, having so deeply experienced a semi collective loss of faith, we now inhabited a slightly less spirited world, when spirit was the slippery magic we relied on to make each show sparkle. In its place was a vacuum—not an empty void, but a powerful rest note, trembling.

At the end of the show, Zach, the character who is the director/choreographer, asks the dancers who are all assembled on the stage, "What do you do when you can't dance anymore?" His question is carefully considered and poignantly answered by different characters, all of whom have built their lives on their identities as dancers, which strikes at the very core of the reality of the lives of those of us playing the parts. Then, in the show, my friend Lydia, who plays the character Diana, sings, "What I Did for Love." It's the culmination of the plot, which explains why every dancer, actor, musician, poet, writer, and artist dedicates themselves to art. The dancers sing the song with shoulders back, squarely facing the audience in an appeal:

Meet us here, walk with us. What does it mean to live a life of passion, to live this life for love?

Twice in one week, Lydia's voice cracked with the first line and ended in gravel, so the girl playing Maggie picked up the next line and sang, "Wish me luck, the same to you," to give Lydia/Diana a chance to recover. But Lydia didn't recover, so Maggie took over the entire song. From my mark where I stood upstage, I could see the spot operators on the light deck suspended from the ceiling, quickly moving the pink spotlight to Maggie in a tense shuffle—our loyal techies, hanging like bats from the ceiling, covering for us.

Lydia took a few shows off, her understudy taking over the part. The girl playing Maggie was not angry to have been thrown into singing a song that her character did not sing; neither was anyone else, not even the stage manager who may have been considering hiring a psychologist specializing in group dynamics. We'd fallen on our asses or had too many blunders in too little time. We lacked the luxury of a full-stop rest. Someone said it was the curse of the blessing of a long-running show.

But maybe it was something deeper, something to do with our collective capacity for intuition, and how, in the effort to make each show real and fresh, we brought to it the stuff of our lives, especially the stuff we lately couldn't make sense of but that was tucked into the private structures of our performances. No one was immune. For over six weeks, we endured a slow leak of our resolve, bumping along, having good shows, not good shows, stepping in and covering up, religiously keeping our shoulders squared to one another's backs because we believed we were the sum of something precious that we loved, that wholly belonged to us.

One night at the end of the show, when the character I

played was dismissed by the director and did not get the job she so desperately wanted, I heaved with tears. And then every night after that, at the same moment of my character's dismissal, I felt the same boundless grief.

The sweet and gentle actor who held my hand later said, "Boy, you're really into it aren't you?" And I looked at him and asked if he didn't feel it, too, an overwhelming loss. And he answered, "Yes, I feel it, too."

Something unimaginable had been sent to us on the wings of a jinx. We sang "The gift was ours to borrow" eight times a week, week after week, unwitting messengers until the night I showed up onstage with a secret my brother had made me swear not to tell, that I never told, even as it revealed itself in a gulp that sent a bolt of lightning searing through my brain.

He has AIDS.

And in the days and weeks that followed, I recalled mishaps that had preceded mine, then carefully watched the cascade of every progressive *splat*, place lost, line dropped, and voice crack, thinking: *What other secrets are alive but hidden here within the souls of friends I know so well, who are so close we can smell each other?*

At the Shubert Theatre in the late fall of 1984, we were dancing in a graveyard.

My Beginning
—
1971

As third girl from the left, my spot on the stage was less rarified than that of someone who stood center stage. Being third meant that I stood at the edge of the spotlight's circle, which for me, provided its own unique and informative sight lines. I could see inside and out—the audience in their seats in front of me, the stage crew hovering in the wings or hanging from rafters, the orchestra conductor shrouded beneath a black screen, my castmates beside me. I was both player and observer—magic on one side, nitty-gritty on the other.

Being third was also a theme, starting with my family position as the third of six children. Neither the oldest nor the first girl, the sibling hierarchy meant I was born into a space less prominent than that of my powerful oldest brother (Laughlin) and sister (Suzanne), who both stood ahead of me. I had an artistic brother (John) close behind me who shared my creative instincts, and after us came two rambunctious younger brothers (David and Patrick), but they fit into the dynamic a little differently because, like John and me, they had little power.

Another thing: My parents were very busy, always urgently doing something that had to be done. The de facto understanding was that all of us needed to accept responsibility for our personal dreams because they had limited availability. They also were somewhat clueless. They thought it was enough to call me from the family room where they watched *Rowan & Martin's Laugh-In*, a late sixties comedy show on one of three channels available in New Mexico. "Christine—quick, there's *dancing*." I'd throw down my homework and run to catch a two-inch, black-and-white image of a gyrating Goldie Hawn, feeling her *right-left-shoulder-kick-shimmy-shimmy* in my own body as if I'd swallowed her wriggling limbs whole. My parents clapped their hands from their easy chairs, never imagining me in Hawn's place, even when I stood in front of them, repeating the *shimmy-shimmy* to shake out the ache of what they couldn't get, or worse, didn't take seriously. Getting to Broadway from Santa Fe may as well have been trying to fly to the moon.

Luckily, I had a body that could talk to me. I'd heard it since I was barely four, sitting on my mother's lap as I watched Suzanne during her ballet lesson. She twiddled in a shy corner, while the expanse of the studio floor filled with sunlight, pooling and gathering in its swirl, the sound of the piano. The music sang in a language that was suddenly as real to me as the ABCs in the books that Suzanne and Laughlin brought home from school. I whispered in my mother's ear, "Why is Suzanne taking ballet when I'm the one who is going to be a dancer?" My mother repeated my words that night at the dinner table, passing Pillsbury brown-and-serve rolls alongside her pot roast, while everyone laughed. My certainty became a family joke, but I knew what I knew, my arms and legs my most trustworthy step-ball-change best friends, and that early instinct—to hold on to my truth in the face of denials—would serve me my whole life.

Still, my dream to be a dancer was subject to a military

life, the United States Navy transferring my father (an aviator, commander of his squadron) every two to three years, shaping my existence with constant disruptions, different schools, new friends, wonderous adventures, and unfinished business. Survival depended upon adaptability and siblings who stood glued to one another when circumstances required it; Laughlin and Suzanne were perennial pillars. Suzanne frequently found practical solutions and Laughlin put problems into words, when my parents often rationed words, especially if they were about something private, like bodies or emotions. I trusted my older siblings' judgment more than my mother's ever since the day she told me to pray on my way to the torture of a new school and its more rigorous curriculum. "But you never pray; you don't even go to church." I looked at her, insulted. Suzanne, meanwhile, taught me long division, Laughlin chiming in, coaching me in popularity, putting on the Beach Boys and saying "Let's dance."

When we lived in Italy, I studied ballet with a Russian teacher, but after that tour, my mother spent most of her time and energy transferring all six kids into and out of schools and new bedrooms; she'd get around to finding me a dance teacher just about the same time my father got his new orders. By the time my parents were sitting in our Santa Fe family room watching Goldie Hawn, I was thirteen. I'd lived in Europe, around the United States, and attended eight different schools. My father had left the Navy to start a new career in Santa Fe, the place where my pioneering great-grandparents and grandparents settled. Santa Fe was to be our new anchor, but moving there was scary—it was permanent—the flip side of a transitory life being that you learn to endure and pace yourself because

Nothing lasts forever, ironically, a lesson repeated nightly as a line spoken by Zach in *A Chorus Line*.

Despite finally living in a real home, for me and my dreams, the move represented a significant loss. We'd previously lived in Albuquerque, where I'd finally been enrolled in a *real* dancing school. The founder, my teacher, was an inspired woman who had once danced on Broadway and whose husband, an Air Force aviator, was often stationed for long months overseas. Her energy went to building a school and her students' skills. While Santa Fe offered multiple venues for music, art, and cultural education, nothing existed for aspiring dancers, so I bundled my hopes into Saturday rides on the Greyhound bus, traveling sixty miles south down the highway for one measly lesson. All the other girls at the Albuquerque studio took classes every day.

My teacher had asked my father if I could live with her when our family moved, but he'd said no, even though the first year transitioning from military to civilian life was extremely difficult. He'd once not had enough money to give me five dollars for the Albuquerque bus fare, my mother whispering in the girls' bathroom that he was "just a little short until the first of the month."

I was careful that weekend, allowing him to save face. It wasn't my father's nature to fail at a mission, and I was old enough to see how his life, too, had changed. He was forty-two, with a wife, six children, and an ambitious plan to start his life over by pursuing a career in commercial real estate. He was on his second career, carrying all of us on his back, while I only shouldered my dream. I got babysitting jobs, thinking it wasn't fair to ask him for something he didn't have.

What he did have, and soon gave me, was an empty office space with a bare wooden floor—a place to practice what I learned each Saturday, executing big leaps and pirouettes to the heavy throb of Prokofiev, or dancing barefoot to Scott Joplin, the Supremes, or soundtracks from movie versions of *Viva Las Vegas* and *West Side Story*. My studio was my portal to a wholly liquid space where music sent me swimming through the air. A dancer knows the world through her body, and without that repeated connection of body to mind, most hours of the day become physically and psychologically stymied, as if you are disconnected from the very source of your life's vitality. At the studio, I found order through the structure of my body, and that filled me with *presence*, an affiliation to something important, like religion but not religious.

By the time our first year in Santa Fe had passed, my father was completely preoccupied with trying to make a living in the private sector, and my mother was cooking for eight each day and traveling to Sandia Base in Albuquerque, where she could shop at the commissary as Laughlin applied for an ROTC scholarship to college and Suzanne studied hours a day, excelling in higher levels of high school math. My father was no longer fun, the way he'd been when our lives in the Navy, despite feeling tough, bubbled with an aura of adventure. He began laying out parameters for our futures, unexpectedly moving past his expectations for Laughlin and Suzanne, saying that my wanting to be a dancer in New York was a *big idea*, but before that, I needed to complete two years of college and maintain a B+ average. I glared at him, layering sheets of steel between us, Laughlin and Suzanne shooting me helpless looks of sympathy. I tried to reason with my mother, but she was no help. Her life had been solved when she married my father, so as I announced plans that had little to do with domesticity, she said, "Oh, Christine, you sound like such a *libber*," proudly using vocabulary she'd gleaned from reading half an article in *Time* magazine. Her pride, more so than the word, telegraphed subtle ridicule; she thought there was something unnatural about females dreaming of things other than husbands and children. Maybe she also thought I had no talent. Whatever, I didn't have her support.

In another year, with both Laughlin and Suzanne forging ambitious paths at college, I hatched my plan. My Albuquerque teacher had taken me to Los Angeles for two summers, where I spent heavenly weeks studying with renowned ballet masters and jazz teachers who choreographed television shows. If I could get admitted to UCLA, I could continue studying with them—I only needed to find a way to cover out-of-state tuition, an amount well beyond my father's financial capability.

I had one option: enter a local contest—America's Junior Miss pageant—sponsored every fall by Santa Fe's local chamber of commerce. Girl contests were suspect to my sixteen-year-old burgeoning feminist sensibility, but I was also practical: The prize was college scholarship money. Besides, Junior Miss wasn't a beauty pageant like Miss Teenage America; to win Junior Miss, you had to have good grades, demonstrate leadership, and be involved in community service.

I entered, not thinking about the ins and outs, just going to my studio every day after school, choreographing my own dance routine, and on Saturdays, showing my dance teacher what I had come up with. I also spent evenings studying for the forty-five minute "interview" with the judges, who supposedly tested you on history and current events. I won in Santa Fe, prepared again, and then won the state title. That's when reality hit, and I suddenly realized that the contest was actually a big deal in the world outside my head. My focus hadn't been on *winning* other than as a step in getting to UCLA, but taking the state title put me in a swirl of adult attention, local sponsors becoming coaches who were serious about prepping me for national competition, which seemed a little *much* in my mind until I arrived in Mobile, Alabama, and was stunned by a sea of hair bands bobbing atop perfectly coiffed dos lacquered with Spray Net. Other contestants were so professionally polished! I went to bed every night feeling stupid that I'd misread the instructions on how to be a girl. I felt the pull of something I resented, sensing that whoever won would be a Junior Miss representing an "ideal" that only existed in magazines.

After ten blistering days, I stood with forty-nine other contestants on metal bleachers as the television cameras rolled across our faces. My parents had come to Mobile and were in the audience, while my siblings and friends were watching on Channel 4 back home. When the "on air" signal was given, Lorne Greene, star of *Bonanza* and the night's emcee, announced ten finalists in a bursting explosion. I jumped out of myself, thinking the bleacher had collapsed when it was actually the earsplitting sound of my name followed by nine others. Then, I was stunned again by more deafening fireworks when Greene named me third runner-up. Chaos abounded, but I was entombed in silence, suspended in the eye of something so big, it was unintelligible: that I'd done it—won enough money to cover two years of out-of-state tuition at UCLA.

Beyond the elation of having the scholarship money, I learned that winning a prize—even if it's third runner-up— makes you legit; journalists shove a microphone toward you, asking what you think and feel. But winning also bestows privilege, and you need to say and do the right thing because a lot of other people suddenly depend on you, like the grown adults back home who later stopped me in the Safeway parking lot, saying they recognized me, that they'd prayed for me. The girl who sat behind me in English class told me the same thing. She had straight A's and a two-year-old son. My winning was proof that, despite a few degrees of separation, there was hope: To them, I represented a chance at life, and seeing myself through their eyes was an experience in perspective, both emboldening and humbling at the same time.

That fall, I headed to UCLA with visions of a collegiate Beach Boys/The Mamas & the Papas lovefest, seeing myself with a book on my lap, riding the Wilshire Boulevard bus to my dance lessons. My ideas dissolved the minute I stepped onto campus, where raging students protested the draft and Vietnam War. I would have happily joined but for the very real tenor of escalating violence. I had spoken out about the war and was worried about Laughlin's draft status but doing that in Santa Fe was nothing like joining the mob growing outside my ninth-floor dorm's window.

My scholarship covered room and board, books, and tuition—nothing else. The forty dollars per month my father sent wasn't enough to cover dancing lessons, so the first year I took a salesgirl job; unfortunately, the part-time work plus the rigor of academics left time for only a couple dance classes a month. I lost momentum, so I chose not to go home over the summer, instead taking another salesgirl job so I could get to dance classes several times a week.

My second year at college was worse—several suicides, more burnt draft cards, and angry war protests followed by dire threats from Governor Ronald Reagan about restricting students' rights. Then insanity arrived early on May 4, 1970, with the massacre at Kent State. The UCLA campus exploded in response; the ROTC building was set on fire; Reagan called out the National Guard, and the entire University of California system shut down in a state of emergency. All classes suddenly offered pass/fail options. By June 1, I had a B+ average, so I took my transcript and headed home, handing it to my father, saying, "I'm going to New York."

I had a suitcase but needed a dance bag, so found my father's old Navy parachute duffle in a military-grade trunk stored in the basement. Inside were yards and yards of silk that weighed nothing but were meant to save his life when he was flying in Cold War missions to places he never mentioned. When we were little, my siblings and I pretended we weren't afraid when he left home, even though we knew some dads didn't come back; my own godfather had died when he missed the tailhook. That's the legacy of military life for kids: They grow up with knots in their hearts, which is another reason my siblings and I stuck closely together. My father laughed when I asked if I could have the bag, and when he said, "Sure," I sewed a big peace sign appliqué right next to the standard-issue American Flag.

My father was a man of his word, driving down I25 from Santa Fe to the Albuquerque airport, barely speaking except when he or my mother drilled a hole in the silence with an occasional exclamation brimming with false confidence—that New York City was going to be "Fantastic! A big adventure!" or that they sure were glad they'd be coming east in the summer because Laughlin had graduated college and was getting married in New Jersey. "We'll have a chance to check in on you!"

"A *big* adventure," my mother repeated, patting his knee.

"Yep." One syllable was all I could muster from the back seat. I was sweating, I was so scared, but even the slightest hesitation would be all my father needed to pull a swift U-turn and head back home. I'd earned a plane ticket and the five hundred dollars he gave me that I'd stuffed into my Keds. So, no, there was no turning back now.

I knew the highway by heart. Traveling south as I had on all those Saturdays, I watched as the Sangre de Cristo Mountains receded and the black lava rock of La Bajada Hill turned to lonesomeness. Always it was the same descent: one-thousand-plus feet down the incline as the sky ballooned upwards, dwarfing the earth as if it were the forgotten design of a lesser god. The landscape looked soulless and abandoned for as far as you could see. In the baked expanse of an ancient ocean, archaeologists found fossilized remains that they measured in eras, pieces of eternity that turned my heart to jelly and made both Laughlin and me feel thrilled and anxious at the same time. We'd grown alike in that respect.

He and I shared the secret fear that we wouldn't ever reach the teeming place called life that was surely somewhere beyond what lay along the highway. I was surprised he was getting married, not for any real reason except that marriage seemed unrelated to solving what we'd confided to each other in recent years: vague feelings of always being on the outside looking in at a world to which we didn't really belong. I wanted to be a dancer, while he was perennially restless in an unarticulated way. We'd been socially adept at making life in Santa Fe work, while the truth was, each of us *really lived* in interior worlds. And from there, we dreamed in the grand proportion of the landscape that surrounded us, frothy with notions that life, in a democratic process, would afford each of us special opportunities. How else were we to endure the constant reminders of our own small allotment of time? Laughlin and I always traveled the black strip of I25 to the Albuquerque airport believing that the highway was the path leading us to the people we were convinced we were meant to be.

I didn't know anyone in the Big Apple. I had no idea what it felt like to stand beneath a skyscraper and see how it pierced the sky. But I had brochures for some of the best dance schools in the country, and most importantly, I had the address where Alvin Ailey taught. He'd become my guiding light ever since I'd seen his ballet *The River* at the Dorothy Chandler Pavilion in LA. Ailey didn't have a formal school or a fancy brochure, which I thought made him better, far superior to anything Balanchine, who left me cold. The dancers' bodies in Ailey's company sang with something I understood: a rashly bold effort at defying gravity that did just *that*. I recognized that Mr. Ailey and most of his company members were Black, and he did have one white girl in his company already. What I wanted most was just the chance to be among them—dancers who'd mastered their bodies as instruments of expression—and finally to be taught by the genius himself: Mr. Ailey.

At the airport gate, my father said to call collect so they'd know I'd arrived. Then he held my shoulders and said, "Take it one step at a time." His face was drawn. So was my mother's. Was it concern or resolve? Perhaps they believed that within a year, I'd be wiser, more mature, and back home, transferring to another university. Regardless, I hugged them tight in a long goodbye because whatever they believed, I knew I wasn't coming back.

The Big Apple

—

1971–1975

A friend from LA, another dancer, met up with me, and although she would leave New York after several months, her initial presence was crucial: We had a type of buddy system initiated by young girls like us who were venturing far from home and needed a companion to mitigate the shock of all we didn't know because we'd only ever seen New York in the movies. My parents knew of the Barbizon Hotel, famous from the days when it housed respectable young working-class women, so we had a reservation for one night. It was the most expensive, smallest room I'd ever seen, with matching yellow bedspreads on cot-sized mattresses only a foot apart. The first morning we set out, walking from 63rd Street on the East Side to the Salvation Army Evangeline Home for Girls on West 13th Street, the place recommended in a flyer from the Joffrey Ballet School. There, we were offered beds in a dormitory for forty-five dollars per week, which included one egg and one piece of toast for breakfast. We'd made it! Twenty-four hours and already a place to live.

The Ailey company was not back from its spring tour, so I started classes at Luigi's Jazz Centre and the school associated with American Ballet Theatre. Then, as soon as Ailey returned, I signed up for admission to his "company class," the only class Ailey taught and that was attended by members of his company. Ailey accepted some unprofessional dancers into the class if they demonstrated enough skill to keep up with those in his troupe. Dancers like me were allowed to sign up for a first class, but then needed an invitation to return. It was a relatively informal process indicative of Ailey's unpretentious accessibility that was unique in the dance world. I printed my name on a sign-up sheet posted on the door of a studio above a church on East 59th Street and apparently made it successfully through the first class because, at the end, I was offered another sign-up sheet, this one kept by Mr. Ailey's assistant.

Classes were generous and democratic, where a young, sunny-faced hopeful like me could stand side by side with the profoundly beautiful Judith Jamison, who moved through space with the suppleness of an undulating wave. I was nothing compared to her, but I was close enough to be her awkward shadow, to hope that by breathing the same air, I might absorb a drop of whatever it was that made her glisten. Dancers work from the inside out, like forensic specialists digging for the essential cores of their bodies, then stretching and slowly placing demands on what is a perfectly engineered structure of bone and muscle. With practice, the body develops its own memory and hones its kinesthetic abilities until they become second nature. Ms. Jamison and all the Ailey dancers had achieved perfect equilibrium, occupying the universe beyond gravity, where every lunge, leap, back-bending curl, or withering collapse originated from some deeply soulful place. Whatever price I'd paid to get to New York, it was worth it to be in the presence of such grace.

After three months, my parents arrived in New Jersey for my brother Laughlin's wedding, and I invited my mother to visit one of my classes. She was thrilled, dressing up and wearing a hat. Mr. Ailey, ever the gentleman, graciously acknowledged her and sat her on a piano stool next to the crazy drummer in the green-and-yellow dashiki. Afterward, she thanked Mr. Ailey profusely; half his size and wrapping both her hands around one of his, she said, "Thank you. Thank you."

My mother had a keen appreciation more typical of a curator or gallery owner than a military wife. She loved all art but didn't take that love farther than the kitchen table, where many Saturdays she listened to the Metropolitan Opera, the music taking her someplace in her head as she scraped the lamb bone, then opened cans of Campbell's vegetable soup to fill the casserole bowl. Later that week in New Jersey, as we were deciding whether to wear flowered hair bands to the wedding, she described the class to Suzanne. She raved about Mr. Ailey, the drummer, the dancing, everyone dripping with sweat. I waited for her to mention me, to tell my older sister how much my dancing had improved under his influence, but she spoke of the entire experience as if I hadn't been there, then moved forward to the wedding, excitedly grabbing a hair band. "The first in our family!"

At the end of the summer, Mr. Ailey held company auditions. He told those of us in the class that he was going to add one girl, possibly two, to his company. At the audition, he kept me through combination after combination while letting others go. Finally, he asked to speak to me and took me out on the fire escape, where he told me that I was good, but that he couldn't put me in his company: "Look in the mirror," he said. "You need to look in the mirror."

I was so startled that I wondered about my arabesque. Did he mean my line had been off?

"Go take some voice lessons. Go audition for Broadway. You don't belong here."

I crept back into the room, gathered my dance bag, and glanced in the mirror, but I saw nothing, absolutely *nothing*, only an eager-faced white girl with freckles and a turned-up nose.

You don't belong here echoed in my head, where the words were lost in confusion. I curled into a ball on my Salvation Army bed and put the blanket over my head. The undeniable power of Ms. Jamison had lifted me on those blistering summer days going to and from the girls' residence. When she opened her arms and spiraled her torso toward the ceiling, I saw the world turning on its axis. She was *the way* forward, she and the other dancers having some holy connection to their identities. And all of it was because of Mr. Ailey and his willingness to teach each of us—including a white lump of wet clay like me—to find authenticity by fully occupying space, starting with our own two feet and from there, daring to leap across any distance to make something true and beautiful. I was stymied by grief, as if I'd lost a parent.

There was no one to talk to. Suzanne was starting an economics program at Stanford across the country, and Laughlin, married, was serving his time in the military as a liaison officer in Italy—luckily not in Vietnam. He was fluent in Italian, having spent a year of college abroad in Bologna. Back then he'd written impassioned letters, as if he'd swallowed the Renaissance whole, but now everything was different, and I still couldn't figure out how marriage fit into that part of him that was reaching for his own small piece of the world. John didn't write; he drew pictures instead.

I numbly kept to my schedule of ballet and jazz classes,

earning money by babysitting and getting occasional checks from my father because money was still tight at home. From my bed in the dorm, I read *Atlas Shrugged*, buying the book for a dime from a street vendor. I stood beneath the Chrysler Building as if it were a sacred temple, then traded out Ayn Rand for Margaret Bourke-White, spending the hours between dance classes at the public library, paging through books of her photos. My favorite was an image of her perched high on a turret of the Chrysler Building. I imagined the courage it must have taken for her to climb out on the ledge of that monstrous skyscraper. But there she was, camera in hand, getting her shot. I read Dreiser, Morrison, and most of Fitzgerald, then a biography of Zelda, all courtesy of the same ten-cent street vendor. Reading filled me with words and stories, a relief when so much of my time was spent in nonverbal pursuits. I knew full well that I was beginning to live out a showbiz story that'd been told many times before, but I'd paid a price to have this one chance at whatever would be my own version. It was the beginning of my learning to control fear through rationalization, distraction, and intrepid faith. Mr. Ailey had to have seen some potential in me, otherwise I'd never have been admitted to his classes in the first place; he had also pointed me toward a place I might belong. His message was always to rise like a phoenix, with dignity and grace. He was *Revelations*; to understand him, all you needed was to see his signature ballet and witness how spirit empowered those bodies to dance. I owed it to him to make good on what he'd taught me.

I found a voice teacher and traded up to a small railroad apartment in the Village for $125 per month. It had a toilet in the closet, a bathtub in the kitchen, and a resident batch of cockroaches. I got a job at Jack LaLanne teaching exercise, cleaned dance studios in exchange for lessons, and did more babysitting.

The NYC streets in the seventies smelled of sweat and urine; dog shit puddled on the sidewalks; and the subways, smeared with graffiti, rattled with a deafening roar. The seats were sticky, a woven rattan. Dance and rehearsal studios were mostly nestled in the honeycomb of the porn district along Eighth Avenue between Fortieth and Forty-Ninth Street where hookers in satin hot pants smoked outside peep shows and pimps in gold-and-purple wide-lapeled jackets wore the most amazing platform shoes I'd ever seen. I was never afraid of violence the way I'd been afraid at UCLA because no one bothered me. I knew where I was going. That's the thing about New York: Life is compressed and concentrated, but in it is a curious sameness. Our faces were different, but I waded through the caverns of Port Authority feeling that all of us were just struggling to make something out of daily life.

I made friends. One was a woman who was ten years older, had two children and a second husband; her first husband had died in an accident. She was getting back to dancing and now wanted to teach, having been professionally successful in her early twenties before her children were born. Watching her dig deep to rebuild her former skills bolstered me. She sharpened my street sense, warning me about scams and the various ways people might try to take advantage of me.

Other friends, girls around my age who had also come to the Big Apple seeking their dreams, became comrades in the daily struggle of life without a safety net. We had checking accounts, but none of us could get a credit card. Banks openly and legally discriminated, not required by law to offer "unmarried young females" the same credit considerations they offered our male peers, so we lived in a pay up front, cash-only world. We never let the phone bill go unpaid, that black rotary receiver being our lifeline, and were quick at basic adding and subtracting, balancing our checkbooks religiously because if we ever accidentally overdrew, we'd lose what minimal access we had to a semblance of mainstream life.

Every Monday began with morning terror—the stomach-churning, throw-up-at-any-minute anxiety that accompanied the unpredictability of another week ahead. The subway was fifty cents. Distance was measured in dimes: Traveling under thirty-five blocks meant I walked. Some days, I ran to the jazz studio so I could mop the floor before it opened; other times, I doused my Jack LaLanne red tunic with cheap cologne when a last-minute babysitting gig prevented me from doing laundry. Most times, I carried my bag of dirty clothes all the way to my clients' apartments, buildings that had laundry facilities, and washed my clothes after the kids went to bed. The strain of daily living drained the blood from my arms and legs, but I still had to learn to execute a triple pirouette. By the time Friday arrived, I pulled the covers over my head knowing that I could lie around Saturday until the afternoon before I made my way to an overnight babysitting job, sleeping on the couch outside the kids' bedroom and staying until noon on Sunday before heading back to Jack LaLanne and the East Side ladies who loved the vibrating machines that jiggled their ample rear ends.

In February, eight months and a lifetime after being rejected by Alvin Ailey, I'd saved enough money to have professional headshots taken and began dropping my 8x10s by the stage doors of shows employing a large chorus of dancers. When that didn't yield any calls, I dropped my picture by every single stage door in the city. Once, I was called in to audition for the girl in *The Fantasticks*, playing in a small theater off-Broadway. I'd had only six months of voice lessons, but the stage manager said I had "good qualities" and to keep studying. He was going to keep me in his file. Every week, I looked through trade newspapers that listed open auditions.

Unlike the more "artistic" dance scene at Alvin Ailey, the studios I frequented were brimming with girls from dancing school backgrounds, marinated in the tricks of makeup and costuming. Many knew when to say just the right thing to make another girl wilt.

"Oh, is that your picture?"

I smiled.

"You're wearing a straw hat?"

I nodded.

"My agent told me never to wear a hat. Oh, sorry, I guess you don't have an agent, but if you did, he'd tell you not to wear a hat."

I learned to avoid girls like that. What I lacked, and knew I lacked, were the many years of semiprofessional training that had carved other girls' bodies into gorgeously sculpted showgirl molds, that had cooled their blood, too, rendering them impervious to the high-stakes pressure of memorizing and executing a complicated dance combination in under five minutes' time. Many were highly skilled kinetic technicians, reptilian in nature. I learned to compete by offsetting their cold-blooded competence with *heat*—a flow of unrestrained connection to the music that I'd learned from Ailey and his dancers.

Still, I knew nothing of Broadway. I'd seen Stephen Sondheim's *Follies* when my family was in town for Laughlin's wedding, and I saw other shows here and there, when I could scrape the money together for a ticket. After being in the city for a year, I landed a summer stock job, which earned me admission to Actors' Equity, the union that controlled all actors' contracts for stock, regional, and Broadway theaters. From there, I built a small life rotating in and out of Jack LaLanne, cleaning dance studios in exchange for lessons, and when I got lucky, getting a dinner theater job, more stock, or a role in a regional theater production, each lasting about six to eight weeks. I no longer received support from my father, and for a short while got by with food stamps and used slugs instead of subway tokens. I went to open Equity calls—auditions for union members who didn't have an agent to get them into "select" auditions. It took two years before I began to make it through to final call-backs with big names like Gower Champion or Bob Fosse, who pulled me aside during the *Liza with a "Z"* final, moving to my ear and whispering, "Are you new in town?" just before saying, "Do this," and clapping his hands in a rhythm. But I had frozen when I felt the brush of his lips and couldn't repeat his clapping sequence, so he rejected me with a sickening smile.

I had little social life, a couple of flings, a summer boy-friend—the relationship ending for reasons I couldn't de-scribe—and last, a real, true, heart-piercing absorption that ended abruptly when the man I was sure I was in love with went out of town for a road tour and never once contacted me.

Life was lonely, but over time, being alone made it easier to endure the manic fluctuations: the extreme highs during the weeks preparing for an audition when all I could do was imagine "getting it" followed by the plunging disappointment five minutes after it was over, when I slung my bag onto my shoulder and headed to the subway, back to my apartment and the desolate stretch of time between bottomless despair and my next chance at being born into a world where I believed I belonged. Sometimes I coped by feeding my fear with cookies, chocolate, and cheese; other times I starved it—as if fear were a tumor growing inside me—seeing how long I could go without food, doing *anything* to control *something* because I could not control the other things that really mattered. My weight went up and down, but still, I was a despot, convinced that with discipline of mind and body, I could shape the future to my will. Truthfully, I merely clung to the pavement, not moving forward, but more importantly, not moving backward, the threat of the "second elimination" looming—the thing I saw happening to girls like me who'd made it through the "first elimination," my term for the girls, like my LA companion, who had left when it became too much to navigate the bleakness of life, trying to make something out of the mere fumes of a dream. The second elimination had to do with having been given a crumb but becoming too exhausted before turning it into a second crumb.

I merely held on with what I had, scraping by one day at a time. Maybe the learned stoicism of my military childhood helped, that and the steam I'd built up over years of being thwarted in my attempt to be a dancer; something, too, about the way I'd been taught that achieving my dream was my sole responsibility and seeing, as a teenager, how my father approached his life transition by refusing to accept failure. Then it was New York itself, a city of strugglers, everyone moving purposely through the streets. I drew on that energy, not to mention the heaven of what it was to be in a studio with music pumping and a community of dancers pushing their bodies to the limits of endurance. It was less a life than a mania held together by the thin thread of hope. I never had enough money to buy a TV, just a radio, which I rarely turned on. Instead, inside my apartment, I weathered the silence, how even in a tiny space, it grew dense like a forest, and before I fell asleep, rustled with hesitant footfalls—the sound of my trudging heart.

Becoming Whole

—

1975

For four years I marked progress in minor increments, making it through another month with rent paid, and every night dreaming that I'd be saved, which is how people who have nothing to lose think. Then, finally, my long-awaited lucky break came, courtesy of a new friend, Sammy Williams, a Broadway veteran who'd taken me under his wing. Sammy helped me get into a private audition for the upcoming national tour of *Seesaw* being directed by Michael Bennett. The job marked the beginning of my relationship with Michael, which, relatively speaking, was minor on his part and stratospheric on mine.

Rehearsals were nothing like what I'd experienced in other theater jobs. They were fluid, with Michael frequently jumping out of his director's chair at the production table to mingle with us dancers, even tease some he knew well. He had a boy's energy, potent and spirited, reminding me of the way the air crackled when all four of my brothers were in the same room. When he stood with dancers all around him, he was the sun. I thought he was brilliant, though I was afraid of him, mostly because he was so powerful, which made me crave his approval, even as that felt dangerous.

The show starred John Gavin, Lucie Arnaz, and Tommy Tune, Tommy being the other great energy in the rehearsal studio. Tommy played a leading character in the production and had choreographed several numbers of the show before it originally opened on Broadway. He was warm, laughed easily, and created a family-like atmosphere, making it seem as if the show's success was dependent on all of us. Best, the choreography was a dancer's dream: innovative, extravagantly showy, and integral to the context of the story. Every chorus member represented a *real* person, like in the opening number where, against a New York cityscape, I played a fresh-faced girl wearing a white dress and *straw hat*.

The one number Michael didn't change from the original Broadway production was the "hooker" number, a scene where the clean-cut Midwestern character embodied by John Gavin stops to place a call in a phone booth on 42nd Street, New York's ground zero for colorful street girls. Michael wasn't sure who he saw in the lead dance role, an acrobatic meringue created by a whipping series of cartwheeling splits, all delivered with sex-kitten playfulness, so he had a group of us learn the choreography, then audition in front of the rest of the cast. Sammy chose the outfit I wore for the tryout—not a leotard but instead a sleek nylon bathing suit that was revealing even as it was baby-girl pink. Sammy said I was good, but Michael made me "swing," meaning I needed to learn all five of the hooker parts and be prepared to go on when someone was sick. Lydia, a spitfire Latina from Spanish Harlem, got the lead part. She had been in the chorus of the Broadway production of *See-saw*, and as much as I was jealous, I knew she was special.

Still, I was disappointed, and Michael knew it because he took me aside, explaining that he'd made me swing because he thought I learned steps well, and that he could count on me to learn every part, be ready with little notice, an important aspect of a "standby."

"But . . ."

"Besides, you're too pretty." He shrugged, saying the words as if I should have known what he meant, when I didn't.

"But she wears a wig."

"I can rely on you. Swing is a big responsibility. I don't like seeing pretty girls in that kind of a part."

Like Mr. Ailey saying I didn't belong, it was another crushingly explicit instance of something unchangeable about me—my face—upstaging some other essence that I had yet to unearth. I knew I could be pretty by the time I turned thirteen, when the fluctuating pattern of pretty or not pretty was defined by the days I weighed less or more than 110 pounds and had on just the right amount of mascara. I privately thought pretty was uninteresting; it was luck, not talent. But in New York, pretty was important, even as it was a self-defeating trap—the nymph ideal turning you inward and pinching off the way you struggled to breathe yourself into your own authenticity. Maybe it was the 1970s, maybe it was just forever, but to be hired or taken seriously, what you looked like came first. That was an aspect of the business that would always plague me.

There was a reason Lydia was good, and the same was true of Nancy L., who played the leather-clad butch-y hooker, and it wasn't about how they executed the choreography. I asked Tommy, who said, "They know something," speaking in his customary abstractions, but what he said connected to both Alvin Ailey and Michael—that there is and must be some essential authentic truth resonating through every expression, otherwise it's just a technical performance. By calling me pretty, Michael was clear about what I had and what I lacked, so I paid attention.

The tour was a six-month immersion with Tommy and Sammy, my mentors. Tommy coached "Use what you have," meaning that if you're looking for your own special quality, don't go looking outside yourself; keep going inward. That philosophy extended to everything creative, and to keep fresh, both Tommy and Sammy practiced a daily ritual in shaping something from nothing. Tommy painted watercolors and Sammy studded ordinary bandanas with rhinestones or visited botanical gardens.

The point was to exercise creative output by doing whatever you could with your hands and your imagination, because setting your brain free in one activity will influence the way you think or do something else. *Artistry is a practice*, an ongoing effort at channeling feelings or experiences and applying them to a medium. It made no difference if they were lousy at painting or flower arranging, what mattered was taking the dive into emptiness and making something of it.

I wrote descriptions of anything and everything in journals, then borrowed the costume mistress's sewing machine and refashioned some clothes I'd bought at a secondhand shop, tearing off sleeves to make new shapes. My daily plunges into shapeless spaces spilled over at showtime, so every performance felt less a repetition of song and dance and more a relaxing into what the song and dance were about. I became more supple, developing greater consistency and confidence onstage, even as I watched Lydia and Nancy project something deeper I had yet to articulate for myself.

Toward the end of the tour, Sammy asked if I could come to his hotel room. He was nervous. "Michael called saying he wants me to attend this workshop he's doing. He might try to create a new show about dancer's lives." Sammy went on to mention other dancers who were participating, dancers a generation ahead of me who were broadly admired and had exactly the kind of New York careers I hoped for.

"You have to go. Aren't you excited?"

"Yeah, a little scared, too. I'm leaving at the end of the week."

I was thrilled but missed him as soon as he left, his absence folding itself into gnawing anxiety about *Seesaw* ending. It had been a six-month retreat, where the exhaustion of daily life and paying bills had been miraculously removed, so I could focus solely on the task of performing eight shows a week and growing through that experience. I didn't have all the answers, but I had new insight into the process of finding them. I dreaded the smack of hitting the wall that coming off the road would be. Closing a show is always and everywhere like that, a deeply wounding feeling that the life you'd earned was only something borrowed. Even if you have a little more money and experience, you are back to starting over because of the shifting scaffolding of a freelance life: an empty apartment, the same littered sidewalks, auditions (if you can get them), and a lonely prayer that you'll find another something to belong to.

Within that looming cloud, I focused on two "Use what you have" bright spots. The first was that my brother John wrote to tell me that he wanted to come to New York. Back in high school, after my father had given me a studio, John asked for a space, too, where he could go to paint. John had strong support from teachers in the Santa Fe art community, and after he graduated from college, he went to Italy, where Laughlin and his wife Carrie were living, Laughlin still fulfilling his military obligation. Laughlin encouraged him to go to New York. "Christine's there." So John wrote to say he was coming.

The second development was that the man I was so sure I'd been in love with, who'd not been in touch for a year and a half when he was on the road, suddenly contacted me right before I signed my *Seesaw* contract. I pretended casualness but was so overwhelmingly thrilled to see him that we quickly picked up where we had left off. He'd never provided a satisfactory answer about why he'd disappeared, but I moved forward, without looking back, which was not so difficult because I had my contract and was headed out of town with plenty to distract me. But he visited me on several occasions during the tour, and despite trying to be coolheaded when he arrived, he always left me spinning.

Brett was a wildly talented up-and-coming director/producer who slept under a poster splashed with Fritz Perls's popular mantra: "I do my thing and you do your thing. . . . If by chance we find each other, it's beautiful." The principle of such strict individualism may have explained the up-and-down pattern of our relationship. But, when *Seesaw* arrived in Chicago, I had a letter from him waiting at the theater. He proposed living together when I got back into town. Sammy hadn't left yet, so I took the letter to him first, and he thought I should try it, and then later, Tommy advised, "But don't buy furniture!"

If I was starting over after the *Seesaw* tour, I hoped cohabitating plus having one brother in town would put an end to the overwhelming loneliness I'd experienced during my first years in New York. I now had some professional momentum that I hoped to build on, plus I was crazy about him, so I said yes to Brett and crossed my fingers that he wouldn't leave the way he'd done before. John moved into my old apartment, and

Christine Barker

Brett and I moved to a Hasidic neighborhood near Orchard Street in lower Manhattan where he'd found a fabulously romantic floor-through apartment. It had high ceilings decorated with rococo plaster designs and a Victorian etched-glass door separating the bedroom from the living room. Even though my parents were happy I finally had a boyfriend, I didn't dare tell them Brett and I were living together because they may have come close to disowning me.

Over the next year Brett developed a small neighborhood theater, and I added acting classes to my dancing and voice lessons, landed a couple of dinner-theater jobs that expanded my resume, plus assisted Tommy Tune on a bus-and-truck tour of *Seesaw* that he directed. Then, Laughlin, having finished his military service requirement, enrolled at Georgetown Law School in Washington, DC—only a bus ride away. He and his wife, Carrie, had recently divorced, though stayed friends, both parenting their two-year-old daughter, Kate.

I made a trip to visit him that fall. The first night he made spaghetti and clams, and we went to an Alfred Hitchcock double feature. Afterward, back at his apartment, we loaded up his espresso pot, scalded the milk, and sank into the mirrored Moroccan cushions on his Turkish rugs. As he smoked, I told him about *Seesaw* and Michael Bennett's workshop for a potential new show, how I was afraid of failing professionally and didn't know how to balance my professional dreams with a personal life. He shared how he had trouble connecting with others at Georgetown: He was older, while most other students had come directly to law school from college, never having faced the draft or Vietnam, been married, divorced, or a parent. Then suddenly, he said, "I'm gay. I want someone in the family to know."

"You are?" I'd had no idea.

He went on to describe a past relationship that he said was meaningful. "Some of it was wonderful, but most of it was terrifying. I was afraid of being found out and being kicked out of school, kicked out of life, basically."

"But how did you realize? Because you loved Carrie. You got married."

"I did." Women adored Laughlin. He'd always had a girl-friend. "And I'm thrilled to have Kate in my life. I'm happy to be a father. I wouldn't trade any of it."

"So, what, then?"

He told me that he was always attracted to men, but it was just sex—some lustful transaction because after sex there was nowhere to go—literally. In real life, he couldn't have a rela-tionship with a man. Sex had to be separate from an emotional connection, family, a job, even personal identity.

"So, what changed?"

"I realized that I could care about a man. Outside of sex. That's when I knew I was gay."

I practically jumped on him, hugging him close, reassur-ing him that he could be who he was. Nothing changed how I felt about him. "Being gay doesn't really matter. You're perfect just the way you are. Really, I believe that with all my heart. I live in New York. Society is changing. Most everyone I know is gay and lives an openly gay life. Same with the people I work with. What matters is imagination, energy, skill, being really good at what you do. You have to come live in New York when you get out of school." Lying on the Turkish rug with a pillow under my head, I expected him to agree, but he only looked at me blankly, as if there was something else that had occurred to him but not occurred to me. He didn't say what it was, so in the end, I was left with the haunting impression that I'd let him down somehow, that the moment was empty when it should have been filled with light.

I buried Laughlin's secret, feeling more glued to him than ever, reaching out with letters and phone calls once I was back in New York. When I looked backward, everything in his life fit together in a way I hadn't previously discerned, even as looking forward was less clear. My faith that he could have a successful life in the city was myopically derived from what I observed in the arts. Still, I believed (perhaps too naively) in progress and that if he could get grounded here, then work and family issues could be managed. I kept him close, and for the first time in my life, the big-brother-little-sister dynamic changed. I felt responsible for him, that we were each looking for our places in life where we could belong, and I was determined to help him.

Over the winter and spring, Michael Bennett's mysterious workshops evolved into official rehearsals at the Public Theater. All dancers in New York City had their ears to the ground; if you didn't know one of the cast members, you knew someone who did. When *A Chorus Line* opened in the fall of 1975 and I saw it at the Public—sold out, but Sammy got me a single ticket—I was riveted, then ravenous: The show was mine. Every dancer felt that way. For me, it was all that theater can be. The show, which takes place at a dance audition, broke new artistic and cultural ground, speaking to realities about growing up, sex, and homosexuality; it spoke the truth in a way that polite society avoided, and it was funny. It was art demonstrating a way forward, and I was determined to belong to it.

Soon enough, producers came forward to finance *A Cho-*

rus Line's move from Off-Broadway to Broadway, but Michael asked for more: a move to Broadway *and* two other companies—an international one to open in London, and a West Coast company to play in LA. It was an audacious triple play, but Michael was now a demigod with an insatiable appetite, and thank goodness, because that meant there might be a place for me.

I eventually got an audition call from Baayork Lee, Michael's assistant, who said that Michael wanted to see me for the part of Val. When I hung up the phone, I knew in my gut that Michael would never give me the part; Val said "fuck" too many times in her monologue; he would think I was "too pretty" to use such language, so, like with *Seesaw*, he'd give me an understudy job. It struck me that the role of Kristine may have unrealized potential. She was played as a ditzy wife—in another context, she could have been the high school cheerleader everyone loved but didn't take seriously. I saw it differently: Why would Kristine go to her audition if she wasn't desperate for the job? Couldn't a girl who had chosen to be married also want something for herself? I believed Kristine was the kind of person who got so anxious that she'd blow her auditions. She just needed people to give her a second chance—a quality I knew I could bring to the part. But I'd have to convince Michael of that, likely during the actual audition.

We weren't given scripts; we just knew that at the audition we'd spend hours dancing, then do some singing, and finally, if we passed all that, we'd be given some lines to read. I called Sammy, whose life had expanded exponentially since the opening at the Public, but still, he graciously invited me to his apartment and taught me the sequence of the opening choreography.

I was manic and scared and so restless, I itched from the inside out, walking to the brink where my life's dream seemed possible, and I didn't want anything, *anything* distracting me. Suddenly, in comparison to getting *A Chorus Line*, my life with Brett looked like charades, with me playing pretend wife, providing free laundry service, meals, and sex, while Brett was totally absorbed in his dream of building a regional theater, a place where he'd said I didn't belong because I wasn't qualified: I was a dancer, and he did plays. Brett was only home on Sundays, his theater running six days a week, and sometimes I felt that if he spent one more afternoon watching a fucking football game, I'd smash the television. Once, right in the middle of the Ohio State versus University of Michigan game as I was chopping onions, mincing parsley, and slicing zucchini, I started banging pots with my wooden spoon.

"What're you doing?" He came into the kitchen during a commercial break.

"I hate this."

"What?"

"Cooking."

In the mess of vegetable curry, he had the nerve to say, "But you're so good at it."

"But it's not *enough*. Would it be enough for you?"

"Well, no, but . . ."

"But *what*? What's the next word? *Say it*." He just looked at me, stunned, and went back to the third quarter of the game, while I sat on the floor and cried.

It wasn't necessarily his fault. Maybe we just typified the stewing gender gap in the changing American culture, plus I was a few years younger than he was. Regardless, the truth remained that I would never have power in my relationship or in my career or even the world at large if I didn't have some professional credibility attached to my name. *A Chorus Line* was that opportunity.

I spent a month rebounding between fear, anger, and doubt. I was manic and alone, but to survive, I knew I had to develop a more productive attitude, convincing myself that the audition would be the best day of my life. I wrote *This is the best day of your life* across my music and on a note-to-self stashed in my dancing shoes. I reasoned that I would be standing on the stage of the Shubert Theatre, with a sea of red velvet seats in front of me, where, over time, in the exact same spot, some of the most talented people in the history of New York theater had also stood. I was *lucky*; *I was being given a chance* to do what I loved and dreamed of. Some people never even got that far.

The call was five hours long, which wasn't unusual for a Michael Bennett audition. We learned different dance combinations, practiced them, then performed them in front of Michael, his assistants, and the production staff. There was a moment near the beginning when I was grouped with three other dancers. We stood in a pool of light, which, on the stage, creates its own universe, voiding everything outside its perimeter and warming your very own spot within it. It is the most intimate, secure spot imaginable, where you and your hopeful heart belong. In the eight counts of introductory music, before I had to throw my arms wide in the opening dance sequence, I felt the sun on my face and a confidence manifesting as words in my head: *I'm home; this is home.* Then I shot out of my body. Step-kick-kick-leap-kick-step.

During a break, after about three hours and a couple of eliminations, I walked to the stage edge and asked Michael if I could please speak to him. I was terrified, knowing he could just as easily say "no" as "yes," or even ask me to leave. Perhaps it was the way I said "please," or maybe it was that I got lucky, because he answered, "Sure," and jumped up to the stage where he met me eye to eye. "I'll do whatever you ask of me, I really will, I promise, but I was wondering, *please*, *may I please* read for Kristine rather than for Val?"

"Why? Why her?"

"She's not a ditz. She's just so anxious to do things right, she blows it. She wants—"

Michael called over his shoulder. "Chrissy Barker"—he called me Chrissy—"is going to read for Kristine, not Val." He jumped down from the stage; the stage managers shuffled their papers. It all took less than two minutes. I was taken to the lower-level basement in the lobby, where a piano had been set up. The musical assistant taught me the script and a portion of Kristine's patter song. I looked at the words and told myself, *A nervous person doesn't speak with periods or commas. She tells her story with modulations of voice, ignoring punctuation.*

I had one audition. Only that one on that day.

Then I waited. Others I knew had callbacks; some even had three. Lydia, from *Seesaw*, had five, all taking place over an eternity that was about six weeks long. In the meantime, I drew a design and embroidered a shirt for Brett. I cut up old denims and made a pair of patchwork jeans for myself. I read Moss Hart, then a biography of Frank Capra, followed by one about Elizabeth Ashley after seeing her in *Cat on a Hot Tin Roof*, though I could barely concentrate during her performance, even as she was sublime in the role of Maggie, writhing on the bed in her silk slip. But I heard nothing back from the audition, not a peep.

Then, late one Thursday on a January afternoon, I headed

home from a day of dance and acting classes, taking the F train to Henry Street, which always felt at least a hundred miles from Midtown. I took off my hat, coat, and boots and walked into the bedroom where the answering machine sat on top of our dresser. I turned the dial to rewind, then set it to "play," and there, in the muck of a winter day, was the voice of Manny Azenberg—Tony Award–winning producer, Manny Azenberg—saying, "Hi, I have a message for Christine. Christine, I have a job for you in *A Chorus Line*. Michael wants to put you in the International company that will open at the Drury Lane in London. Call me back at . . ."

I slumped to the floor. If I'd had a working beeper, I could have accessed the machine from a Times Square phone booth earlier. Now it was after six p.m., too late to call back. I got up and played the tape again, taking it slow because I might not have heard it right. I rewound the tape, played it again; the words were the same.

I sat on the floor again. I waited through three breaths, then rewound and listened once more, just to make sure I had it right. And when I *was* sure, I lay on the platform bed and stretched myself long, from one end of the bed to the other, just to feel myself big. I tried to repeat the words, to tell myself what had happened, but no syllables came, just a ricocheting, jumbled ecstasy beating between my ears and out my heart. I kept the news to myself, for *hours*, knowing that Brett wouldn't be home until late, and not even sure if he'd be the first I'd tell. I had to hold it close and call it mine before I released it to the world. I had a *real* job dancing in a hit, groundbreaking show. I wanted it to be the role of Kristine, but whatever it was, I was cast, which meant I was *something*.

To know that you are *something* makes all the difference in a life.

Lying on the bed, I wondered about all the big and little moments, the seemingly insignificant choices that became blistering lessons. I could map my life with one straight arrow connecting a thousand points of gritted teeth when I faced the unbearable balance between disappointment and hope. Most times, I was a failure. But not today. Today, I was who I'd believed myself to be, and I stretched my arms and legs reaching for all four corners of the world because for the first time ever in my entire life, I felt *whole*.

On the Other Side
—
1976

Everything changed in an instant, as if a fairy godmother had waved her magic wand, a timeworn cliché, and yet that was precisely my experience. The vast reach of a publicity blitz put *A Chorus Line* on the covers of national newspapers and magazines, while the Broadway cast made television appearances. Macy's even sold *A Chorus Line* towels. That I was now associated with such a production suddenly qualified me as legitimately belonging to a rarified group. When I told Laughlin that I'd been cast as Kristine, he immediately bought a ticket to Toronto, where the production would have a tryout before going to the big opening in London. That he acted so quickly and decisively was a sign of his absolute support. Brett couldn't rearrange his schedule of plays, so instead planned to come to London, and my parents thought they'd wait until the show returned stateside, saying they'd bring my younger brothers, which was understandable given the cost of the trip. Suzanne had to figure out her last semester of law school, although I knew with certainty that she would come as soon as possible. My grandmother in San Francisco wrote a note, saying that I had the hide of a rhinoceros and the soul of a butterfly. I don't know if that was an original line, but I liked it.

After signing my eighteen-month contract, I traveled home to Santa Fe for a vacation, knowing that once rehearsals began, I wouldn't have a break for at least a year. Daddy asked about my salary.

"Six hundred dollars—not including living expenses."

Suzanne, who'd left Stanford after earning a masters' degree, was now top in her class at the University of New Mexico School of Law. "Oh," she said, "you mean six hundred a month."

"No, a week."

"Wow." Daddy was impressed, my salary adding validity to my budding career. But probably, for both my parents, the most important thing I'd brought home was a promise to marry Brett when I returned from the tour. He had proposed after I signed my contract and arrived in Santa Fe to ask my father if he could marry me, something significant to my traditional parents.

I'd brought home a full-package deal—career and marriage—something to make everyone happy, the burden of all expectations finally settled. My parents toasted Brett and me with champagne, a wedding in the future even as I couldn't wait to get back to New York, where the next part of my life, a chapter just for me, would begin.

Rehearsals were held in the Midtown Manhattan basement studios of the New York City Center theater. Lydia and a couple others I knew from *Seesaw* or other jobs were also in the cast. New to me was T. Michael Reed, otherwise known as Tom, a seasoned veteran and our dance captain. Unlike a lot of other dancers, he was extremely articulate and well organized, whether scheduling rehearsals or breaking down a step: *The right foot is turned to a forty-five-degree angle, the shoulder is . . .* His exactitude inspired trust, an important factor when physical exhaustion and frayed nerves took over after repeating a step for the hundredth time because it still wasn't perfect.

There were five cast members from California, which was unusual, but the show and Michael's expanded reputation had been enough to draw talent east. Olive was a particularly colorful creature among that group. If Mick Jagger had had a ninety-three-pound baby sister, she would be that girl. She had blue-black hair cut into spikes, a lanky androgynous body, and a style that was all electric, exuberant disorder. She was a fascination, not to mention hysterically funny.

Because the show was not notated—meaning the physical movements of the choreography had not been translated into written language along with the positions of dancers on the stage—the Broadway cast joined both the International and LA companies in rehearsals to teach us the complicated formations and dance steps that were part of the "Montage," a section midway into the show when all seventeen characters are onstage dancing through intricate patterns. The rehearsal space was a swarm of activity, with two dancers shadowing every member of the original cast in a process of kinesthetic cloning. The idea was that once we learned the big dance sequences and our character's positions on the stage, we would split into our three separate casts.

Every day was an exhausting eight-hour whorl set in motion by Michael's vision, which generated feelings of deep love for the work and one another and other times bubbled with pressure-cooker angst. Everyone, from the top down, felt insecure about Michael's extremely ambitious time frame. He'd launched his multipronged effort to have three companies running simultaneously *before* the show had won the coveted Tony Awards that normally are crucial to the advance ticket sales that support a production's finances, particularly those of touring companies. To complicate matters, *A Chorus Line* was competing against *Chicago*, Bob Fosse's new musical that would open on Broadway only a few weeks before. The rivalry between the two titans was palpable, not to mention that of competing producers who had enormous investments at stake.

By most standards, the timeline was impossible, but Michael was more force than man. Splashed across the front of every program was "Conceived, choreographed and directed by Michael Bennett." The show was his moment in history, his chance at redefining the American musical; his energy was Herculean and his power unbounded, lording over the producers just as he did over us—his serfs—his dancers. His personal involvement in every single detail blurred the few boundaries that existed between director, performer, script, showtime, and reality—a dynamic fed by the personal ambition, hope, and insanity of every one of us.

The burden of success would be carried by those executing the story—the dancers—and none were more burdened than the dancers in the original cast. When they arrived at City Center, generously coming to teach us their parts even as they had a show to do that night, we felt the gravity of their presence. Every one of us knew that *A Chorus Line* came to fruition because of their fullhearted willingness to share their stories and participate in the workshops that resulted in the script, lyrics, music, and choreography that we were now learning. We felt we owed them, especially those in my company who were younger, less-seasoned performers, Michael's version of a farm team. We faced each day with solemn dedication, knowing we were meant to internalize the original cast's precision and nuance, then create it anew. Every day, we committed our souls, believing that, at the root, the show was theirs. We broke our backs to earn their respect.

On a floor buried beneath 53rd Street, the captains of Broadway worked their magic—Oscar-winning composer Marvin Hamlisch, playwright and author Jimmy Kirkwood, up-and-coming lyricist Ed Kleban, and top Broadway producer Manny Azenberg anchored themselves at the production table while nineteen times three of the best professional dancers in the United States exploded at the sound of the rehearsal pianists pounding their keys. Assistants Bob Avian and Baayork Lee paced the perimeter of the room, eyeing our movements like hawks, while at the vortex flamed a gleeful Michael Bennett: "Step, step, leap, kick, step, AGAIN!" With both arms outstretched, he was a modern-day Mephistopheles. You could feel his charge bouncing from dancer to dancer, multiplying the sense that you were part of something seismic and eternal that was worth pledging your soul to. The building rocked on its foundation.

Michael was less accessible than during the *Seesaw* rehearsals, and whenever I was around him, a choking shyness wrapped itself around me. Still, I burned with gratitude, and one day when only Michael was sitting at the director's table, I approached him. He looked at me with eyes that were dark and cold. "Oh. I just wanted to say thank you. Really, Michael, thank you for giving me the job and the chance to be here." He looked me up and down, and I thought I might cry, which was totally absurd, but then the hard edges of his face dissolved into something soft, and he said, "Sure. Yeah."

That thank-you was the third time I had ever spoken to Michael one-on-one, but I took another chance and approached him again a few weeks later when I asked him if he would consider a small costume change. During the show, many girls wore beige tights, while my character Kristine and some others wore black tights. I asked if I could wear beige tights. He raised both eyebrows at once: "Why?"

"Because the backdrop is black, the wings are black, Kristine's tights are black; she drowns in all that blackness, and . . ."

"You can't get fat."

"I won't."

"You won't?"

"I promise. I do. I promise you."

"Okay." Then he turned and had someone make a note for Theoni Aldredge, the costume designer, about my wearing beige tights.

Beige tights were revealing, whereas black tights could hide some weight. Michael hadn't ever seen me heavier because I'd kept my "super-girl body" during *Seesaw*, weighing in at 106, then keeping my weight there for my *A Chorus Line* audition. But the truth was that weight was always a terrible predicament for all of us who made a living in tights; all it took was one relaxed weekend binge before being faced with weeks of starvation.

Luckily, the fear and awe Michael inspired in me was tempered by the comfort of the dressing room, since once the companies divided into their separate groups, the International company had its own rehearsal time and space. Several of us girls and some boys shared the dressing room, not minding the lack of privacy, changing our clothes and laughing like a ragtag gang of siblings. Olive told us the story of her audition, where Michael asked about her life and she said she used to be fat, which sent all of us into paroxysms, and Lydia said, "Girl, you're so skinny now, you look like you left your butt at home.

You could wear your dance pants backwards and it wouldn't make a difference."

Olive good-naturedly shrugged before one of the boys piped up about grass—what were we going to do about that?

Most everyone, *especially* Michael, openly smoked grass, though we dancers only smoked after work. It relaxed us, moving the blood through aching muscles and having fewer hangover effects than alcohol. Everyone was planning to take along a few joints to get us started in Toronto, knowing that within a few days we'd meet a stagehand or musician who could supply us. The issue was how to pack our grass without getting caught in immigration and customs. Lydia proposed we hide joints in our steamer trunks, which the company planned to ship along with the set and lights. "No one's going to break open those locks and inspect the drawers," she argued.

But Olive, with remarkable aplomb, said, "Get them to take it for us. They smoke. They know we smoke."

"The administration? The managers?"

The room grew quiet. Olive's practical suggestion was indicative of her different background. New York dancers normally had very little to do with the production side of a show and rarely crossed the boundary that we believed separated our interests.

But another Californian, one of the boys, added, "Good idea."

Olive waved her hand, "Christine, you talk to them for us."

"Me?"

"She's right," Lydia said. "They'll listen to you. You're the quiet, serious one."

"I'm not quiet. . . ." I protested, stung.

"Okay, you're not quiet, you just think a lot."

Then Lydia took the room as if I weren't there: "Barker's a thinker. She's always the Equity Deputy, telling us our rights and reading or figuring things out. We go way back, right, Barker? You know how to talk to them. Go talk to Martin."

"The stage manager?"

"Yeah."

"Yeah," the voices echoed. What Lydia said was true. In general, I was more cerebral than most other dancers, but also, I had a practical side that helped me know when to switch strategies, while most of them had no filter, responding to anything and everything with spontaneous abandon—a trait that made them good performers, but sometimes got them into trouble. Lydia also spoke from a place of loyalty. I had rescued her early on during *Seesaw* rehearsals when Michael was deciding whether to cut an entire scene and dance number for which Lydia had a speaking part. Her lines were being rewritten every day, and one day, she flubbed completely trying to get the words off the paper. Michael grew edgy and abruptly ended rehearsal. From where I sat on the sidelines, I understood that Lydia couldn't *read* the words quickly enough to deliver them. In our room that night, I went over it all with her. I also covered for her, taking over her role in the hooker number when she felt paralyzed by homesickness. Last, we were connected because everyone paired us as "nice" girls, and once we knew Olive had come from LA and didn't know anyone, we made it a point to include her in our friendship. Besides, Olive was wacky, and we loved wacky.

I accepted the grass-deputy job but put it off until it was nearly time to leave town. "Martin, could I speak to you, please?" He sat at the long production table.

"Sure." He put down his pencil and script.

"Privately?"

"Oh."

I had never talked to him, just listened as he gave out reams of instructions or read some of Michael's notes after Michael had left for the day. Martin and his assistant, David, had not come from Michael's usual staff of stage managers, which was a first—for such important positions, Michael hired only those he knew well. The word was that, despite having never worked on a musical, Martin and David were Manny Azenberg's absolute best team, having held together several difficult productions when the stars threw operatic temper tantrums, the kind of drama that could upend life in the wings. In this case, Manny's power seemed to rival that of Michael's, seemingly because he was financing the production and had vast experience in mounting a show in London.

I followed Martin into an empty music room. He turned to face me and smiled, something accessible about him, which I wasn't expecting. I expected all business, a piece of cardboard, the typical management type. He had strikingly blue eyes that were bold—even challenging. He was big, not big in his body, even though he was tall, but big in his *presence.* "I feel a little awkward," I said, suddenly feeling foolish, "but I've been appointed the grass deputy."

"What?" He looked shocked.

"A lot of kids smoke pot and they're planning to take some to Toronto."

"Not a good idea." He punctuated each word like a school principal.

"I know. That's why . . . why they want me to talk to you. Maybe we can figure this out together," I suggested. He folded his arms, so I pressed, a little more sweetly: "Well, no matter

55

what you and I agree on here, I'm pretty sure a lot of them are going to take at least several joints to get started . . . before they make some contacts. It's to relax at night after the show." He had not moved, so I added, "God knows Olive will probably have roach clips instead of barrettes in her hair when we go through customs."

That got a grin.

"What do you want me to do?"

"Take it. Get it in for us."

"What?" He was aghast, and I had the feeling that he was pretty straight, at least as far as grass was concerned.

"Here's my proposal: I collect everyone's stuff, put it into one bag. You stash it in the Mylar or the lights. You supervise the trucks and moving the set, don't you? Isn't that your job?"

He looked at me very carefully then and asked, "What's in it for me?"

"If you do this for us, we promise no one will carry any-thing—*anything*—on them. We will be well-behaved scouts at all points of entry, even Olive. You have my word."

"Your word?"

"My word." He laughed out loud and shook his head, which was slightly insulting, so I added, "You're going to be the one responsible for getting us onto the plane, into another country. Don't you take care of stars? Everyone says you do all of Manny Azenburg's plays and keep the stars in-line."

"No hard stuff. No pills, no coke, NOTHING else. One baggie total."

"Deal." I offered my hand, expecting him to shake.

"Not yet."

"What?"

"Who sent you flowers?"

"Who— How'd you know I got flowers? That's none of your business."

"I've never seen anyone get flowers at a rehearsal, and you're right—I do big shows with big stars, and *none of those big stars* ever got flowers at rehearsal." He rocked back on his heels, smiling again. "I'm just curious."

"Yeah, well, don't say anything because I'm engaged and I don't want any trouble, especially when I'm trying to learn the show and make it okay to be on the road for eighteen months."

He laughed louder.

"Jesus Christ! Do we have a deal?"

"Yes. We have a deal."

A businessman had sent me the flowers, someone who was very rich and had been introduced to me when he'd attended an "invited dress rehearsal." I assumed he was a Broadway "angel," a potential investor. We'd had a brief conversation where I smiled a lot and took very seriously the idea that I was a "representative" of the show, as had been mentioned in a pre-rehearsal pep talk given by the producers. The businessman suggested getting together when the cast was in London. I had no intention of exploring *that*, but the next day, when the doorman handed me the flowers, I had to admit, my cheeks flushed. It was a wooing of an entirely different magnitude, another indication that I really was in a new and different world. I thought I'd kept the bouquet secret, only showing Lydia and Olive. But apparently, Martin made it his job to know *everything*. He probably tipped the doorman every week in exchange for tidbits of personal information.

Olive may have seemed like a completely spontaneous combustion of craziness, but actually she had a refined understanding of the power of image. I thought of myself as a dancer hired to play a part, whereas she thought her job was *to be* the part, never appearing anywhere without being dressed and coiffed to convey a persona. Olive had memorized every Marilyn Monroe, Judy Garland, and old-screen-starlet biography, considering their examples as proper templates from which to build her brand. She convinced me to meet her one morning at Boyd's, an Upper East Side beauty shop that she couldn't believe I didn't know about because even in LA, people knew about *Boyd's*. Rehearsal didn't start until noon, so we had plenty of time. The makeup artist sat me in a plush chair, redoing my face and teaching me how to create "smoky" eyes and use multiple layers of blush to enhance my cheekbones. Olive easily spent hundreds of dollars without hesitation. And so did I when I saw what the makeup artist had done to my face.

"What's all that?" Brett asked as I unpacked my purchases later that night.

"Makeup. Hair stuff."

"Oh—the new you?"

"It's more for the stage. For my character."

"Rather than worrying about makeup, you ought to explore your character for who she is, where she's been before the audition, why she needs the job. That's the way an actress would approach the part."

"I've done that." It wasn't as if I hadn't had *any* acting classes. I didn't want to start a fight. "This is just makeup and hair stuff."

"It's important to know that once this show ends, the dancers will probably never experience the same level of employment. What kinds of jobs are there for dancers?"

"I'm going to take classes at the Royal Academy of Dramatic Art when I'm in London. Remember?" Brett had recently been obsessed with the artificiality of Broadway, declaring it an avenue for "star tripping"—not real or honest enough. He had a point, but I could argue that *A Chorus Line* was as real as real got, and that most dancers probably had never been given the chance to develop other skills, something I was determined to provide for myself in London.

On another day, Olive and I went to Bloomingdale's. I'd probably been there only three times in the five years I'd lived in New York. She helped me pick out a pair of trendy jeans, tight across the butt and flared at the ankle. She wound a blue suede belt around my hips. "Now, just wear a leotard on top. You remind me of Julie Christie," she said.

When I came home with new clothes, Brett was testy again, but rather than try to placate him, I ignored him, his increasingly brooding moods annoying me.

On the day the company left town, Brett saw me off at Shubert Alley, where a Greyhound bus was parked and ready to take us to the airport. I told him I loved him, but the words came out in a cough, and I burst into tears. I suddenly felt so awful, sobbing and clinging to him, feeling badly that we'd been fighting. By the time I calmed down, I was the last one to get on the bus, and the only seat left was next to Martin.

"Is it cancer? Where's Cecil B. DeMille when we need him?" Martin handed me a handkerchief. It was white linen.

"I was saying goodbye to my fiancé."

"I know who he is. He runs a downtown theater."

"How do you know?"

"Because I was at Manny's office the day you came in to sign your contract, and he came with you."

"I don't remember you."

"You wouldn't. I walked out of Manny's office just as you

walked in. I knew who you were because I had your picture from the cast list. Manny was expecting you and told me you were coming in. He was surprised when you walked in with Brett. He'd never met Brett but knew who he was because Manny follows all the downtown ventures. He didn't know that you and Brett were a number. Did Brett go with you so he could meet Manny?"

"What? No, he went with me to help me sign the contract."

"You needed help?"

"Well, I . . ." I put my bag between us and tried to rearrange the things inside, even though they didn't need rearranging. "I wondered about the 'favored nations' clause."

"Everyone gets paid the same salary, regardless of role."

"I know."

"So why aren't you in any of Brett's productions?"

"I'm not right. He does small, intimate plays."

"I give you two weeks. You'll be over him in two weeks."

"Fuck you!" I turned my face and looked out the window. After the grass deal, I'd warmed to him, even more so after he'd comforted the girl who played the role of Sheila after Michael very publicly announced that she was going to lose ten pounds before we opened in Toronto, *even if he had to starve her himself.* He was so loud, publicly shaming her, and when she ran from the room, Martin followed her, somehow getting her back up on her feet and back in the rehearsal room. I liked him then. But now, I zipped my dance bag shut and kept my face to the window.

A few minutes later, he tapped my leg and whispered, "Your shipment arrived safely."

"Already?" He nodded, then took out a book: *Portrait of*

a Marriage by Nigel Nicolson whose cover, from what I could read, described the author's parents' complicated relationship with each other and the same-sex partners they also loved. Apparently, Martin was a reader. He noticed me noticing. "Have you read this?"

"No. I'm more into Frank Capra."

He laughed. "No wonder you gave me *your word*."

"It happens that *my word* means something."

"Well, I thought a little Vita Sackville-West and Virginia Woolf was appropriate before going to London."

"Oh, did you pack some stones to weigh down your pockets?"

He laughed again. "I'll loan you this after I'm done. It's about love and marriage, infidelity, bisexuality, but mostly love."

I reluctantly found that comment interesting.

Toronto

—

1976

The second night in Toronto, the dressing room group plus Tom stopped by my hotel room to pick up their goods as facilitated by Martin. We passed joints back and forth. Tom, drinking red wine, confided about life in the military and hiding the fact that he was gay. Most of the boys told stories that were dark, about being beaten up in their hometowns, bullied. Their stories were deeply disturbing and underscored how we in the theater world lived in a different—albeit fragile—bubble of tolerance, which often fueled our hopes for change. Then one of the California boys revealed that his father was gay. His parents had divorced, yet he'd grown up in a tight circle of acceptance even as that acceptance didn't extend to the larger world. He was the first gay person I'd ever met who had a family who embraced him. And that reality haunted me—that only one man of everyone I knew had escaped the consequences of familial backlash.

I loved my new friends and all that we shared—not pedigreed backgrounds, but iron wills. We each had something important to show the world—that's what got us out of the tumbleweeds and to the Big Apple in the first place. What was new for each of us was that we'd been told by the most important man in the world—Michael Bennett—that we were special, and that was *everything*. Every second we shared onstage was rapturous proof that we'd transcended some element of the ordinariness that had formed us, and we weren't about to cede one inch. Onstage, we lived and breathed as one.

Martin showed up at a hotel room gathering a couple nights later. As stage manager, he held a position of authority, and when Michael wasn't around, we were accountable to him, so at first, we were reserved in his presence.

"So, why'd you want this job if you've never done a musical?" I asked.

"Why would I want to do *A Chorus Line*? Work with dancers?" Martin's tone made it seem obvious, when it wasn't obvious at all.

"Are we so different from actors?"

"Yeah. You are." Everyone was dumbfounded, so he added, "Dancers are an entirely different breed. You think with your bodies." I wanted more of an explanation, but the boys preferred to ask Martin about the gay bars in Toronto. They called the men they picked up in bars "tricks," a term new to me, and Martin gave a quick rundown, then somehow segued to a story that grabbed everyone's attention—something I was realizing he was quite good at—about a bar in the Meatpacking District in New York: "It was like a seedy hotel, with a skinny hallway and shabby carpet, the kind you don't want to look at too closely—that's why the queens wear platform shoes, right? So anyway, you're supposed to choose a door, not knowing what's behind it, so I tried one, pushed it open, and there was a guy standing there, stark naked, all tied up with thick ropes. He said in a deep voice, 'You can do anything you want to me, or I'll do anything you want.' So, I said, 'HUG ME,' and ran out!"

Lydia fell to the floor, snorting in hysteria, which made the rest of us laugh even harder, as Martin concluded, "Is that what you're interested in? Because I can't take those kinds of bars seriously."

Except for Tom and Martin (who were older by seven and eight years, respectively), most were like me, twenty-five or younger. We were heady, spirited, maybe emotionally immature, and maybe all of that helped make us good performers. None of the boys was in a serious relationship. Martin and Tom, on the other hand, both had live-in partners and secure gay identities within their established lives in the theatrical profession, something I was becoming increasingly aware of as not possible in other professions. Tom and his lover were monogamous, but Martin and his companion, Keith, had an open relationship. "Don't you want to belong?" I asked.

"Belong? I don't belong to anyone. And you shouldn't belong to anyone, either. You belong to yourself." He poked me in the chest when he said it.

"Well, maybe that's the wrong verb—"

"Barker. You think too much." Lydia passed me her joint.

"Well, maybe it's just a thing: to want to belong, to feel connected. Maybe 'connected' is a better word than 'belong.'"

"Barker's got a point, though," Lydia added. "Right, Mr. Martin?" She had married after *Seesaw* and completely "belonged" to her husband, Tito, and their Puerto Rican culture. The only other girl in the group was Olive, and she didn't have a boyfriend.

"What about you?" Tom asked.

"I have a fiance. He's coming to London to visit." Martin looked at me, waiting for a fuller reply, but I ignored him despite fearing his instinct—that my relationship with Brett wouldn't last—had some truth to it. I told Tom, "My oldest brother is coming to Toronto, and maybe my sister."

Those first nights, after everyone left, I worried about Laughlin. The boys were free with their stories, and on Martin's side, his humor, though Tom's discussion of military life, and Martin's descriptions of Harvey Milk and Stonewall demonstrated how grossly naive I'd been about the potential consequences for a gay man "coming out."

A week in, I asked Martin to help me secure one of Michael's house seats for Laughlin, who was arriving as we were to start previews. Somehow, Martin picked up on something I'd said, one thing leading to another as the others left, and we were alone in my room. I suddenly confided Laughlin's secret, Martin listening empathetically and adding perspective on what life might be like for someone with Laughlin's history, a man who'd served in the military, was a father, and was now pursuing—at a highly acclaimed *Jesuit* school—a career in law, when, "It's essentially against the law to be gay. You see the precariousness of that, don't you?" Martin prodded. He promised confidentiality, and I trusted him because his information and perspective were essential to understanding my brother's predicament. Not lost on me was an obscure similarity in how Laughlin and I both buried aspects of our identities within the challenge of social expectations, though of course, Laughlin's homosexuality was much more dangerous than my feminism. Martin was now the keeper of a private truth, which was unexpectedly relieving, some dark shape morphing with the element of insight.

When Laughlin arrived, he dropped his bags at my hotel and got himself to the theater because I had to be there early. Martin met him at the box office and gave him his ticket. During the show, I looked but couldn't find him in the sea of seats;

then, before I had even washed off my makeup, he burst into my dressing room. "God, I was so close to you. I felt I could reach out and grab you. Jesus! I almost grabbed the guy next to me and said, 'That's my little sister, that's her, the third girl from the left.'"

I wore a pleated antique voile blouse (that Olive helped me buy) over a pair of tight blue jeans, swung a new leather bomber jacket over my shoulder, and because I had a job and he was in school, we spent a big chunk of my week's paycheck at a swank restaurant. "To you. To your up-coming opening in *London*. To my little sister." Over the weekend, my picture was in the Sunday supplement of the newspaper. He saw it first, ripped it out, and put it in his pocket. He was selfless in his pride, vestigial childhood bonds coming forward that turned my success into a shared experience. I was happy that he was the first of everyone I knew and loved who saw the me I'd become, and significantly, that my new self was being launched within the context of *A Chorus Line*, a theatrical phenomenon that laid bare the very essence of his personal dilemma. Much of the show's success was attributed to its refreshing frankness, how characters talked openly about their bodies and identities, unselfconsciously mentioning topics that were taboo or spoken of in whispers. The show was cutting-edge, and I hoped that seeing it would give him confidence in his future as a gay man. We talked nonstop the whole weekend. I introduced him to Martin and Tom, and when he left, I felt sure that he would begin to find a way out of the trap his life had been.

The show opened in May, a week after Laughlin's visit, and was an astounding success. Still, Michael considered the entire Toronto run a tryout for London, so we had rehearsals starting at eleven a.m. the very next day. We were dizzy from

Tom's pirouette drills when Michael came running down the aisle from the back of the house screaming, "Stop! Stop!" The pianist lifted his hands, and we froze, Michael yelling, "We just won the Pulitzer Prize! We got the Pulitzer Prize!"

On stage, no one moved. We were rooted in stunned silence, feeling the reverberations of Michael's voice echoing across the red velvet seats at the Royal Alexandra. Then Lydia pulled me close and whispered so no one else could hear: "Barker, what's the Pull-it Surprise?"

For six weeks we played to sold-out Canadian audiences, lines forming outside the stage door, hands reaching across barricades asking for autographs, the faces of adoring strangers carrying us from one thrilling, exhausting day to the next. Warming up in the wings, we admitted that we were bone-tired, but from the first eight bars of music that started the show, the audience's roar buoyed us. No matter how spent we were, their rapt attention lifted us off our feet. I was dripping-sweat drained every night, at times more elated than I ever thought possible, other times so wrung out, I was no longer sure where the show ended and I began. On days when I felt overwhelmed by the dazzle and pressure, I prayed at the altar of Michael Bennett, whispering, "I know you put me here because you believed in me," and waiting for the Lazarus effect—the power of Michael saying I was special. Then, on other days, when I felt on the brink of losing it entirely, too weary to put my body through the paces, I stirred the pot of indignation. I heard Martin's question on the bus the day we left New York, "Why aren't you in any of Brett's productions?" which brought up waves of resentment that I wasn't good enough to be taken seriously, a double whammy coming from someone I loved, and pushed me forward when I thought I couldn't take another step.

Then, one day, sitting at my dressing room mirror, I reached for my lipstick and was paralyzed. I couldn't remember my first line. My head flooded with visions of falling during the opening number. My chest caved; my limbs turned to dust. I tried to paint my bottom lip, the way the artist at Boyd's had done, but my hands shook.

It was early; "Places" hadn't been called, but I went to the wings anyway. The wings, entrenched in metaphor, were revered as magic portals: the passageway from the real world to that of the stage. Our wings were dark, bound by tall partitions wrapped in heavy black fabric, the floors and ceilings all painted the same deep black, so every plane merged in a dimensionless space. I did a few pirouettes, my toes tingling as if they'd fallen asleep. I stood with my back up against the downstage flat panicking when Martin appeared at the stage manager's podium to check the headsets.

"What are you doing here?" he whispered.

"*Oh.* I'm just . . ."

"What?"

"I don't think . . ."

"What?"

"I can't."

"What?"

"Do it."

"Why not?"

"I don't know. I'm afraid."

"Of what?"

"Everything. I feel like my tights are too thin; this leotard doesn't fit. I feel like . . . I'm standing on top of the first row of the audience. I can see them, though they don't know I can, and they're all looking up, right between my legs. I feel so exposed."

"They're not looking at you. They're looking at the character."

"I can't."

"Yes, you can. Go inside the words. Think. Hope. She needs the job. What if she gets the job? Ride that path of possibility. Live that chance."

He bent over and put his arms around me, the darkness of the wings accentuating the reach of his whisper. "You are so beautiful. You have no idea what you look like out there. I can't take my eyes off you." He shocked me, and I suddenly felt light-headed, putting my hands on his chest, where the vibrations of those words still resonated. He put his lips to my ear, saying he would stand at the back of the theater, under the red exit sign that we'd been taught to spot. He backed away, called, "Places," and the others arrived in the wings; at the blackout, we ran to our spots on the stage, and after the opening number, there he was, standing at the back of the house, as promised. That night, I played to him alone.

Later, we went back to the hotel together in a cab; he was uncharacteristically quiet. I wanted to say something, but still wasn't sure *what* had happened in the wings. "Why don't you drink?" I asked and put my hand on top of his. He did not move it away.

"Because I drank too much."

"Why not smoke?"

"Grass makes me paranoid."

"Really? I love the way it makes me feel."

"I've had debilitating panic attacks." He spoke

matter-of-factly to the plastic panel separating us from the cabdriver, describing severe anxiety. Then, when he'd finished his explanation, he turned his whole body toward me, and I felt his heat, something primal and voracious.

From that day forward, I looked at Martin differently, believing I was in on one of *his* private secrets, that part of him liked women, which was confirmed on another night when he said he had come to New York from California with a girlfriend, and that they'd lived together. At some point, he started living a gay life, all of which reminded me of Laughlin. Over time, I also learned that other friends had had gnawing stage fright, teeth-chattering moments of self-doubt, and that Martin had been integral in getting them back on their feet, too.

He seemed a genius in his own right. Martin's reverence for the power of theater to transform life was palpable. His specialty was being on the inside of that process. Backstage, he was blunt when he wanted to make a point but otherwise personable, communicating amiably with everyone—dancers, techies, musicians, boys, girls, younger, older, gay, straight. He was at the nexus of both the technical and artistic aspects of the show, making sure that all the light booms, stage sets, and amplifiers worked; that the tech crews were in their places before our feet ever hit the stage. During performances, he "called" the show from a booth at the back of the house, wearing a headset to cue the conductor, light operators, or techies doing the set changes. Artistically, as the director-in-residence, he watched and timed every performance to ensure pacing and tempo so that characterizations, line readings, and comic beats were maintained. Socially, he was our resident adviser, responsible for keeping us on track when going clubbing until all hours of the night eroded some voices or the repetitive task of doing eight shows a week frayed our nerves, leading to squabbles in the dressing rooms.

We began to spend time together during the day. He had a way of intellectualizing both the artistic tasks of being a good actor and the challenges of living a professional life—two very different skills that I'd had a whiff of during *Seesaw.* He understood what it was to live life in extremes: the daunting experience of the endorphin-fueled high during performances followed by the off-hours withdrawal, a fall that could make ordinary life feel mediocre and empty. I felt how living under the bright lights became isolating, the world of public pressure and expectation closing in. Not that any of us wanted a "normal" life, but you crave what you give up—its dependable consistency. Our strengths were also our weaknesses.

"We're not *realpeople*," Martin said, using a term often mentioned in dressing rooms.

Realpeople lived a normally incremented day: breakfast by eight and dinner at seven. *Realpeople* held regular—not freelance—jobs with steady paychecks, lived in homes with yards, had car payments, insurance bills, lives shaped by predictability, which by its very nature contrasted with an artist's life. In the dressing room, we did not think of ourselves as *realpeople*, and even as we had a name for that group, we didn't have a name for ourselves, only believing that we were something other.

"You don't think of yourself as—"

"*Realpeople*? I'm gay. That fact alone separates me," he said. "And don't get confused—you're not *realpeople*, either."

"But here we are—doing laundry."

He laughed, and I watched the rhythm of his constancy; even in the way he measured the detergent and folded his black socks, he was solid, like he was wrapped around a rock. The dryer went round and round, and he sat next to me, reading the newspaper's film reviews aloud, adding his own funny comments, then saying, "Let's go see *The Man Who Fell to Earth*!"

We dropped the laundry at his hotel and arrived just in time for the matinee. The movie theater was empty, except for us, the air-conditioning blasting. Martin put his hand on my arm. "Jesus, you're freezing!" He took off his clean black socks, handing them to me, and I slipped my hands inside, pulling them over my arms as if they were long opera gloves. Then I leaned into him, at first for warmth, but then because it was the most natural thing to do.

If Lydia had said that I thought too much, she was right. But somehow, I had to make sense of my new existence, living a lifetime in the two-hour span of the show, then spending the remaining hours of the day preparing, studying, writing, observing, resting, being an artist. Our work was about compressing life and communicating the fullness of an experience. While I continued to feel underprepared about how to sustain such intensity eight times a week, Martin framed the task, giving me direction and confidence, telling me first to trust the genius of the script, that delivering a good performance had less to do with "acting" than with having the courage and endurance to stand before an audience and honestly live what it means to be a dancer, in that moment. "Too many newcomers in this profession are obsessed with being celebrities. Forget about being a 'star.'" What made me "good" in the show, he said, was how I lived my vulnerability openly, in real time showtime. "That's the quality you will be able to take to other acting parts." Michael had always insisted on authenticity, directing us to project an in-the-moment sensibility, which was exactly what Martin was talking about when he said to trust the script. Still, I was a dancer, more accustomed to letting my body do the talking. Acting was new, and being consistently "good" on cue eight times a week was a superhuman task, even as it was exactly what I wanted to learn to do and was what would make me truly professional.

As I grew closer with Martin, Brett seemed ever farther away. He had done the "right things," sending me a telegram on opening night with lovely, inspired words, and we talked on the phone regularly, but as I tried to describe my ups and downs, he reduced my feelings to terse summations: "Sounds like you're really gaining experience."

"Do you get what I'm saying? This is *important*." When I hung up the phone, I felt lonely, wondering if he was incapable or uninterested, but he was more intuitive than I gave him credit for. Soon he began making comments that I talked a lot about Martin: "I can see that Martin is having a big influence on you. Reminds me of the influence Tommy Tune had on you, when you were in *Seesaw*." My relationships irritated him, even though the men were gay. He was dismissive, "When you go on the road, you're always under the influence of one of the *guys*."

I bit my tongue at his inflection, my fury flying to the time he had said, "You don't want to be a fag hag."

"A what?"

"Fag hag: A girl who hangs around fags because she can't get any straight men interested."

Those were indelible words I'd return to repeatedly when articulating some basic but essential premise that separated us—his presumption of authority. That he was ignorant and arrogant enough to use a term meant to shame Laughlin, Martin, Tom, and all my friends was despicable, convenient, and typical, because the late seventies dynamic for every female I knew was this: Straight men stood at the top of the pyramid and employed whatever tactics they needed to keep it that way, which likely was harder in the theater business because gay men were among the most talented and successful. Gay men were also the only ones willing to mentor girls. Girls wanted to be taught, to learn, rise in the ranks. Mentoring, for most straight men, meant sex, which girls—even if they choose to put up with it—didn't prioritize. Girls wanted careers. My friends and I thought most straight men in the business were hypocrites, predators, or idiots, and lately Brett seemed no different.

Martin took me seriously. He talked about *everything*—feelings, appearance, emotions, opinions, politics, economics. He didn't hide or try to ingratiate himself—something that I began to see was a bad habit of mine. He unapologetically stood his ground and navigated the world from a spot that was wholly his. True, he was perennially restless, insatiably busy, always craving some new experience, but he'd folded me into his life in a way Brett never had folded me into *his*. When Martin discovered that Toronto was *the* place to buy leather, we went to a tailor, and each of us had leather jeans made. He introduced me to Nina Simone and played her on his tape deck. I didn't know who Claes Oldenburg was, so he took me to see his sculptures on exhibit at the museum. "Is this too much?" he asked. "I mean, you have a show to do tonight. Do you need to spend the afternoon resting?"

"No. I'm good." I loved filling up on all the things I'd never known. One day he said, "We have to get you a credit card," which even a few months ago, I hadn't been able to get. He went with me to the bank to fill out the application. Toward the end of our run in Toronto, at a dinner between shows, he curled his foot under my leg. "What are you going to order?"

"I think I'll start—"

"By having an affair with me?"

"You're asking between the soup and the salad?"

"With you it's more like three leaves of lettuce. *No dressing, please, and a stalk of celery on the side*. So, what do you say? *Yes?*"

I wanted to say yes, but "No" came out instead.

"Okay."

"I—"

"Yes? *Yes?*"

"I can't be a trick," I said, using the term he and the boys had taught me.

"I know."

"I just can't—"

"I know."

"So, how can we—"

"I don't know."

"Then, what are we talking about?"

"I'm not sure. But *something*."

It just happened, though of course, it didn't *just* happen. But there we were with this contradiction between us, and if we couldn't label it, how did we solve it? We had dinner; he stroked my wrist under the table and talked about the upcoming move to London, where his contacts had found me an apartment near to the one he was renting. We went back to the theater in time for me to take a quick nap before the evening show, which I couldn't do because I was so agitated about saying no instead of yes.

Before Brett, I'd had a boyfriend, several affairs, and a couple of spontaneous single-night flings, but like many girls, I was careful sexually. We had to be; we couldn't risk our careers by getting pregnant. I hated when I heard phrases like, "She's inhibited," or, "To be free, women have to be sexually free," which missed the point entirely. Every girl I knew was just as horny as every guy; we weren't *inhibited* about sex; we were *inhibited* by the consequences. The pill still had significant side effects, weight gain—the kiss of death for dancers—being among them. The Dalkon Shield and other IUDs often resulted in infections, sometimes infertility; abortion had been legal for only three years. We used diaphragms or sponges and developed habits of doing everything but having intercourse because sex was complicated and never free. Even with Brett, sex was not free because no man wore a condom. There wasn't even a discussion about *that*. Sex always carried a kind of power that had consequences for girls, and that reality separated us from all males—gay or straight.

The other *very* significant thing about sex related to how people looked at girl dancers, how they looked at our bodies and didn't see *us*, and how that was confusing for them even as it wasn't for us. When your body is a commodity, you develop keen boundaries; that's what I meant when I told Martin I couldn't be a *trick*.

Sex, to me, once you figured it out and could coordinate the interruptions of putting in a diaphragm or whatever, was great, a delicious kind of enmeshment. I liked the totality of it, and that it *meant* something wholly outside words. It was like music in that way. Even when a guy and I stopped seeing each other, there was always an acknowledgement in the way we looked at one another, something permanent in the level of intimacy we'd shared. In the best way, sex was communion, and I didn't want anything less, *especially* with Martin because I was pretty sure that whatever it was between the two of us, it was getting pretty darn close to communion, even without the sex.

Lydia was taking a nap in the dressing room, and I thought about confiding in her, then reconsidered because I was afraid that she would say it was time for me to go home to Brett. But then my dilemma spilled out when Olive and I were warming up, just the two of us at the backstage ballet barre.

"It just feels so awkward, when normally I don't feel that way. Do you think gay men think about protection?"

"No *man* thinks about protection. That's a girl's job."

"Right. But there's hepatitis, syphilis. It's not just girls getting pregnant."

"Just go with the flow; do what you feel like, then figure it out."

"If I did what I felt like, I'd mount him like a horse and ride him right here."

"Then what's stopping you?"

"That I *really* like him. It doesn't feel like a 'being on the road' kind of thing. And . . . "

"What?"

"Deep down I'm worried that I won't be as good as a guy."

"Yeah, there's *that*."

Olive went back to stretching her scarecrow legs, and I didn't elaborate my other fear: being left. If the sex wasn't good the first time, Martin likely wouldn't come back for more, and even if we got over that, he would still, at some point, leave. I would never be enough for him sexually, when to me, he would be everything. I thought about Laughlin and Carrie. I thought about Keith and his open relationship with Martin, which still confused me. Why wasn't Keith, Martin's partner, enough? Martin said he'd protected Keith in his will, so why wasn't sex with him enough to make them a couple in the way I thought about coupling? I wanted to believe that something private could exist between two people that was wholly and solely theirs, that even if they were apart, they could rely on that thing between them. That's what I thought love was, or, at least, what I wanted it to be.

My brain and my heart were all twisted, and I was hot every time I stepped into my tights. So, a night or two later, I let go, making out with Martin in the wings until David, the assistant stage manager, called, "Places," which we heard through Martin's headset.

After the show, he had friends of friends to entertain, so we enjoyed a couple more days of slinky do-si-dos and high-stakes flirting while I was trying to get unconfused about what it meant to be involved with him. Except that was impossible because it was all just a mishmash of heat and fear and magical rationalizations on top of glorious performances on the stage. And then, out of the blue, he said he had to talk to me. And I thought, *Oh God*. But he said, "Look, I need something. I have a doctor's appointment tomorrow. I've got a touch of the clap."

"Oh. Okay."

Silence. Then, "I've had it before."

"So—what do you do?"

"I have to get a shot. And it's cut with adrenaline. Last time it induced a panic attack. I thought I was suffocating. Literally being stuffed in a coffin."

"I'll go with you."

I didn't know if "the clap" was syphilis or gonorrhea, not that it mattered. I figured getting the clap was an occupational hazard for gay men, sort of like getting pregnant was for girls. Venereal disease was not something addressed at my family dinner table, but I'd read enough Isak Dinesen to know about its reach.

Martin picked me up; we took a cab to the clinic and sat in two plastic chairs in the waiting room. When the doctor came out, Martin introduced me, and I became aware of a secret society of professional gay men. Martin went in alone, and when it was all over, he said only that it wasn't as bad as the last time. We stopped for a coffee, then went to the theater early so he could finish some of the prep work for getting the set to London. In the cab after the show, he was uncharactistically sedate. "How's the tush?"

"Sore."

"I'm sorry."

"For what?"

"For your tush. Come on. It's over."

"I'll walk you to your room."

"How about I walk you to your room and stay awhile?"

"I don't want you to."

"Okay."

"Thanks for coming. Look . . . I don't like it when I'm not in control."

"Okay. But you can't always be in control, and I was happy you asked me."

"Happy?" He was meanly sardonic.

"Happy." I left him at the elevator.

Meanwhile, Suzanne and her boyfriend had become engaged, and in the spur of the moment decided to fly to Toronto before the show left for London. Spur of the moment decisions were totally unlike Suzanne, but evidently not unlike Jeffrey, her fiancé. Still, when they arrived, I saw the exuberance that now enveloped her. Martin joined us for dinner and entertained them with his repartee. Later, he said, "They're such perfect *realpeople*."

"Stop."

"No, I mean it. And in a good way. Look at them. They're happy in a way that we never could be."

"What do you mean by that?"

"That they can fill in those blanks: law school, marriage, children, a home."

"But we can have that, too, if we choose it, just in a different way."

"That's the point—in a *different* way. You hear yourself? *Different*. We're not *realpeople*."

"Maybe not, but why do you, of all people, set boundaries on what's possible?"

The doctor had prescribed six weeks of celibacy, which cooled Martin's libido, plus the run in Toronto was coming to an end. Frankly, I welcomed the reprieve because I didn't know what it meant, really, to be involved with a gay man, so I focused on what we shared, joining him at the theater during the day, watching and listening to him and his longtime assistant, David, who was straight and thoughtfully reserved. Martin had always said that what made them such a good team was that they were opposites. On the night we closed, I witnessed all that they'd organized: backstage swarming with crews who dismantled and packed the set, costumes, and lights the minute we dancers exited the stage. It was an all-night, military-like operation, leaving no trace behind, almost as exciting to see as the show itself.

Meanwhile, we'd been apprised of situations with other

American casts in other shows whose members sat in cold rooms while customs and immigration agents ran their hands over the hems of coats, looking for drugs. We were already in the public eye, having had substantial publicity broadcast across London announcing the imminent arrival of "The smash hit of the seventies!" (*Sun*, July 20, 1976). Martin was worried and enlisted my help in spreading the word about not taking any contraband with us, and he especially wanted me to keep my eye on Olive, who'd used the time in Toronto to enhance her appearance and collection of accessories.

She showed up at the airport in pink silk pajamas, the straps of her tank top falling off her coat-hanger-thin shoulders. She wore Jackie O sunglasses and sashayed through the corridors, carrying her fire-engine red, 8-track cassette tape player. I was a Girl Scout in comparison, purposely wearing a white blouse and cardigan. Still, something worked because we made it through Heathrow airport without a glitch, and Martin took me out to celebrate with dinner in the West End.

At one point, he took my hand and said, "We're here. We're in *London* and we're opening a hit show at the Drury Lane." I could only nod. It was too big, a life experience that even as you're living it, it's outside of you. At some future date, you'll try to remember it *exactly* as it was, but you won't have the vocabulary; you may as well have gone to Mars.

The Drury Lane
—
1976

The Baker Street flat Martin had arranged for me wouldn't be vacant for several more weeks, so he invited me to live with him in a large floor-through with two bedrooms that he was sharing with David and David's girlfriend, who was coming to live with him, and who, like Keith, would be arriving after the London opening.

Although I'd traveled throughout Europe as a child, I had never been to London. At first sight, both the neighborhood where we were going to live and the Drury Lane Theatre lived up to my storybook imaginings. Martin's apartment was on a block lined with perfectly symmetrical, two- or three-level attached buildings, punctuated by short black wrought iron fences and gates leading to tall, mostly painted wooden doors—though the door to Martin's was a handsomely stained walnut. We put our suitcases down and found that the house cleaners had prepared the flat for two couples as both rooms had king-sized beds.

"Is this going to be alright?" Martin asked.

"Sure." The sex thing didn't feel as pressing because of his imposed celibacy, and the fact that once rehearsals began, the grueling schedule would temper any yearnings—libidos were often dulled during times of extreme physical stress, and now that we'd arrived, we faced frontline pressure: Michael intended to obliterate the British notion that American theater was inferior.

Before leaving Toronto, a friend of Martin's had candidly asked, "Are you lovers? What's your relationship? You're so close, but I can't figure it out."

To which Martin replied, "We don't know." And that was the truth of it. We didn't debate if we were a real love story or a misguided melodrama playing out on the fertile grounds of a road trip. Even if it "wasn't complete" in the way love and sex were understood as inseparable, his attentiveness to the parts of me that I deemed sacred provided me with more emotional completeness than I'd ever experienced with another man. Perhaps that was pitiful; but I chose to believe it was wonderful. Added to that was how quickly we settled into a quirky kind of domesticity, one of us finishing the laundry, the other picking up the milk. I do not know how he was with men, but with me, Martin was romantic. He was comfortable with intimacy, like he wanted to share skin, to meet you at the itchiest spot on your soul. Someone said he adored me, and I believe he did, the two of us existing within the magical world of opening a hit show in a legendary city at the most important time of our lives. It wasn't real, except *it was*.

Before we left Toronto, news had broken that Michael Bennett and Donna McKechnie—the featured dancer in many of his shows who played the lead character in *A Chorus Line*—were getting married, which struck some, including Brett, as "completely absurd." Michael was a gay man who lived an openly gay life. Yet historically, many gay men married. Martin could list current famous men—among them Leonard Bernstein— who publicly had a wife and children but who privately had gay lovers. In the late seventies, everyone I knew was questioning and exploring the nature of sex, relationships, gender, and identity, perhaps laying the foundation for future generations and what was to come in terms of sexual orientation, same-sex marriage, and greater gender equality.

But at the time, with marriage limited to unions between men and women, I wondered if gay men considered marriage because it was an essential passport to social citizenship. Marriage conferred legitimacy upon an adult, which many gay men needed to be successful in society. (Perversely, the same was true for women.) Anyway, in the art world, gay men could marry women without giving up men. Martin even said offhandedly that maybe he would get married, that he'd lived this way for five years with Keith, and maybe that would change.

Maybe, too, gay men considering marriage had to do with fatherhood, which was rarely mentioned, even though some gay men admitted they wanted to be fathers. And why wouldn't they? There was no doubt that Laughlin was a happy father, devoted to his daughter, Kate.

As far as women were concerned, would a straight woman marrying a gay man be a bad idea? Its premise would be transactional, but so were many heterosexual marriages—a perspective I argued after Brett's comment that Michael marrying Donna was "completely absurd." History was full of women who'd married men for convenience, social acceptance, or financial security. Before we'd become engaged, Brett and I professed bohemian views, even saying that marriage was a bourgeois idea. I was surprised after signing my *Chorus Line* contract that Brett proposed, but I accepted. Now, with my life expanding, I began to think that his proposal was prompted by his need of my promise to return, and that I agreed because doing so gave us both some security during what we knew was a major life transition. Part of me wished he'd asked me a year earlier in the swooning heat of our relationship, when I was so ready to be madly in love with him because I believed that some crucial part of life—love—had finally happened. By the time I arrived in London, though, I stopped thinking about marrying Brett or anything that distracted me from focusing on the show and the here and now. My job was my first-ever chance at fulfilling my dream. Even as I looked forward to Brett's visit, I was aware of my intense connection to Martin, which in another context may have been distressing. But there was no reason to spend energy trying to understand the triangle or evaluate a blurry future when I was barely twenty-five years old, in London on my way to the Drury Lane, where someone, standing under the exit sign at the back of the house, saw me to an even greater extent than I saw myself, and I liked to believe he adored every bit of the girl he saw.

The Drury Lane epitomized London's theatrical history and magic, dating back to 1663. Some parts had burned down and been rebuilt over the years; the backstage area was historical, charming, and very outdated. The vast and drafty caverns behind the stage were so immense they'd accommodated elephants along with Sarah Bernhardt. The theater was also haunted. Lydia had packed a rosary and refused to use one dressing room that she swore smelled like *him*—the lavender ghost.

And though we'd been warned about it in advance, none of us were prepared for the "raked stage," meaning the floor was on an incline, with the highest point upstage and the lowest point ending at the orchestra's edge. A rake design is meant to enhance an audience's perception of the entire stage, but it is not made for dancers; in fact, "real" dancers did not dance on raked stages, and no musical on Broadway that had "real" dancing had ever had a raked stage. The other *Chorus Line* casts did not face this challenge, a fact that we didn't dare mention, Michael wanting London at his feet and expecting us to overcome any minor issue of physics, even though human knees and ankles aren't engineered to absorb additional forces when leaping and landing.

Some of us girls started out rehearsing in flat jazz shoes, thinking we could ease our way into our two-inch dance heels, which already required a physical adjustment, as heels force the center of gravity forward. Dancing in heels on a raked stage accelerated our downhill forward momentum, so with one, two, three steps and a leap forward, we had to lean back with our upper bodies to stop from crashing into our knees. A pirouette begins from a position on two feet, but our feet were often on different levels, which played havoc with our ability to set a turn. Even so, Michael didn't want any complaints; he wanted us to solve the problem because from the first downbeat of the music, he repeated that he intended to set London on fire. The show had won nine Tony Awards in May, and in New York was sold out for a year; the LA production was also a hit and sold out; London was Michael's final conquest in his march to total dominance in the world of musical theater. We *knew* that, so we shut up and endured, knowing our careers, and likely our futures, depended on him. *One-two-lean back-leap.*

Within days, mounting exhaustion, physical pain, and mental stress shredded our nerves; we danced and sang through gritted teeth and tears. Fueling the intensity was a new distinction that we clung to with die-hard covetousness: Michael said we'd become his favorite company, an honor always bestowed on the original cast who was *family and blood* to him. But some original cast members had joined the LA cast, making that company a hybrid version of the original, plus there'd been high drama and jealousies over the Tony Awards: who won and who didn't. We were separate from all that, and, as a group, younger, more purely bonded in our collective admiration, hence our determination to never, ever let Michael down, even as three of us fell flat on our asses and another took a bite out of the stage with his two front teeth.

Tom drilled every detail of the choreography until we reached a near breaking point. "It's too much," Lydia said, tears streaming down her face as we unwrapped the wax paper enfolding our cold boiled eggs. Eggs were the only thing we could get to eat from the tiny, one-person kiosk across the street from the stage door—our food choices being plain boiled eggs, beans on toast, or Scotch eggs, something seemingly invented in World War II that resembled miniature land mines: eggs hard-boiled then deep-fried in a wad of dough. We hadn't been in town long enough to set up our apartments, find grocery stores, or buy or make food that could nourish us when what we needed more than ever was a healthy diet. We arrived at the theater early and left late when stores were closed, London's West End not being the twenty-four seven commercial environment of Times Square. We were exhausted, hungry, our bodies hurt, and we were anxious about the opening.

At night, I smoked a joint to put my body to sleep in the sexless bed I shared with Martin, which was bearable because rehearsals were worse than crushing, and I was usually back at the apartment first, in the shower, and asleep by the time he got home. My body was racked with blisters and bruises, but when Martin climbed into bed, he reached across and pulled me close. We cuddled, and I often awoke with my hand cradled in his.

"I'm so happy waking up to you. You're so beautiful."

"Are you saying that so I'll get up and make your granola?"

"Yes."

"Then I'll make your granola."

"Jesus! What's that?"

"Oh." Trailing from my butt to the side of my quad was an inky-black bruise. "Looks like a map of California."

"More like Madagascar. Come here. Let me get a closer look."

"No way!"

He laughed, but then added, "It's the rake, isn't it? Who else is beaten up?" Martin was anticipating that we'd make it through opening, but that he'd better be prepared because there would be injuries over our six-month engagement.

"Think my beige tights'll cover it?"

"No. Put makeup on it."

As opening night approached, the company manager reported the plans for the opening night party and what would be expected of us. Martin told me to make a date with Tom and the others because he didn't like opening night parties and never went. Even though I begged, he stood firmly by his choice, so I reached out to Tom, the California guys, and Olive. Lydia's husband had arrived for an extended stay, and she would be with him, which was a blessing, because she was really frazzled. I worried about her, remembering the *Seesaw* days when her emotional fragility overcame her.

The show was a blur; we were numb—too pumped and too worn out to feel anything—but we got all our laughs, no one fell, and the audience was out of their seats at the end. Changing out of my costume, I was too tired and too relieved to feel any excitement about the party, but I found a three-word note from Martin and a small, folded piece of paper with a gram of cocaine inside.

Coke was a popular but expensive elixir, and because of that, its use varied greatly. For me and most of my friends, it was a treat—a widely accepted party drug that went along with other extravagances we could rarely afford, like champagne and caviar served at galas on silver trays held by black-suited butlers. When Tom and the others arrived at my dressing room to escort Olive and me to the party, I showed them what Martin had left. We all shared the contents and rallied. "London, here we come!"

The venue was loud and dark, crowded with tons of people we didn't know, and disappointingly, the food was terrible. At one point, Tom saved me from a tall Englishman with very blue eyes who was so drunk he kept pitching forward toward my breasts, his face once landing on my shoulder. He drooled trying to finish his sentence.

"So glad you showed up. He's so drunk."

Tom twirled me out onto the dance floor. "That was Peter O'Toole."

"What? No . . . really? Show me." Tom inched us closer to where O'Toole slumped, and indeed, from the distance, I took in his height and the blond wave. "He does have very blue eyes, but my God, he was drooling."

A few more spins around the floor, and Michael cut in on Tom, raising my blood pressure a thousand percent.

"Michael. Wow, thanks again for having me here." He smiled, and I added, "I hope you were happy, that the show was what you wanted it to be."

"I'd be happier if you gave me some coke."

"What? I—"

"Martin told me he gave you some coke."

"He did, but I gave it to Tom and the kids."

"So, you don't have any?"

"I'm sorry. I gave it to—I didn't know . . ."

Michael turned and left me on the dance floor, the lights of the disco ball swirling like I'd landed in a cheap soap opera. Michael's drug usage was common knowledge and widely accepted; we'd all been aware of times he was high during rehearsals and how his moods could change, but I was totally unprepared to be in a position where he might ask me for a line.

I wanted to go home then. I was too tired, too disappointed, and very sad about what had happened. Martin wasn't home, so I fell asleep, but in the morning, he handed me the newspaper, and shockingly, my picture was in it, and Olive got a good mention.

"How was the party?"

I started with Peter O'Toole, then told him about what happened with Michael, about how he left me on the dance floor when I didn't have any coke for him.

"Oh Jesus, I told him to go to you."

"What? You didn't tell me that. I didn't know. I shared it with Tom and the others."

"I thought that Michael could get to know you."

"Because I had coke? You were pimping me out?"

"No! I just thought if he knew you a little better, he—"

"He'd be interested in me?"

"Yeah."

"I want him to be interested in *me*, not in whether I have drugs in my purse."

"You're so naive."

"Don't ever pimp me out again."

"I was just trying to help."

"That isn't help."

"Well maybe being so idealistic isn't helpful, either."

"You're so cynical. And he wasn't even gracious; he didn't say one word about the show."

"The show was over."

"Only for the night. And, you know what? It's a choice to have standards."

"Oh Jesus, are we back to Frank Capra?"

"Who are you if you don't have standards or hope, especially if you're a girl because let me tell you, gay or straight, men always make the rules." The words jumped out. "I'm a girl!"

"Oh, give me a break—"

"No, look at me. I'm a girl, not a man. Don't try to fit me into your male way of thinking or ascribe to me your man-way of transacting through the world. Don't you dare erase me because you don't fully understand how girls are different and how we have terms, too."

Later that evening, Martin apologized, saying he'd been upset and had called Keith, and Keith had told him he was wrong, that he shouldn't have done what he did. I accepted Martin's apology. Then he started calling me "sweetness." "Okay, sweetness." And that was his new name for me.

Meanwhile, I was sad about Martin's judgement and didn't know how to interpret Keith, whom I'd never met. I was impressed by Martin's acceptance of his opinion, which illustrated a deeper basis to their relationship, one that maybe I'd been ignoring because it was confusing to me, and confusion served my interests. Still, I was reminded that on the most basic level, Martin moved through the world differently than I did: He was a player, and that had helped make him successful. I didn't know the game well enough to play, and what I did know turned me off. On top of that, I was worried about Michael, not knowing if he'd take it out on me at some point.

Soon after, Martin and his friend Jack Ward moved me into my apartment. I liked Jack. He was funny and kind, agreeing that the location of the flat was fabulous and entertaining us with British quips as he and Martin took down heavy old-fashion drapes and rearranged the furniture. Soon, I had light and a full view of the quiet symmetry of the buildings out my window, all lining up in a smaller version of Martin's block. "Now, let's get you some fresh flowers," said Martin.

I barely had time to enjoy the larkspur and delphinium Jack placed in a teapot brought down from the high cupboard since, soon after the opening, Princess Margaret and her entourage confirmed they would be attending the show. Her presence required that the cast follow strict guidelines and receive "protocol lessons" taught by members of the court administration. The sequence of events was explained: A line of palace guards dressed in poufy, striped pantaloons and helmeted hats would march onstage. Once positioned, they would raise their long silver horns and blow a heraldic tune. From that moment, the clock began ticking; the performance must *commence immediately*. Princesses don't wait.

When the show was over, the princess would be escorted to the stage, where we must be lined up and ready. Michael, who would be arriving from LA, would be introduced to the princess and then take her down the line of dancers, introducing each of us, which seemed unnecessary but was supposed to make us feel that we had been properly welcomed by the court and all of England. Michael was panicked that he would forget our names, so the plan was that Martin would stand next to him and whisper names as they traveled from one cast member to the next.

The second court administrator who arrived gave us our etiquette lessons. He wore a dark suit and was classically crusty. He told us no one was to offer a hand to the princess, but we girls could curtsy if we wished. Curtsy lessons ensued, but we reminded Mr. Eh-ta-kit (as we nicknamed him) that we would have on our finale costumes, not ball gowns, and thus would have no skirts to grab and hold as we bowed. "Yes, yes, of course," he said. But it was clear that he had no idea really that we would be in spangled leotards and fishnet tights, so he continued with his miming of a lady-in-waiting lifting her skirts as she placed her right foot behind her left and bowed. We were also instructed that we were not to speak to the princess or her entourage, unless, of course, we were spoken to first. In that case, we could answer, but must remember to say "ma'am" or "sir" as part of our answer.

On the night of the performance, the poufy heralds marched onstage, lifted their horns, blew their shrill announcement, and marched off. Blackout! We ran to our marks. Afterward, we lined up as rehearsed, and the princess appeared, along with Michael in coattails and sneakers, beaming. The escorts following behind the princess murmured things like "Jolly good show," but when Princess Margaret spoke to someone a few bodies ahead of me, Lord Someone (whom Martin thought might be Lord Snowdon but later Jack said he probably wasn't Snowdon because of the princess's impending divorce) suddenly found himself parked in front of me. He smiled. I smiled. Pause. Pause. No movement ahead, so he spoke, "Are all forty-eight states represented here, miss?"

"Oh. I beg your pardon, *sir*, but we have fifty states in the United States."

"Oh my goodness. Since when?"

"I think since before I was born, *sir*."

Martin turned in his tracks, having heard my voice. His eyebrows formed a perfect *V* all the way up to his hairline.

Later at my apartment, Jack howled, and Martin couldn't believe it, saying, "What were you thinking?"

"He asked me a question. I answered. I said 'sir'."

Both thought it was hysterically funny.

"Everyone else was tongue-tied, but you just piped up like you were sitting at a family dinner."

"Well, frankly, I was a little surprised that he didn't know history."

"It's not his history."

"Oh, right. I didn't think about that. I expected him to be a little more informed; he's royalty, after all."

"That doesn't mean he's educated," quipped Jack.

After the opening, the princess's visit, and living on adrenaline since we'd left New York for Toronto, we faced the growing burn of sustaining a high level of performance eight times a week. In the warm-up area, weariness dissipated every plié, and our otherwise rounded voices sometimes grew shrill. Daily irritations like the tube not running after the show and the scarcity of cabs (not like Times Square) made it difficult to get home, and the lack of familiar food or conveniences amped up the pressure of maintaining our weight, energy, and focus. Lydia's husband had returned to his job in New York, and she called in sick a few times. When she came back, she cried for almost an hour before the matinee. What set her off was the man in the kiosk across from the theater: "I kept telling him, I want my coffee *light*. They're English, don't they understand *English*?"

Worst was the damp cold, which intensified the consequences of the raked stage. The house, where the audience sat, was heated, but the elephantine caverns of backstage weren't fitted with heating ducts; a single radiator hissed in a dark corner stage right. We sweated through the opening number, then stood on the white line for the next hour and a half, freezing. We started wearing double tights and asked Martin to contract the costumer about adding sweaters to our costumes. Heaters with large blowers were installed in the wings but only turned on intermittently because their loud industrial whirring made it tough to hear our musical cues. Early autumn settled in like cement; we were a dispirited, frayed lot. I wished I was living with Martin and that we were lovers. It was suddenly so anti-climactic, and I started to feel left behind when we hadn't ever really begun.

And then we were told that Michael was coming back to check in on us. He'd been in town for only two days when he came for the princess's visit, so he didn't hold any rehearsals, just gave notes to Martin and Tom who came around and told us what Michael had said. Plus, in six months we were to be replaced with a British cast, as mandated by British and US Actors' Equity, so Martin and Tom had been reporting on the progress of auditions, Tom expressing some qualms about British dancers who didn't have the same training as American Broadway dancers. He suggested that once the cast was finalized, he'd have to teach them to dance.

The day that Michael arrived, I had gone to the theater early to watch the auditions. Tom had suggested that I could help him once the cast was set. But when I arrived, it appeared that auditions had ended early. I couldn't find Tom and everyone else was gone, except for Martin and Michael, who stood near the wings and were engaged in a playful kind of banter that reminded me of the boyish antics of my two younger brothers, who would tease, pinch, and slug each other for fun. In this instance, though, Michael and Martin were kidding about the British actor who was the front-runner for the role of Paul, the coveted male role of a young Latino who tells the story of his father's discovery of his homosexuality. I couldn't hear all their words, but the intent was clear—Michael was in hot pursuit and Martin was ribbing him about it. Their shenanigans occupied all the space, so they didn't see me, and I turned around and headed for the door. We girls had our issues with "casting couch" situations, but sometimes, the boys had it worse. Sex was always a form of power, and seeing Martin play along was disappointing.

After the show that night, Martin informed us that Michael called rehearsal for the next day at ten a.m. Silently, we shared a cab home, my bones heavy with dread.

Michael screamed for the first half hour, baring his teeth like a rabid dog. I was afraid he was high. At one point, he turned to me, saying, "I can drive a truck through your lines, your delivery is so off." Then he lit into others, his rage growing with each lacerating criticism. He didn't want to hear about the rake or the cold or anything else. He worked us to death; even the rehearsal pianist looked at us with pity, taking his hands off the keys as we stumbled again and again through the opening sequence, a few of us falling. After dancing for several hours, Michael lined us up on the white line, just like in the show. He didn't want to hear our scripted lines; he wanted us to answer his questions as our real selves.

Olive was center stage. Her turn came before mine. She stepped forward, squinting and shielding her eyes, trying to see through the spotlight glare that beat down on us like an FBI interrogation and made Michael, who stood at the back of the house, invisible. Michael asked her where she was from.

"Akron, the *rubber* capital of the world. Like tires. Rubber." Even as the words slipped from her mouth, we *knew* she'd made a mistake. Her emphasis on rubber and breaking the syllables apart was just her impulsivity meant to lighten the air because that's what funny people do: They let the words slide straight from their brains to their tongues, without a filter.

But Michael roared from the back of the house, "GET OUT!" And he continued bellowing as he literally ran down the aisle. "GET *OUT.* GET *OFF* THE STAGE."

We served at the pleasure of Michael. If he did not want you, no Actor's Equity union contract or fancy employment lawyer could protect you. You were gone. Olive hadn't learned the lesson that I had from years of navigating my father's absolutism: Never openly challenge a powerful man, especially in public. Her words were innocuous, but that wasn't the point. The point was that Michael was punishing us, and we were meant to absorb the blows. By daring to alter the tone, Olive had threatened his authority, which is all he needed to eviscerate her.

Being fired like that could break a person. Maybe one of us had a college degree. Maybe a couple of us had gone to good high schools. But we didn't have skills that translated to the real world, and most of us didn't come from families who could provide a safety net.

I had heard about, but never experienced, the lethal cruelty of a Michael Bennett attack, the frenzy of unbounded violence, feeding on rage. When it happened, there was nothing I could do but watch, and then turn around that night and do the show, trying not to think, trying not to wonder whether the same could happen to me, even as I stood next to Olive's understudy in the same pink pool of light I used to share with Olive. I kept my mind blank, and instead, nailed myself to the ground, determined to do the best show I had ever done because I still had a chance, and if I committed to each performance as if it were my last, I could hope that my job would be there again tomorrow, the next night, and the night after that.

Back at my Baker Street flat, the scene lived inside me, the howl of his scream, and it paralyzed me, bizarrely conjuring my brothers' descriptions of my father's stories about practicing tailhook landings, of how he watched as my godfather went down in a fiery red explosion when he hit the deck of the aircraft carrier. There was nothing left of him, not even dog tags. And all the while, my dad was hugging the clouds, leveling his grip, because in the flight pattern—which cannot stop, which goes on no matter what—he was next in line to position his jet and capture that thin tinsel wire.

I had been next in line to Olive, but this wasn't war; this was business, and every one of us was replaceable. Still, I was sick each time I thought of Olive starting out at the Royal Drury Lane in London and (as I would later learn) ending up working at a box factory in LA.

London

—

1976

The first week after the incident, Olive's absence was a presence, an undeniable shadow circling her understudy. No one felt secure or special any longer, and that pall of fear sent us to our private retreats, shrinking groups of friendships within the cast. Privately, Martin confided that Michael had threatened his job the same day he'd thrown Olive off the stage, but Manny Azenberg had stepped in to resolve the situation. Martin hadn't done anything wrong; in fact, he'd been holding the production together when the cold and the rake were daily threats. Michael was merely asserting his power, sending the message that no one was safe, even if you were good at your job. Michael's penchant for destruction unleashed something in Martin, who considered the show a sacred thing, not something to beat and ravage in fits of uncontrollable rage. Martin also seemed to have mistakenly believed that Michael considered him part of his team.

The added stress from Michael's visit was a contributing factor to one dancer throwing out her back and another hurting his neck. Knowing that injuries were inevitable until we got off the raked stage, we stoically tried not to develop dread, the mental sinkhole usually appearing on Wednesday mornings when we were only two shows into the week and still healthy but faced two shows on that one day, a twelve-hour uphill stretch. That's

when the air thickened to mud and even thinking about flinging our arms and legs into that wall of sludge became mental
agony.

What helped motivate us was that we were momentarily
rich—almost all of us earning more money than we'd ever had
in our lives; and for people like Lydia and me, that was a ticket
to a better future. From the beginning, I had set financial goals
and helped Lydia do the same, arranging to have deductions
from our paychecks placed into accounts at the Actors Federal
Credit Union. Lydia was saving so that she and her husband
could buy a house in Queens; plus, she sent money to her mother who lived in the projects of Spanish Harlem where Lydia had
grown up. My plan, too, was to afford to live somewhere decent
once I returned to New York—married or not, I expected to
support myself. Part of my plan also included tuition money
for classes at the Royal Academy, more education that would
help secure my future.

Still, neither money nor a leading role was enough to keep
Lydia tethered. London was too starchy, the antithesis of her
Puerto Rican roots. She suffered abject homesickness, and
some days couldn't put on her tights, crying hysterically at
her dressing table. I coaxed her. "Think about your house in
Queens. C'mon, just get through it tonight. Maybe you'll have
an upstairs AND a basement."

But as the "Fifteen minutes" call blared over the backstage
intercom, I ran from our dressing room to find Martin, and, as
he had too many times with only ten minutes before curtain,
he grabbed Lydia's understudy and furiously poured her into a
costume in the final seconds before "Places." Martin believed
Lydia wasn't going to get over the hump, so in a couple of
weeks, she sat with him as he phoned Michael, and Michael

kindly let her out of her contract, his demeanor notably opposite of what it had been on the day he fired Olive. Lydia was
relieved, her old self again, joking and fanning herself with her
ticket home, until I put my head down on my dressing table
and cried.

Her leaving seemed a kind of failure that scared me as much
as Olive's firing. Two other dancers were now wearing knee
braces under their costumes, and everyone wondered, *Who's
next?* Martin spent his time trying to repair what had been a
seamless cohesion among the cast, a kind of kinetic chemistry
that was now unraveling. With me, he was distracted, which
heightened my feelings of insecurity. If initially I had been his
Pygmalion fantasy, something that he no longer had energy
for, I was still the girl in the process of becoming real. I wanted
nothing more than to feel the dewy deliciousness of my awakening and have him there beside me. But we were out of sync,
a precarious fragility exposed when I thought what we had was
carved in stone. Then, several disquieting nights arrived all
with the same pattern: Martin calling me very late from a red
phone box on the corner.

"Did I wake you? Can I come up?" He'd come from the
bars, which hadn't been fun. The first night, he harped about
Michael's threat, the humiliation of it becoming a trigger, un-
stoppering some deep and toxic past. He spoke with urgency,
"I don't care who touches me, just so long as I am touched."
And I understood the long-term damage inflicted on everyone who'd survived the abuse of a culture that degraded and
shamed you for being gay. Clearly, gay people only had the
social outlets of bath houses or bars. He called on several more
occasions, staying for an hour or so and then, exhausted, leaving for his apartment. I might not see him the next day until

half hour, when he'd make his rounds through the dressing rooms, and I'd hug him without a word.

I shared his pain as best I could, and if I were still in my "awakening," I was now in it alone. Furthermore, Keith would be arriving for his London visit, as would Brett, two more lumps congealing in my throat. But I stuck to my plan, plunging myself into interviews with teachers at the Royal Academy and setting start dates for private lessons after Brett's visit.

Every day, I went to the theater a little earlier, and most times, was the only one there. I loved sitting on the bare stage and breathing in the animated stillness of the old, empty playhouse before heading to my dressing room to begin the process of leaving behind my personal life so I could immerse myself in that other, better me. I'd seen enough to know that fear makes you small, so I rolled my hair in hot rollers, put on my tights, then my second pair of tights, warmed up by elongating my spine against my legs, making space between bones in the way that every stretch is a metaphor for what needs to be accommodated by both mind and body. I breathed through my concerns about Martin's wounds, confusion about what we meant to each other, and frustrations with Brett: that I'd always paid half the rent, half the Con Ed bill, and half the grocery bill. Even in London, I sent him my half share every month to maintain the lease on our apartment. Having a home was important to me, but why didn't my financial contributions—equal to his—entitle me to a full and equal share of a professional life? That's where it got sticky: I was supposed to be a part of his life, but why couldn't the reverse be true? Did a demanding career and financial independence undermine the value of what made a girl feminine or attractive? I put on my shoes and buckled them tight, hearing Tommy Tune's advice: "Use what you have."

With an eight p.m. curtain and two p.m. matinee, the Drury Lane became my cathedral, a place where I could channel whatever was in my head or heart to the story that lived inside the show. The few steps from the wings to the stage provided a seamless entry, and from there, every line delivered or sung resonated with personal relevance, the script itself providing a road map so that each time I stepped beyond the white line into the no-man's-land at the edge of the stage, I felt the surety of a *you are here* marker. I opened myself to the expectant darkness, admitting with my first line, "I don't know where to begin." And each time, in response, the warmth of an attentive universe came back to me.

When Brett finally arrived, I was anxious to the point of nausea. After the show, he told me I was wonderful, and I knew he meant it. Then later, at the flat, he came up behind me to hand me a glass of wine, and I suddenly felt him, his height, the solidity of his frame against me, the way I *knew* him. "Come here." I knew he wanted me to sit on his lap. I had once loved the feeling of his strength and was willing to surrender because of the safety it implied. I didn't have to do too much or be too brave because he liked me small. I moved away. "What?" he asked.

"Nothing. Nothing. I just want to be able to look at you, talk face-to-face." And then we had a lot of sex, and he made his plans, getting tickets to all the other shows playing in London.

His small theater had been a resounding triumph. He had discovered scripts and mounted productions that attracted Broadway and film producers, not to mention stars. He was cocky, saying he could attract headliners because, "Commercial theater is just not very good." I wished a bit of his cockiness would extend to me and my career, but as much as he had said I was wonderful, he never added anything about looking for something we could work on together.

I went to the Drury Lane, and Brett saw shows all over the East and West End. We never talked about our future, except for him telling me about the new apartment he'd rented for us with the money I was sending. "You're going to love it. You'll turn it into a fabulous home once you get off the road."

I pretended that I didn't hear him.

Martin hadn't met Brett and I hadn't formally met Keith, so Martin decided the four of us should have a *quick* dinner between shows on a Saturday. I dreaded it but found Keith to be mild mannered and quiet, accepting of me and the closeness Martin and I shared. Martin had confided that he'd told Keith all about me. Keith only spoke when I asked him direct questions, which left plenty of room for Martin and Brett to compete for the alpha male position. Maybe it was over my soup and their burgers, Martin stopping midstream. "You eat meat?"

And Brett replied, "Of course I eat meat. And have sugar in my coffee, too."

To which Martin turned to me and said, "I'm going to remember that."

I kicked Martin under the table. I hadn't eaten meat for several years. Vegetarianism was popular among dancers, and although I gave each of them a pass for being carnivores, I was frequently annoying about sugar, removing it from the breakfast table and reminding them to read food labels.

The conversation turned to New York, where they both knew the same people, so they bantered and dropped names,

Martin taking an unfair swipe: "How many seats in your theater?"

"The number of seats doesn't matter. What matters is the work," he said, and he rattled off stars who'd performed at his theater.

Each cemented himself to an opposite side of the same avenue, and thank God it was over in little more than an hour. Afterward, Brett gave me a big, huge kiss in front of Martin and Keith, going off to another show in the West End, while I went back to my dressing room to rest before the evening performance. By the end of the week, I was exhausted and looking forward to being alone so I could fully immerse myself in my lessons. Brett hadn't arrived with an engagement ring, which didn't surprise me, and underscored the fact that marriage didn't come up once.

Once Brett left, I started my lessons. To my new teachers, I was legitimate. According to them, my background in the disciplined world of dance was enough to qualify me, which exemplified the more inclusive attitude of British theater. My teachers' perspectives made me feel less like a dancer learning to sing and act and more like a professional striving to explore the full range of her ability and craft. In the first weeks, they described what they believed was within my scope and recommended the types of parts I ought to explore: slightly over-the-top characters with a whiff of physicality or zaniness; for example, a working girl, a waitress, a detective, someone who was slightly off-center from the typical professional. The other type of character was a young woman grappling with significant circumstances. They suggested that I may someday have the capacity to play leading roles, but that I needed to grow into that responsibility by concentrating on cameo parts. Their assessment provided me with a potential shape to a career that might even include film, something I hadn't ever thought about.

When I called Brett and enthusiastically told him I'd been assigned a classical monologue—Millamant's dressing-table scene from Congreve's *The Way of the World*—he said, "That's good. She's assigned in a lot of introductory classes," which was insulting.

Martin, along with Tom, had become heavily involved in rehearsals with the newly hired British cast, plus Tom was notating the choreography of the show for Michael, something that needed to be done if the show was to expand into the future. Tom's Marine Corps experience infused him with precision, his dance charts looking like war-game grids, with each character marked in a specific spot at a specific point in each number. I asked him if he had time to work out with me so that I could keep up my dance technique, ever mindful of the rake. "Actually," he said, "why don't you come to Cassie rehearsals? I have to teach the dance to the British cast members, and I could use an American dancer to help demonstrate." Wow. That was an idea. Cassie was the lead part in *A Chorus Line*, and her dance solo would be a juicy challenge.

One Saturday matinee, about a month after Brett had gone back to New York City, I suddenly felt as if I were bursting, the sensation building as I spent Sunday in a suffocating panic. I had a list of doctors provided by our company business manager, so after not sleeping at all, I called on Monday morning and got an appointment before Wednesday's matinee.

Not one girl I knew in the show, in any show, in any class, for the entire time I had been living in NYC, was on the pill. We couldn't afford the five-to-ten-pound weight gain courtesy of the high doses of hormones. Relying on other forms of contraception was complicated by the fact that many of us never had regular periods—I once went a year without—the consequence of extreme physical demands on our bodies. If there were a "safe" time, none of us knew exactly when that was, another reason why it was frustrating that no man would wear a condom.

In the less than three minutes it took the doctor to walk out of the exam room and come back with the results, I pretty much determined that if I had sole responsibility for birth control, the choice to end a pregnancy was mine alone. When he confirmed the fact, I asked, "Is abortion legal in London?"

"Yes, miss. It is."

"Then I need to have one immediately." I signed my name for the one Saturday appointment that was still available.

In high school, a friend of mine got pregnant, so her parents allowed her to marry at sixteen, and she quit school. I knew two girls who'd had abortions during the time it was illegal in the United States. One had died; the other had been taken by her parents to Mexico. I had followed closely the contraception and abortion battles leading to *Roe v. Wade* and had always believed in the right of a woman to make her own choices. Still, abortion was never discussed in my family—my parents likely believing we had immunity from such problems.

But I wasn't immune, and leaving the doctor's office, I turned the wrong way up Harley Street, then backtracked toward the Tube, which I took straight to the theater. I cleared off my dressing table, scrubbed it, then rearranged all my stage makeup, throwing out old lipsticks and noting what needed to be replaced. When that was done, I headed down the stairs to Martin's office.

"You're here early."

"I need to talk to you. Close the door."

"What's wrong?"

"I'm pregnant."

He just stared. "Are you sure?"

"I saw a doctor on Harley Street this morning."

"What's his name?" Martin got out a piece of paper.

"I need Saturday off, possibly Monday."

"Okay. Do you need money?"

"They want half in cash, up front. Then, they'll bill me."

"I can get cash, if you need it. Don't take out money against your credit card." He didn't flinch when I told him the price, which was almost a month's salary at my pay grade.

"I probably can come up with most of the first part."

"Just do what you can and pay me back, or you know what—forget it; just tell me what you need."

"I'll pay you back."

"I don't care about the money. Whatever you need is yours. Just go get it done."

"Martin . . ."

"Don't tell him. Don't you dare tell Brett until it's over. He'll try to talk you out of it or ask you to wait, and you can't wait. You can't. Where do you go?"

"The office on Harley Street. A car and driver will take me to a clinic out of town. But I have to get home from there on my own."

"Where? Never mind. I'll get the address. What time?"

"Four, four thirty."

"Okay. I'll find a way to come get you." Martin turned in his chair and began writing everything down. "Are you okay?"

"No. I'm scared." I wiped a few tears away but told myself

not to go there until after the show, feeling that once I started crying, I might not stop.

"Don't get talked out of it. You can't leave and come back. Don't be naive. It's you—the girl—who always loses."

On Saturday, at five a.m., I climbed into the front seat of a black Mercedes sedan as two other women chatting in Spanish slid into the back, each perfectly made up with heavy eyeliner and red lipstick and wearing Ferragamo shoes—as if they were going out to dinner at an expensive restaurant.

We drove in the rain for an hour, and by six a.m., arrived at a beautiful estate. The driver continued along a private, tree-lined driveway, which led to a white-columned country mansion. Inside, nurses in white uniforms and caps held clipboards, and one escorted me up a marble stairway. *This is how rich people have abortions*, I thought. The nurse spoke to me in Spanish, assuming I was Spanish because Saturday was the day women came from Spain to have their pregnancies terminated, but I was too terrified to remember any of the words I'd learned in high school.

The last thing I heard was her repeating, *"Tres, dos, uno,"* as she inserted something into my IV.

Then I was awake in a room. There was a tray of cookies and some tea. The nurse entered, smiled, motioned that I could get up. She brought more food, then left me alone. It was 3:08 p.m. by the clock. I looked out the window, held on to the railing of the bed and did a few plies, stretched out my legs and back. When the nurse entered again, she gave me a sheet printed with instructions in English and pointed to my clothes.

By four thirty Martin was waiting in the grand foyer, the yellow sunshine falling in sheets behind him. He hugged me, took my hand, and led me out to the waiting car. I didn't know his friend. "A former trick who has a car," Martin described to me under his breath and shrugged.

The trick took one look at me and nodded. "Looks like quite a day camp for girls."

"Shut up," Martin warned.

They drove me back to Martin's flat, where he had made a bed for me in the living room, and Keith had put out tea. Martin left for the show and Keith went out. I was numb, just repeating to myself, *It's over; you're going to make your way back from this*, but then the residue from the anesthesia took over. I fell asleep, and much later woke up to laughing voices—Keith's and others, but not Martin's. It was the sound of a group of men having a wonderful time.

I felt fine the next day, so told Martin I was going back to my apartment, and though he tried to talk me out of it, I insisted.

The story was that I had a bad strep throat. I called my teachers to cancel the week of lessons and went back to the show on Tuesday. I was nervous, but ironically, no one seemed to notice anything different about me, which was a relief because I felt ravaged, the feeling having less to do with the abortion than a raw and stony clarity about the *facts* of my predicament. In the first few days, I relied on discipline and ultimate trust in my body, doing extra warm-ups, resting during the day, eating well.

Ten days later, during my follow-up exam on Harley Street, the nurse asked, "How are you feeling, miss? Do you have any regrets?"

"No."

"Oh." She seemed disappointed. "Some women who come in do have regrets, and we recommend they talk to a counselor."

110

"Thank you. But I have no regrets. None at all."

Getting pregnant was bad luck. I did not feel guilty; I felt stupid and angry that sex was between two people, even though only one suffered the consequences. Men already controlled my appearance, my weight, and my livelihood, but I'd fight to my dying day before I'd let any man decide when I was going to be a mother, especially because having a baby would likely end my career. No business, let alone show business, accommodated mothers; I couldn't take a leave of absence, for example. Brett and every other man would never have to make such a difficult choice, but if they did, I was sure they would choose as I had.

I again went to the theater earlier and earlier, sometimes warming up with insane jumping jacks and burpees, exercises we learned in middle school PE. My head was full of humming heat, my brain sizzling in a frying pan, especially as we sang, "What I Did for Love," which took on the additional weight of a very personal choice. Later, I began having imaginary conversations with the children of my future, as if they were real and reasonable adults hearing my story. I told them I couldn't bring them into the world until I had the means to give them a chance at a good life. I'd get there; I just wasn't there yet. I felt a palpable connection to them, even though they were only ideas talking to me.

After that, I went on the pill and called Brett to tell him I'd had an abortion. We floundered, at first trying to discuss the specifics on the phone, but then he said he was "hurt" and resented "being left out," which was when he blew it because the first thing I needed to hear was that he would have been willing to support me and the baby. His voice got louder, mentioning his feelings, never saying that he'd have been willing to leave his theater job—something that would have been necessary if we were going to rely solely on his income. So, there it was: The consequence for me was a consequence he was not willing to accept for himself.

Within six weeks, I weighed 117 pounds, so in deference to my career, I stopped taking the pill. I had rehearsals with Tom, voice lessons to practice, and lines to memorize for my acting teacher. In a way, the personal removed itself from my daily life, and I wondered if I were growing cold or bitter. But I told myself that I'd lived a similarly solitary life during my first years in New York. Now, I had my monologues or the show, places to let my feelings out.

I didn't go home for Thanksgiving, though Suzanne and Jeffrey were getting married. I couldn't take the time off and was secretly relieved, knowing the gap between my old life and the new was too wide; it was better to stick with my lessons. My singing improved technically but rarely felt organic, while there were times in acting when my fear of forgetting lines was replaced with a gushing fluency and a connection to both the character and myself. Those moments were intoxicating.

So was dancing with Tom in the Cassie rehearsals. We were a natural pair, like ice dancers, because of the way our bodies matched up. Once I learned the choreography, he rehearsed it with me, not by watching, but by physically shadowing me. He had laser accuracy and was taller, stronger, and quicker, his shadowing pushing me in a stretch from wing to wing. The music set the pace, but he set the distance and the nuance—every jeté or arm movement powered by a thousand silent yearnings. A dance is a physical monologue for which there is no other vocabulary, and Tom shared with me the love and surrender to the language we knew best.

Gypsy Life
—
1977

After we closed in London, we returned to the United States, becoming a traveling group of show people, setting up and packing up in Baltimore, Detroit, Miami, San Francisco, and Washington, DC. The 18-wheelers arrived at the rear entrance of each new theater and the crew swarmed, carrying the Mylar and mirrored flats, the lights, and our costumes. We lived in residential hotels or short-term rentals, spending one to four months at each stop, an experience of nomadism that, with each uprooting, gave me more mental space. I had the luxury of my work and an unknown place to wander, my books and sewing, while Martin and other friends in the cast took the pulse of each new city by visiting the gay bars.

At one point, Martin suggested I take a weekend off to see Brett as we hadn't seen each other since before the abortion. "Choose a place equidistant so you both travel about the same distance." Martin reasoned that I could call in sick over a weekend, so I phoned Brett, who agreed to the plan. We settled on Atlanta, a Peachtree hotel that I heard about and idealistically suggested because the name portended springtime, renewal. I wrote Brett an impassioned letter, saying I hoped we could move forward, that all along I had imagined a relationship where we were a dynamic couple, each of us a successful professional working hard in our individual careers, harkening back to the sentiment in his Fritz Perls poster.

On the Monday of my return, Martin kept me company in my dressing room. "So, did you meet up at the airport? The timing work?"

"Yep. Thanks again for letting me off." I was brushing on blush, looking at both my face and his in the mirror.

"So?"

"He'd run from rehearsal to the airport, just making his flight. I wore my new dress."

"I like that one."

"We bought a new chair."

"Furniture?"

"We never bought furniture before. Only some plants. You'd like it—clean Scandinavian lines."

"So?"

"Hand me my shoes." I pointed to the new ones sitting on the floor.

"How often do you get these?"

"Every couple of months. I'm hard on my feet."

"The red dress, right?"

"I guess it was great—you know—being in a hotel, having maid service."

"So."

"He didn't have time to change. He'd run from rehearsal; his hair was greasy, his shirt a mess, and he had dirt under his fingernails." I buckled my shoes.

"Okay, sweetness."

"It was so disappointing. Am I awful?"

"No. He could have done something to make you feel that you're special."

I was trying to miss Brett, but what I was missing was reassurance about the type of partnership I aspired to and had described in my letter. At the same time, my more practical side worried that life on the road had tainted my perspective, made it easy to forget what days, weeks, and months would be like when my contract ended and I'd be back in New York, unemployed, without the community of the show. Life shrank quickly when you didn't have a job that boosted your confidence eight times a week, and I knew well how easily life with Brett could grow thin with his seemingly insignificant needs. *Can you do the laundry? I won't be home until late but will you* . . . The blandness of his requests, even as I was paying my half of the financial share, horrified me and felt more sickening because in the past, that domestic trap had come naturally. I'd been confused, thinking it was love, the pairing of love and confusion always an ongoing theme.

In Baltimore, my family visited for a weekend, John traveling from NYC, joining my parents who arrived with my younger brothers from Santa Fe. For some reason, my father couldn't join my mother and brothers at the matinee performance, so he attended the evening show the night before. In my dressing room, he hugged me, and I felt a heave in his chest, like he was crying, but my father never cried. "I'm so proud of you," he said, "I wish your grandmother was alive, and I could tell her about you." He looked at me with admiration, something I'd never expected.

My brothers remarked how amazing it was to sit in the audience and see me on the stage, and my mother was thrilled, too, even as she commented on the girls' leotards: "Your leotard is cut up so high on the thigh. In fact, all the girls' leotards are cut high. That's *new*. You didn't used to wear your leotard that way."

"It's the leg line; the costume designer emphasizes our legs."

"Oh. Well, it didn't used to be that way."

"That's true; it didn't." The more revealing leg line was a substitute for what really worried her: my confidence. She was keen, correctly sensing how my independence may raise issues with Brett, with marrying. For the rest of the visit, she looked at me with distance, and for the first time, I welcomed that, because if she couldn't be completely *for me*, then at least she might stop nit-picking.

After Baltimore, Martin and I shared a two-bedroom apartment in Detroit. "C'mon. We have to see the new Renaissance Center. It's opening the tower, the big new renewal project to bring back Detroit." We also went to some dazzling, eye-popping drag shows. I absolutely loved them, especially visiting the dressing rooms—red and gold and blue glittering gowns hanging like aerial gardens, rows of wigs and shoes snaking across tables, jar upon jar of rouge and powders, all of it illuminated by hot white lights and a network of mirrors reflecting front, back, and sideways, the dazzle of transformation. And the queens—every one of them—beautiful, though I was particularly fond of one with an inviting, smoky voice.

Later I said to Martin, "You know what I want?"

"What?"

"That voice. Her voice."

"You can bet she didn't get it from singing in the choir."

"I'm sure she paid dearly for a sound like that. But still, that's what I'd like."

"Okay, sweetness."

"What? You think a girl can't be sweet and have a voice like that?"

"No, I don't. I think that kind of gravel is some hard-earned agency."

On Easter weekend as we were getting ready to head to Miami, Keith and some friends of Martin's arrived. On Sunday, our day off, Martin and I had to get our trunks packed, but I'd insisted on celebrating the holiday.

"Oh . . . like *realpeople?*"

"You don't like Easter eggs?" I was getting a cake in the oven while he organized his piles: jeans, denim or corduroy shirts, and always only black or blue socks.

"Are these Peeps in my socks? I love Peeps."

Keith came in from their bedroom. "I found chocolate eggs in my shoes." He held the extra suitcase he would take back to the city for Martin and me once we filled it with our winter clothes.

The others—Maurizio, Phillip, and Jack Ward—Martin's friends from various ports, were camping out on the foldout couches, moving back and forth between the showers and the kitchen.

"Jelly beans. We got jelly beans!"

Maurizio, a hairdresser from Miami, said that if the boys wanted their haircuts, he needed something more upbeat, so Nina Simone was traded out for Latin salsa, and Phillip, a construction engineer from San Francisco, stuck his head under the kitchen faucet while Maurizio set up his barbershop. I put eggs on to boil.

Hair piled up on the floor of the open kitchen/dining area, and I warned Maurizio that I didn't want strands in my frosting, which elicited a few gross jokes that I ignored. A knock on the door got louder, and Martin said, "It's probably David. He gets bored being with Nancy," referring to David's girlfriend who had been given an understudy part after London and wasn't very social. David walked in, saw the hair on the floor, the frosting and coconut on the table, everyone mamboing to the Tito Puente beat, and Martin threw his arms into the air: "Welcome to Christine's gay bar!"

"What?"

"It's just funny. All of us and you, sweetness."

"But—"

"I didn't mean anything. It's just the way it is, our family."

Yes, indeed. I spread the frosting thickly around the perimeter of the cake. It *was* the way it was, but I heard a distorted echo of Brett's "fag hag" accusation.

Jack Ward had been reading on the couch, trained, as he said, to tune out all the riffraff from his weekly transatlantic crossings as an airline steward. "What else did you buy?"

"A chicken."

"Lovely. I'll take charge of that, shall I?" He washed his immaculate hands in the sink, then rinsed and dressed the chicken.

"Did you get kits to dye the eggs?"

"Yes."

"But let's set some aside for deviling, shall we?"

"Deviling . . . yes!"

"Look what I have." Maurizio pulled out a bag of feathers, sequins, beads, and glue, remnants from some of the drag shows where he'd been a hairdresser.

As soon as Phillip's hair was cut and Maurizio had given him a shave, he put on his tool belt and went to my room to figure out the problem with the lock on my trunk. When he came back to the kitchen, he said to me, "You should find a stagehand in Miami—"

"She could have any stagehand, or any man, for that matter," chimed Martin. "You should see how they drool over her." And he looked at me then with the full weight of what befuddled him: that I was physically loyal to Brett, a fact he found appalling even as it held him in awe. The only man who ever tempted me, still tempted me, was Martin. And he knew it.

He'd called this group *our family*. All of them, plus Tom, offered me true affection and had made a place for me in a world to which I could never really belong, the hard part about it being that it was also the only world I'd experienced that respected my sense of personal agency. Gay men understood a lot about straight women like me, relating to how we were expected to divide ourselves in half. I wished for a time and place for all of us that would be less boxed in by rigid identities, groupings, and expectations—not just for me, but for them, too. I looked around the table, knowing that the way I straddled two worlds kept me in a chronic state of aloneness, but that was the trade-off. Martin and Tom were the only people in the world who kept me moving toward my dream, believing that it was not only legitimate, but also viable.

We went from Detroit to a short stop in Miami and then to San Francisco, where we were booked for a three-month engagement. On the first Saturday, the new head of the film/television department from my agency called, asking if I could come to LA.

"On Sunday?"

"Yeah. There's a party on the beach in Malibu. I can introduce you to people." I asked if there was an audition. "No. It's different in LA," he explained. "The people here need to see you first."

"Oh, so my credits don't really count?"

"Well, sure, they're interested that you're a dancer and have that look and all. Why don't you just come down?"

"Let me check the rehearsal schedule. We haven't officially opened."

"I thought you could get off. This is a chance in LA. It would be fun for you."

"Sure, but I can't just leave town without asking the stage manager."

"Okay. Leave me a message."

I left a message later saying that I had rehearsal, then seethed with Martin and Tom. "I've paid 10 percent of my salary, every week for an entire year, thousands of dollars that, so far, only got me that phone call!"

Around the same time, Jimmy (James) Kirkwood, who coauthored the book of *A Chorus Line*, showed up backstage at the Curran. He wasn't part of Michael's team, having his own success as a writer of books and plays, but always dropped by a theater if he was in town where the show was playing. Early on, I'd told him I liked his books (*There Must Be a Pony!* and *P.S. Your Cat Is Dead*) which had made an impression because he said most dancers didn't even know that he was a published writer. In San Francisco, I ran into him backstage near the mailboxes, where he talked about what he was working on, and then he asked me if I write. "Sort of."

"Well, here's my advice. Stop talking. Don't talk." He winked and walked away.

A few weeks more and Brett arrived for a visit; I hadn't seen him for two months, since the Peachtree weekend, but this time he looked great in a freshly pressed shirt, and he brought gifts, though no engagement ring. He stood like he always stood, a sameness to him that made me feel he was ready to pick up where we left off—not at the Peachtree, and not in London, but from where we left off in the days before I ever got my job. Suddenly, and without premeditation, words stumbled out of my mouth: "I can't . . . I don't . . ." I had to sit down; it was so wrenching: a swoosh, like being pulled backward, a very sure feeling that he'd always win, and I'd be smothered because my dream was inconvenient.

When I said I couldn't continue, he fell apart, which was awful, and all I wanted was for him to leave so I didn't have to see the painful mess that had become of us. I said I'd pay my share of the rent until I returned to NYC and had the chance to move my things out of the apartment I'd never lived in. That way, he had at least four months to adjust.

Martin was at the theater when I arrived.

"You're early."

"Brett and I broke up today."

"Long time coming."

"That's what you think; I'm stunned."

"But you'll be better. You'll see."

But I didn't get better; I only had less of a burden. Some part of me would always be sad about the failure of our relationship.

My grandmother, who lived in San Francisco, was a big comfort, and Tom allowed me to invite her to one of my Cassie rehearsals. She brought my aunt Marion, her sister. When rehearsal was over, I stepped off the stage, dripping with sweat and out of breath. They each wore hats, silk dresses, and held white gloves in their hands.

"You were lovely. So lovely," said Aunt Marion.

Nana Helen, known for her dramatic flair, added, "I was at

the Colosseum in Rome when Isadora danced. We wept, it was so beautiful . . . and now . . . here you are."

Tom told Michael during one of their phone calls that he'd taught me the Cassie dance, so Michael said he'd like to see the work when we got to Washington, DC, the next and last stop on the tour, when our contracts were set to expire. I didn't know what to think—only that I had to dance well.

Then, a month before the end of the San Francisco run, a new understudy for the lead role of Zack joined us. He was tall, with a romantic, movie-star look about him. I didn't pay too much attention until I accidentally bumped into him backstage. His dark hair fell in a curl across his forehead.

"You're Christine," he said.

"Yes. I play her, but that's my name, too, just spelled differently."

"I'm Chad."

After the abortion, my libido had waned, but suddenly and rashly, having freed myself of any obligation to Brett, I took the plunge. I was tired of being lonely, and it was comforting to be in bed with someone. Chad started rehearsing the Cassie scenes with me when I told him I had to do them for Michael once we arrived in Washington, DC. Martin looked at him and looked at me and shrugged, then stopped dropping by my dressing room. Another signal, besides our contracts expiring after Washington, that life on the road was coming to an end.

Transitions

1978–1979

At Kennedy Center, I danced and read lines for Michael, who said, "Okay. Why don't you start working with the musical director on the song? I'll give you a 'floating' position. Stay with the company through Philadelphia and then return to New York. I'll pay you a base salary of two hundred dollars per week in New York to keep working on Cassie and be ready on a moment's notice to fly to any company in case of an emergency."

His words were sun-showers raining down, making everything I'd done in the last year worth it and appeasing the growing panic I'd begun to feel about returning to New York, jobless and without a place to live since I'd broken up with Brett. Tom was thrilled and hugged me. I immediately called Laughlin, who was finishing his last year of law school at Georgetown. "Fantastic!" he said. "Why don't you come with me to Italy over Christmas. You'll need a break before going back to NYC, and invite Chad—that's his name, right?—if you want." So, I invited Chad, who accepted; extended my contract through Philadelphia; and bought my ticket to Rome.

Tom had finished the dance charts of the show, which were being duplicated so that every cast now and in the future would have them as a guide, and Michael rewarded him with a supervisory position, traveling among the three *Chorus Line* companies, adding new cast members as needed and keeping each production in good shape. He left before we closed in Washington, both of us celebrating together what we hoped were new futures, and confident we'd see each other in New York. Martin, on the other hand, who'd been increasingly restless since we left Detroit, was more aloof, seemingly because he was focused on his new job—a new Manny Azenberg production that would get him off the road and back home for at least a year. On our final night in Washington, before "Places" was called, I ran to him, but he waved me away with typical avoidance of anything remotely sentimental. He wasn't ever going to give me a card, much less a trinket, I knew *that*, but I stood my ground, holding out my arms to his refusal. What we had wasn't just a flimsy structure built on the residue of showtime magic. But he turned his back to me, calling "Places!" into his headset, so I marched to my spot in the wings, whispering, "*You coward!*"

I settled in an apartment in Philadelphia with Chad, not wondering if our relationship was serious, just happy to have companionship. He had decided to give his notice and leave the company when I was leaving because Michael didn't offer him the role of Zack when it became available in the touring production, and he didn't want to remain an understudy. I wondered about his decision to give up his job but assumed he knew what he was doing. We finished our contracts and flew straight to Italy.

Being with Laughlin was heaven. He took us to the mosaics in Ravenna and told me the story of the day he first saw *David*—how he cried because he'd been so overwhelmed by the celebration of a man's body. He calmed me when I said I was nervous about returning to New York, not knowing where to live, feeling exhausted from a year and a half on the road and literally having done over six hundred shows without more than a week's break. Laughlin's answer was to tour me through art and history, as if they were his personal companions; he didn't have answers to all his life's conundrums, but his pursuit took him to places where beauty and imagination had transformed the dark ages forever. He inspired me to look to the world, the immensity of its undertakings—a bit grand and abstract, but still, thought-provoking and expansive—while Chad was often grumpy, overtly frustrated by Italian timetables (completely unreliable) and the lack of English-speaking people. I ignored his moods, thinking they were a waste of energy when we had this singular opportunity to immerse ourselves in an entirely different world.

He offered to find an apartment for us to share if I wanted us to live together in New York, and I accepted, feeling reassured that he understood what I wanted for my career. Overall, it seemed a companionship worth exploring. He was, in many ways, opposite of me, a dynamic Martin frequently attributed to the success of his personal relationship with Keith and professional relationship with David. We arrived in NYC in early January when it was bitter cold and empty. In the eighteen months I'd been gone, friends had moved away or to LA and my old haunts had changed. I was starting over, even though it was from a slightly different place.

At first, the rhythm of daily life was disorienting. No longer on vacation and without the routine of an eight p.m. curtain or a two p.m. matinee, I watched dusk arrive before the moon rose, the planets marking time. I quickly got to dance classes and scheduled voice lessons, trying to re-create a connection to my creative life as the days began to shrink with a vacancy of loss. I felt severed from a source of vitality, like someone had died, or I'd lost a limb in an accident. The feeling was all-consuming. When I asked Chad if he, too, felt that life was muted without the camaraderie and work of the show, he said, "Not really."

I clung to the fact that I had an agent and the Cassie stand-by job, which—although hard to admit—had begun to feel like a slippery bargain. I was offered no formalized rehearsals and no one in the Broadway staff knew me. The isolation was terrifying, given the responsibility. It was a physically demanding role, something that required daily workouts and practice. But I existed outside the show's universe, only tethered to it by a daily fifteen-second phone call to a person I'd never met, asking him if an emergency had arisen. It was up to me to stay in performance shape and rehearse the dance, song, and lines. I considered renting a studio space because the stage manager said I could only occasionally come to the Shubert; the stagehand's union controlled the hours the stage could be used outside of performances. When I did get an hour, Chad came with me, moving the single work lamp from the floor and rehearsing the lines with me before I practiced the song and dance to the tinny sound of my tape recorder. Afterwards, I took Tom's charts and walked myself through all the various Cassie positions onstage during each dance number, marking, *The right foot is parallel to the wing, the left shoulder is . . .* and praying that if I ever went on for the part, I would have several *real* rehearsals with a full cast and at least a musician playing the piano.

It took six weeks for the nightmare to swoop in. On a Tuesday night, I suddenly had to do a matinee performance in New York the next day, then fly out that evening to stand by in Cleveland for the weekend. At the Shubert, I was given a fresh pair of tights, a red leotard, and a dance skirt. I brought my own shoes, and Tom, who was in town, came. I had never rehearsed the dance onstage with the spotlights or the mirrors that flew in from the rafters, so Tom warned never to venture beyond the white line because the edge of the stage disappeared in the lights, making it easy to fall into the pit. I had never sung with the orchestra. Tom was anxious about the lack of real stage preparation, and just as I began to pray in the wings, I overheard a cast member I didn't know whisper, "She's *too young*." Later, Tom said that I'd danced beautifully, and the scenes were okay, meaning the rest was crap. I hadn't rooted myself to the ground, claimed my space. I told Tom that I'd felt overwhelmed having to check every second to make sure I was standing on the right spot, so the mirrors didn't land on my head, or I didn't fall into the pit, the technicalities distracting me from playing the truth of her. The orchestra was so loud. My voice got tight, the pressure building inside until I was claustrophobic, trapped in a box of spinning red lights.

In those days, no one ever talked about anxiety, the mental stress on young performers, who, like athletes, could cave smack in the middle of very public, high-stakes competition. But that's what happened to me. Performers rehearse over and over until we are overprepared. We know our spots, where our feet land, every change in a light cue. That's our insurance, the safeguard we put in place so we can fully give ourselves to the music, intention, choreography, and words, and ignore everything else that isn't the story we're telling. Without that scaffolding in place, I was exposed, so naked, standing before a thousand people, and I couldn't get control.

It was humiliating, and I carried that psychic devastation to the airport, where it shadowed me in Cleveland as I repeated the failure. I couldn't shake off the shame; there was no time to process, to talk to someone, anyone, who might know something about the total collapse of faith, and what that meant when you were expected to always and everywhere PERFORM with flawlessness. So perhaps it was that I was too young, or maybe too green, but it was also that I was *human and alone.*

Michael's business manager fired me as soon as I got home from Cleveland, and I accepted the news with blistering relief, knowing that I couldn't make the job work under such isolated conditions.

I called my agent, who, interestingly, didn't think it was such a big deal, and said he'd start getting me into commercial auditions and some soap opera casting offices. Still, I was haunted. Martin listened quietly when I told him. He, at least, understood, giving me a pep talk and then later helping me get an audition for his new show, *Whose Life Is It Anyway?* I was still raw, and it was my first ever audition for a straight play. Martin said later that I came off as shy, a bit too timid for a young nurse dealing with a paraplegic. I knew I disappointed him, especially because he'd talked to Manny Azenberg about me.

Two months back in from life on the road and I was back to the cliff edge of self-doubt and auditioning, where you had *one* chance, never an opportunity to go back or redo. Auditioning is a freakish process, most times leaving you an orphan because had it worked out, the job that materializes is the most substantial thing you could ever know. I added an acting workshop to my voice and dance lessons and dusted off my sewing machine, making elaborate velvet pillows and practicing the

"Use what you have" mantra, trying, day by day, to rebuild my confidence.

Chad met with a writing partner to work on developing an idea for a new show. He had no interest in commercials or film work and was focused instead on bigger things like producing or directing. Unlike me, he'd never invested in getting an agent; he had a good voice, which he thought was something he could rely on if other opportunities in the business didn't come his way. By spring, without something concrete to show for our efforts, I turned inward, packing my disappointed and discouraged self into deeper feelings of doubt, while he got angry, an emotion he relied on to lift his spirits. I'd never been around a person who processed life that way, seen how anger fuels a form of entitlement, which seemed to me a twisted form of confidence. Still, we kept ourselves busy with our individual projects, then together, began restoring furniture that we bought at a local thrift shop.

My agent eventually pulled through with an audition for a soap opera, a part I believed I could play. My classes had helped me regain some of my footing, and Chad coached me. He also picked out my outfit: pink high heels and a white knit dress that clung to my body like spray paint. I read for the casting director and several producers, who then asked me to wait in the hall. In my second reading, I wasn't nervous the way I had been when I auditioned for Martin and Manny Azenberg, this part less restrained and having room for me to add some physical flair. The casting director said he'd call my agent, who reported back, "Whatever you wore and did, man oh man, you turned their heads around. The casting director said that when you walked in, you stopped them cold. Evidentially, you're not quite right, but one of the producers said they ought to get you on the show, even if they have to write something *new*."

The feedback filled me with hope and renewed faith, although nothing ended up materializing. Then I booked a commercial, and a second one, as Proctor & Gamble, Coke, Pepsi, and Dr. Pepper were suddenly mad for dancing commercials. Chad had stopped working with his writing partner and took a singing part in the chorus of a new show that tried out in Philadelphia, then closed after a few performances in NYC. Through the fall and winter, I got odd jobs here and there with dinner theater productions, then finally had a chance at something truly dazzling—*Amadeus*. I read for Constanze, Mozart's childlike wife, a part that called for the spirited zaniness my London teachers said would suit me. I rode my bicycle from the Upper West Side down Broadway to the audition, which was my way of getting pumped, feeling rash and boundless as I walked into the theater. I loved, *loved*, every second of my audition, teasing Mozart from beneath the piano and trying to hide under his bench. In the end, the role went to a well-known actress when I was so sure it would be mine because, in that half-hour audition, I felt that I was back to who I believed I was.

Resilience came slowly, one brick at a time. I missed Laughlin, who was caught up in his last year of law school, and sometimes I spent long afternoons with my brother John, who was now living in a downtown loft owned by the artist for whom he worked. I'd sit on a gesso can while John painted. As children, when Suzanne and Laughlin were off at school, John and I had had our imaginative games. I always thought we shared the same artistic gene, but in many ways, he was the stricter version of an artist, and watching his hands as he painted, I saw the abandon I felt when dancing, his wild scribble-scrabbles kinetic and expressive.

Other times, the stretch of a single ordinary day could make me so twitchy, I wanted to claw at my skin. The soulful place where I had thrived was gone. Without consistent, steady work reaffirming my vision, twenty-four hours could be an eternity of claustrophobic emptiness. I scratched at imaginary itches on my neck, feeling physically desperate for something to fill me up. Then, one Friday evening when Chad and I were doing laps at the Henry Hudson pool on the West Side, he said, midstroke, in the lane next to mine, "Maybe we should get married."

Oh. I did another lap, a lopsided flip turn, and freestyled my way through the lane. After I finished, I called my parents to ask if I could get married in our backyard, and when they asked me about Chad, I said, "His mother has been a postal worker his whole life, so there's no problem with me pursuing a career," which seemed the most important thing to say. Later, Suzanne told me that when they got off the phone, they looked at each other, saying "Chad who?"

In six weeks, we were in Santa Fe, and I was putting on a white silk dress that I'd found in a Phoenix mall when doing a quick singing and dancing gig. Laughlin walked into my bedroom, blurting, "Don't do it. You can stop right now."

"What? The judge is in the backyard. Why are you saying this *now?*"

"Because no one did it for me."

"You had second thoughts about marrying Carrie?"

"Obviously," he whispered, still no one in the family but me knowing he was gay.

"But how can I? It's too late."

"No. It isn't."

My father knocked on the door. "Ready?"

Laughlin shook his head, and I was furious, just like when Martin told me on the bus that I'd be over Brett in a couple of weeks. My gut flip-flopped on both occasions, only this time I said, "I do."

How could it be that I'd suddenly agreed to get married, and to a man I didn't fully know? In a couple of years, I would shudder, remembering the pervasive feeling that life had walked out on me and I couldn't get it back; I remembered abject desperation and struggle for meaning—any meaning—to fill the void that permeated my existence.

But I was in the thick of it then, so nothing revelatory occurred to me. Back in New York, Chad and I made cards, saying, "We were married." Then, in the late fall, Michael called.

"Do you want your part back? No Cassie understudying, just Kristine in the Broadway cast."

"Michael? Yes! Oh my God. Thank you so much. I'm so grateful. When do you want me to start? And it's your call, but may I please wear beige tights?"

"Are you fat or skinny?"

"Skinny." I lied. I had two weeks to get off six pounds.

Michael saved me, increasing the conundrum that Michael Bennett would always be. I was indebted to him and touched that he'd called me himself. I prayed he'd reached the same conclusion I had about the Cassie fiasco: that it was right for me to have tried, even though it didn't work out. After me, they never again hired someone as a swing unless they were also a member of one of the casts. I had no hard feelings.

On the night I walked through the Shubert stage door, the doorman handed me a telegram: "FINALLY on Broadway. Love, Martin and Keith."

Broadway

1980

Yes! FINALLY on Broadway, I'd been delivered from the depths, the stars aligning as Laughlin landed a job in the city after working as a law clerk for the United States Court of Appeals for the Tenth Circuit, meaning two of my brothers were blocks away, plus I was married, so I had a partner to buffer the manic swings of life in show business and share in the effort to create something out of nothing.

I didn't look back, riding the bus along Broadway to the theater and getting off at Times Square, which was seedy and filthy, but by the end of 1979, was sandwiched between areas of renewal that burst with the imaginations of developers and clever New Yorkers. New York, emerging from bankruptcy, was suddenly experiencing its own big bang, astronomical expansion coming from all sectors. The energy lifted me, made me eager to be a part of the city's resurrection, a physical manifestation of my own deliverance. Landlords turned their Upper West Side buildings into "co-ops," and in the blocks between SoHo and Times Square, building codes enticed buyers to purchase "raw space" in industrial or commercial buildings. Such buildings were situated in partially abandoned areas that the city was too poor to fix. From my seat on the bus, I saw an urban homesteading rush, a perfect opportunity for a girl like me who'd come from a pioneering family who'd settled in the West.

Laughlin was thinking the same thing. Now an associate at a white-shoe law firm with offices on three top floors of Rockefeller Center, he pounced first, proposing to John and me that "The three of us go together and find a big space that we could develop into three apartments." We'd grown up alongside the ghosts of our grandparents and great-grandparents, knowing of their land swaps and real-estate deals, some of which led to properties our father now managed. Laughlin's proposal was a family tradition that made sense to us.

I took the idea to Chad, who was excited about the prospect of a loft conversion because it would give him something to do, even though he was nervous about the financial obligation. He'd blown through a lot of his income and savings, plus, his unemployment claim had lapsed. Despite being married, we'd kept our finances separate, adopting a system whereby we each contributed equally to our shared expenses, then paid for everything else individually. Ironically, buying a loft was facilitated by our separate finances as ownership in a co-op allowed for partnerships among individuals who had separate and differing levels of interests. I didn't know anything about such legal and financial structures but learned when we started looking at unconverted spaces in SoHo and along Broadway between Madison Square Park and the Village, wide open floor-throughs filled with light in fabulous looking buildings built in the twenties and thirties.

John eventually found an opportunity that could work for two apartments—a U-shaped space on the top floor of the mansard-roofed old Gilsey House hotel on Broadway, a few blocks north of the Flatiron district. Laughlin agreed that the layout and size were suitable for John and me (and Chad), and he was less interested because the building was nestled among some homeless hotels. But John and I were scrappy artist types who'd never been able to afford more than an iffy neighborhood, so when John showed Chad and me the building, its fresh coat of white paint looking like icing on a giant wedding cake, we were sold. Plus, the loft space had windows and a skylight structure that opened to the roof, with a full view of the Empire State Building, all we needed to convince ourselves that we could navigate whatever it took for the city to clean up the neighboring blocks.

I was at rehearsal at the Shubert when John left an emergency message with the doorman. When I called him back, he said, "We have to come up with the down payment and get the money to the developers tomorrow. They have another buyer!"

I begged Michael, who was mellow on that day, explaining why I had to run to the Actors Federal Credit Union two blocks away. He said he'd recently bought 890 Broadway, at 19th Street, and was converting it to rehearsal studios, so, "Okay. But twenty minutes."

I threw a coat over my leotard and tights, not even changing out of my dance shoes, then sprinted across Shubert Alley. I withdrew nearly every cent from my account, folding the cashier's check into halves, fourths, and finally eighths and stuffing it into the toe of my shoe, where it stayed even when I rehearsed the finale, kicking my legs high. The next day, at the development company, I unfolded the check once, twice, three times before presenting it to the banker, whose face drooped in generous folds like those of a pug. With a googly-eyed expression, he hesitated before touching the now slightly soiled check, warning, "You know you have to meet residential requirements in six months, right?" The deal was that the developer carried the balance of the purchase price until the building received its Certificate of Occupancy, because no bank would provide a mortgage unless the property was deemed "residential."

"Yes."

"Because the people who previously owned this unit defaulted, which is the only reason you got the space."

"Yes."

"So, everyone else in the co-op is expecting you to meet the deadline, which is in six months." He looked at John, Chad, and me with pity and shook his head at the crumpled check. But no matter, we had just the right amount of imagination and ignorance to make it work.

Before he moved to New York, Chad had worked construction jobs. Our plan was for him to supervise the project, which we agreed would be a bare-bones effort to meet the minimal residential requirements, such as constructing a couple of walls and installing updated electrics and plumbing for two bathrooms. We were happy, and Chad, who hadn't had a paying job for more than a year, thought the timing was good.

My father loaned John and me a small sum to cover some initial building costs. We didn't ask or expect more because he had his own business problems, plus college tuitions for David and Patrick, our younger brothers. Our mother, meanwhile, invoked the Great Depression, warning, "It's too much. You'll starve. You won't have enough left over to buy a loaf of bread."

Martin had recently bought into his building that had turned co-op; he'd been in and out of town since *Whose Life Is It Anyway?* closed, getting some directing jobs. Unlike Laughlin, who had clearly voiced his opinion about Chad on the day of my wedding (though he was slowly thawing), Martin had never said a word about my husband. I still trusted him and asked for his advice.

"How are you going to put it together?"

"We buy the unit, then physically divide it into two spaces, one larger than the other. In terms of ownership, I have the largest stake, a majority interest, then it drops down to John and finally Chad. Chad wants a minority position."

"So how did you put it together?"

"It's based on each of our financial commitments to both the down payment and the proportionate share for all ongoing financial obligations." Laughlin and Suzanne had been instrumental in coming up with a plan and drafting legal documents which acknowledged our ownership positions.

"And Chad's okay? He's working?"

I explained about Chad and the construction, so Martin suggested I go to the Actors Federal Credit Union, where I had a good track record, and explore whether I could get a construction loan, just to ease the finances. I hadn't thought about that, but the credit union was a lifeline for actors because commercial banks would rarely loan us money. "I'm at Manny's office this week. Why don't I meet you there, and I'll go up with you?"

The loan officer said I might need a cosigner, and Martin, without hesitation, said he'd sign. I looked at him, wondering suddenly if he'd anticipated that I'd need help, and when he signed his name, passing the paper to me, I said, "Sister Mary Angelica would have given you penmanship detention and made you stay after school."

"Darn. I would've rather had the priest." And with that, I had a construction loan.

Martin headed to Manny Azenberg's office without so

much as a hug, and I headed down Broadway toward the loft, getting two steps before my heart collapsed. Martin had signed his name, formally acknowledging that he was my safety net in what was surely a gesture of love, that thing between us, so difficult to label, so unknown to others, yet a small essential sliver of our lives.

Over the next six months, apartment 8E hummed with manic energy, the kind of creating something out of nothing that I trusted. Two separate front doors off a foyer-type entrance were installed, electrical lines run through walls. We were giddy the day two fifteen-dollar pull-chain toilets we'd found on Canal Street arrived. I spent non-matinee days working at the site, then going to the theater by five p.m., operating like an old-fashion money changer, depositing my paychecks so that I had enough every month to pay the loans and co-op maintenance, then setting cash into piles to pay the unemployed actors who were our building crew. During the construction, Chad and I partnered well. We liked the drama of activity and effort, seeing something materialize before our eyes. Then, in the middle of a Sheetrock frenzy, I hit the jackpot with a toilet paper commercial that doubled my income and made me believe the universe was on my side. For a brief time, I had *everything*, my own version of the American Dream: a home with an unobstructed view of the Empire State Building, where I shared the same sky with Margaret Bourke-White, and I walked the same blocks along Broadway as characters I admired in books on my way to my other home, the Shubert Theatre.

Life in the Shubert's dressing room number five was a bit more complicated than when I shared dressing space with Lydia and Olive during my touring days. My Broadway roommates were more seasoned young women with careers and proclivities. Nicky repeated her nightly drone, "Red leather, yellow leather," trying to keep her tongue from knotting. She stared in her mirror as if she were watching a mechanical toy that looked just like her, applying her mascara, layering it with a thick brush, then opening a large safety pin, the kind my mother called a diaper pin, and separating each lash, one by one, with the sharp tip. I was always afraid she might stick the pin in her eye, but her hand was steady.

Nicky liked heroin, though mostly used methadone, and got through the week by clawing her way to Saturday night. The time between the matinee and evening show on Saturday was hardest for all of us, but particularly for her. No matter what she did between shows—that I never asked about because I usually slept— if she could get through her "red leather, yellow leather" exercises, she could get through the whole show, which she needed to do, having not earned a whole paycheck in weeks. We only got one show off per month without being docked, and she needed money.

"I'm going downstairs to get some tea. Can I bring you back some?" I asked, thinking she may be a bit low on energy.

"Yeah. Two sugars and some cookies, if Alice has them."

Alice, officially our costume mistress, was mother of us all. Her large space in the basement was the only place in the entire backstage area that was always warm. She kept a supply of tea and cookies, and was a confidante, discreetly stowing a second pair of everything for when we unexpectedly got our periods, as well as sewing the buttons on our vests and instructing the dressers in repairing the sequins on our finale costumes. In all my years, she was the only person I'd ever seen Michael Bennett defer to.

I handed Nicky the cookies and the tea. "Okay?"

"If I had a BB gun, I'd shoot that guy." The sound of bag-pipes cut through the metal grates on the window outside our dressing room. Every weekend, some (supposedly) Scottish guy dressed in a Royal Stewart–plaid kilt serenaded Shubert Alley with the same three-song whine.

"How about a couple of Advil?"

"Okay."

Nicky had her job because Michael had known her for a long time and loved her, and so did I. When she was good, she was stupendous. She had that rare ability to stand onstage and be completely present with nothing separating her from the audience. Doing that over and over, eight times a week was where the drugs came in: They took the edge off, giving you a certain abandon, unless you crashed.

"Red leather, yellow leather."

"No Mo-Mo Mouth tonight, Nicky," warned Kaye, my other roommate, who was new and less tolerant of Nicky's edginess in the dressing room.

"Mo-Mo Mouth" was the horrible, awkward disaster that happened when your lines didn't come out right, when a word suddenly tumbled into the wrong sentence, and other words showed up where they weren't supposed to be, creating a great and terrifying unraveling. Mo-Mo Mouth could spread like wildfire, and admittedly, Nicky was a weak link.

I'd originally met Kaye when we were both booked on the same commercial. Her boyfriend was a musician, and although I didn't know her well, she'd asked if she and her boyfriend could come see the loft. Chad and I had moved in by that time, living in the wide-open space with our few pieces of furniture. They visited one afternoon; then the following Saturday night, the four of us had a post-show dinner. After a bottle of wine, they invited us to join them at Plato's Retreat, an adult's-only sex club, where they had a midnight reservation. I'd never known anyone who'd attended and had the impression it was a straight version of one of the more decadent gay bars in the Meatpacking District that Martin described. Over shrimp scampi, they described taking off their clothes before going to the "mat room," where you could join an anonymous group, watch other people have sex, or have sex yourself, knowing that you were being watched. I was caught off guard by their invitation, so blithely asked. "Is it crowded? I mean, how close are people to you? Like, when they're watching you have sex?"

And Kaye responded, "Once some guys got really close; I could feel them breathing, so we asked them to move back." Her answer suggested they'd been more than once.

"What about drugs?"

"The usual—quaaludes, poppers, coke," her boyfriend said.

Chad looked at me as if accepting the invitation was my decision, which technically it was because he'd run out of money, and I paid for things on the nights we went out. I used the several-hundred-dollar admission fee as an excuse: "Thanks, but we're on a really tight budget."

They laughed. "I guess you're busy being an urban pioneer, spending your money on *homesteading*." We all laughed then, toasted to home and mat rooms, but the next day, I expressed my dismay to Chad, who shrugged, saying, "It's for fun."

"That isn't what I'm asking. What I want to know is, do you see that as a way for *us* to have fun?" When he didn't have a ready answer, I pressed. "Did you want to go?"

"I don't know."

I thought he did know, and worse, I suspected that he

didn't perceive it as anything other than a drug-infused sexual extravaganza for consenting adults.

"I'm your wife," I said, and stared at him long and hard.

We lived in a world without boundaries, the 1980s social culture testing every limit. What, I wondered, was sexy about having public sex? Kaye's description sounded like exploitation masked as free expression because what was she, other than an object, some beautiful piece of communal property as the patrons of the club stood by and watched her boyfriend fuck her? What was in it for her? Being watched? In that case, why not do porn and get paid for it? At least then she'd have some control over her most personal self.

I had hoped that marriage would provide a bulwark from the increasingly inescapable prevalence of sex and drugs, especially in the workplace. Salacious but true stories abounded about Bob Fosse's bacchanal sex parties, where attendance was "suggested" for the dancers who worked for him. And, at the Shubert, a new understudy wobbled onstage night after night. She was dangerously high but, according to Tom, untouchable because she was Michael Bennett's drug source for pills. I'd stopped smoking grass before we bought the loft because it started making me paranoid, and coke, too; neither was pleasant or worth the expense. I didn't care what or how others chose to "party," I just wanted it separated from work so I could build a life doing what I loved to do.

By August, the city was a sweltering swamp. We kept all the windows to the loft open because we couldn't afford an air conditioner. I'd resumed my schedule of classes since we'd finished the renovations, and beyond the show, was going to an increasing number of commercial auditions. Chad, meanwhile, was completely without prospects, very unhappy, and complaining about everything. He'd stopped giving me his monthly share of expenses months ago, never telling me that he was nearly broke until I asked, and he answered, "What difference does it make? You got that toilet paper commercial."

"The difference is you didn't tell me. You just assumed you didn't need to address it." Now, three more months had gone by. "I'm worried," I said. "Are you thinking about possible next steps?" We had friends; *everyone* had friends in the business who figured out ways to bridge the gaps between gigs—taking off-the-books waiter jobs or doing construction, like the actors who'd served as our crew at the loft—and when the gaps became extended periods of time, they became more serious about their careers' timelines. Most of them had to transition to another aspect of the business or another career entirely. But he waved away my concerns with an air of bravado.

"Do you have any ideas?" I pressed.

"I don't know."

"Then help me understand how we're going to solve this problem of applying for a mortgage." Now that we had the Certificate of Occupancy, the developer wasn't going to carry the balance of our loan.

He only shrugged and started to walk away.

"I thought we were partners. That we were sharing this."

"Don't you have a matinee to go to?"

I was furious, retreating to the bedroom to get my bag. I understood his disappointment about work. I was not immune to those kinds of problems, but nearly two years had gone by since he worked in the business, and recently, he'd blown off an agent who'd arranged an audition for him, Chad saying the job was beneath him because it was basically a chorus job.

Coming home after the matinee and getting off the elevator, I could hear him belting out a song, his voice a simmering volcano. August bled into fall, the leaves turning colors. He sang constantly or had recurrent bouts of asthma, complaints about dust, and other sensitivities that incapacitated him. I often visited John in his apartment next door. He was sympathetic when I said, "I don't know if Chad's lost or paralyzed." But John only affirmed that he was going to stay out of whatever was going on, adding that he was a partner in the loft and didn't want his ownership jeopardized.

In late September, Chad developed an interest in photography, borrowing space in a darkroom, setting up lights around the loft, experimenting, sometimes using me as a model. He was good at it, and it seemed to feed his soul. And then, he dropped it.

The less he did, the busier I got, working on a scene from *The Crucible* in acting class, auditioning for commercials, running to the theater, and, more often, sleeping on the floor of my dressing room between shows instead of going home. Then, one October matinee, I fell, crashing onto my hands and knees during the opening number. I scrambled to my feet, the actor playing Zach, ad-libbing, "Are you okay?" while I answered, "Yes, yes," as the music played on.

But Tom, who was in town that month supervising the show, met me in the wings. "We need to talk. Meet me in the warm-up area before tonight's show."

And when I did, he said, "You moved too quickly through the transition. Set your fourth position. Ground yourself to your mark and focus on your spot."

I wanted to throw up suddenly, hearing both the literal and metaphorical in Tom's advice.

I'd accrued a week's vacation, so I called Martin to ask if I could spend a quiet week in the Hampton's at the house he and a couple of friends had bought. I planned to sleep, read, and walk the beach. I explained it to Chad, thinking I might go out alone, but he said he'd take his camera and shoot pictures of the dunes. The first three days I slept an average of fourteen hours a day. When I wasn't sleeping, I devoured *The Right Stuff* or went for a walk. The following Monday, I went back to eight shows a week and reached out to the television agent who'd called me long ago in San Francisco, asking if he could get me some film auditions.

"I need to see new pictures." Pictures were an entree to meetings with casting directors, and his attitude was somewhat dismissive, making me think he still hadn't forgotten my refusal of his invitation when I was on the road.

Pictures cost thousands of dollars, so I took the ones Chad had taken of me during my "retreat," and a couple taken by a photographer I'd met, a friend of a friend who had snapped a couple of shots in exchange for my helping his daughter with tickets. "Your eyes are dead in these," the agent said, pointing to one from the Hamptons. "Yeah, but this one is good. I like this one." He held out the professional photographer's image. "But look, when I put the pictures together, you look like two different people. Which girl are you?" Of course, he was right, even as I decided to be polite and not mention the white powder circling his nostrils.

At a certain point, Martin called and suggested that Chad transition by pursuing a job in a production company, where he could learn the skills of a company manager—basic bookkeeping, handling the logistics of moving a cast and crew from city to city. A company manager job seemed promising, so Chad, with some investigating on his own and input from Martin and others, got a job that would take him on the road for several months.

I prayed it would work out, and before he left, we caught another break when the co-op developer who carried our mortgage re-extended the offer because mortgage rates had climbed to an average 13.74% and were predicted to go higher when Ronald Reagan took office. We and several others in the building wouldn't qualify for bank mortgages, now at nearly four points higher, something no one had anticipated when the developers originally structured the deal and young professional people or artists like us invested everything they had.

As it turned out, Chad was away over the Christmas holidays—holidays being the busiest time of year for theaters and actors, when no one can take time off. John went home to Santa Fe, and Laughlin and I were left in the city. His daughter, Kate, who was now six, came for a weekend before Christmas. She had begun visiting Laughlin on a regular basis, with Carrie, Laughlin's ex-wife, bringing her down from Boston. Carrie and Laughlin had remained friends and were perhaps even closer, Laughlin having confided that he was gay.

On Sunday morning, I met Laughlin and Kate at the Central Park Zoo, Kate squealing about last night's "storm."

"There wasn't a storm last night," I said.

"Oh yes, there was!" She'd been taking a bath when Laughlin came running into the bathroom yelling, "A storm is coming. Take cover!" And he threw pots of water in her direction, showering the walls and splashing the floor, the two of them laughing hysterically. That spontaneously imaginative person who wasn't afraid to make a mess or break some rule if it meant he could make you laugh or feel special was

Laughlin through and through. It thrilled me to see him with Kate, bringing to her the kind of turn-around moments that he always brought to me.

I had a show to do later in the day, but on Christmas morning, Laughlin arrived at the loft, where we sat on the floor under an emaciated Christmas tree I'd bought on 14th Street and decorated with ornaments I'd sewn from fabric scraps. Laughlin handed me a present wrapped in white tissue and tied with a wide, red satin ribbon—a *real* ribbon, not papery but thick and lush, like something you might tie in your hair. It was sumptuous, another Laughlin surprise, this time on Christmas, when it was impossible for him to do anything small—even in the years when he was broke. When he handed me the present, I felt a shift, some expanded atmospheric release, time flip-flopping so that it wasn't about the present, and it wasn't about Christmas. I felt the change when I commented on the ribbon, saying that it was real—*real satin*—and he answered, "That's my friend, Perry."

I noted not the name but the cadence of his voice as I began to untie the ribbon and feel its silky truth between my fingers, and then observed how "Perry" played on Laughlin's face and danced between us. When he spoke about Perry, he spoke brightly and without hesitation, as if some upward moving thing had caught hold of him.

January
1981

I wanted to believe that the magic of Laughlin's news coupled with Chad's new job would gracefully put my personal life back on track, but a few days after Christmas, as the clouds thickened and took on the color of ash, I couldn't find the floor during ballet class. It felt slippery, like it had been sprinkled with baby powder, though no one else in the class was bothered; they were wheeling with the waltz: *One, two, three. One, two, three.*

I left class before it was over, something I never did, but I had to get outside and breathe the air. I didn't love ballet—no Broadway dancer loved ballet—it was simply that ballet class was the safest and most expeditious way to keep your body in strong technical shape. And for me, the music and methodically structured class always brought a kind of relief, a reliable place where my head caught up to itself, my body leading the way. But as soon as I was outside, the bile rose in my throat: *I thought we were making something of ourselves and doing it together. We must keep moving forward and making good choices!* The phone was ringing as I unlocked the door.

"Christine." It was a voice I didn't recognize. "It's Perry, Laughlin's friend."

"Hi."

"Your brother tells me your Christmas sweater didn't work."

"Oh. Hi. It's so nice of you to call. I wasn't expecting to— I've just come in the door. The sweater is beautiful; I've never had anything like it. It's just *me*. I think I'm allergic to angora." I was stiff, my words plain when I wanted them to be funny.

"Laughlin said that when you put the sweater on, you started scratching like it was infested with fleas. That your neck turned red and there were practically blisters popping out."

"Laughlin exaggerates. He just does that to make a good story. Don't argue with him, or you'll lose. He's very persuasive."

Perry laughed. "He made it sound as if I'd unleashed the furies on you, so I want to make it up to you and take care of it right away."

"He's just giving you a hard time; really, he's a tease."

"Really?"

"Really."

"I'd like to know more about that. Can you come to the showroom sometime soon?"

"Sure." *Can I come to an up-and-coming almost-famous designer's showroom and look at clothes?* "I'd love to come. Should I call your secretary?"

"No. I want to pick something out for you myself. I have my date book in front of me right now. When can you come?"

Anytime. I can come anytime. "Afternoons are good. Except Wednesdays. I have a matinee on Wednesdays."

"Okay. Well, how about Thursday?"

"You mean the day after tomorrow?"

"Is that a problem?"

"No, no. That's fantastic."

"Good. Thursday, then, the day after tomorrow."

"Okay! This is really— What time is good for you?"

"Come at three. It's 575 Seventh Avenue, but enter near 40th Street and Broadway, on the Broadway side, and come up the stairs. I have the second floor. The showroom is to the left and my office is to the right. Come to my office."

"Okay."

"See you Thursday."

"Yes, see you Thursday."

The Exchange
—
1981

The building at 41st Street had once been a bank. I walked up the wide, sweeping marble staircase, the color of polished ivory, which led to the second floor, where a hallway stretched from Broadway on one end to Seventh Avenue on the other. Perry said the door on the *right*. If there were a recurrent motif about life in New York, it was exactly this: a door, which, upon opening, could present you with a once-in-a-lifetime possibility, a new job or an association that promised to move you up the stairs to heaven. No matter when or where, I never turned a knob without whispering, "Open sesame."

Inside was a counter, behind which sat a delicate girl with an orchid face. Beyond her were windows lining the entire east wall. Assistants sketched on large boards, and remnants of tweedy fabrics and blue paisleys littered the floor. Perry, who looked more handsome than in his pictures, was out of his chair in seconds, walking through the jumble of activity as if nothing were there, and I thought: *He's Puck; he either possesses some rare agility at negotiating the buzz or, in fact, he is the buzz.*

"Let's go next door to the showroom, shall we?" He called over his shoulder to the secretary, the girl with an orchid for a face. "Take messages and I'll call everyone back."

In the showroom, clothes hung on racks—things he said he had picked out in advance.

"Now, let's see. How about this?" He handed me a wide-legged pair of pants. "And put this with it"— a cotton sweater with one bold cable—his signature whimsical twist on classicism.

"Well, look at you," he said with a pleased grin when I came out of the dressing room. "A Broadway dancer and actress." He pronounced Broadway the way they did in Fred Astaire movies, filling the word with helium and accenting the wrong syllable.

"You know, you're perfectly proportioned. Will you try something else?"

"Sure, I'd love to, but I only have a sweater to exchange."

"You have a huge credit, and all these clothes are *samples*. They're going to hang on racks unless someone like you wears them." I wondered what Laughlin had paid for the sweater but felt too awkward to ask. Perry shoved the hangers down the bar, looking at me, looking at the clothes—every piece beautiful, singular, expensive, making me think of Diana Spencer, transforming her look with clothes and grabbing all the headlines, an engagement to Prince Charles imminent. "You know, maybe you'd rather have something more fun. What do you wear when you go out at night after the show? Aren't you married?" His hand circled his jaw, trying to envision my place in a world of celebrity engagements.

"My husband is away, but even when he's home, I don't go out very much. Sometimes I have commercial auditions in the morning, or a morning ballet class."

"You don't go out? Not even to Sardi's?"

"Sardi's?" He'd definitely been watching too many old movies, which made me shy, sensing a mismatch, like he may have expected someone else, his comments so clichéd and Hollywood-esque. I wanted him to like me, especially if Laughlin liked him, so it was a balancing act: ignoring the awkwardness of putting on different outfits so he could judge how I looked juxtaposed with the allure of something beautiful against my skin when what both of us were doing was sizing each other up. He had the advantage. When I walked out in a white linen shorts suit, he clapped. "That is *perfect* for a little sister." I knew he was an only child and that he'd been depressed when his father had died recently, so his saying "little sister" touched me, making me think he wanted a sibling like me.

"Tell me about your commercial," he said. "What was it? Dr. Pepper? McDonalds?"

"Both."

"But Laughlin says you don't eat meat."

"Nope. Unless I'm being paid; then I'll eat anything. They give you a spit bucket. You just take a big bite, chew enthusiastically, and when the director yells 'Cut,' spit it out." Whether it was the description of my spitting or the pragmatism I voiced, he flinched. I looked down and saw not a scuff or mark on his shoes, knowing that I was hard on my feet, needing new dance shoes every six weeks. His Southern manners were impeccable, and he looked a fixture in the showroom, a clean, untouched perfection to him, the blond wood floor, and walls of thousands of mirrors.

"My best—or at least my most lucrative—commercial was for toilet paper."

"Oh." He paused, handing me a pleated linen skirt. "So, what's going on now? Something new in the works?"

"Not really. I've tried for some soap opera contracts or parts in straight plays, but I'm sort of stuck."

His constrained demeanor broke then as he animatedly declared, "Don't say things like that. You should never say negative things; speak in the affirmative. You should only say what it is you want, and let your mind follow the words. Say things like, 'When I get a soap contract.' That's how you make things happen." His almost-evangelical words sounded genuine. "You have to surround yourself with only those thoughts, and people who will support you in getting where you want to get."

The early eighties were bursting with positive-thinking gurus, Erhard Seminar Training, and other kinds of self-help philosophies. Some actors were devout Buddhists or Christians, all of them believing in the innate ability of a person to bring into reality whatever they could fully imagine; the more detailed the visualizations, the better. To me, their beliefs were related to the dancer mindset: imagining physical lines before achieving them in real time and space. But Perry took it a step further, speaking of success as something that could be acquired, like a commodity. And who was I to doubt him? Maybe part of my problem was that I was standing on the wrong side of a juncture, my choices clouded by negativity, when all I needed to do was cross the street. Still, I was struck by "who will support you in getting where you want to get," the subtext baring the basis of our exchange: that these clothes were a trade; he needed my approval.

"I think you should try on the balloon pants and the little cranberry jacket. There is a hair comb that goes with it, too." Perry went to the phone at the other end of the room and called his secretary. "Julia, can you find the hair comb that Lisa wore in the show?" He turned to me then. "If Sunday is your day off, are you free to go out Saturday night?"

"I— Yes, I think so."

"How about if your brother and I pick you up at the theater

and take you out?" He dialed a number by heart and dropped his voice into the black receiver. "Mr. McClatchy." McClatchy was my brother's middle name. I'd never heard anyone call Laughlin by his middle name. "She's here right now. Let's the three of us go out Saturday night after her show. We'll go to Dorine's in SoHo. Here, he wants to talk to you."

"Hi. A great time." I paused as Perry walked back to the clothes rack, then whispered, "But Perry has all these clothes out, and I only have a sweater to exchange."

"Do they fit? Do you like them?"

"Of course. They're PERRY ELLIS."

"He's generous. He wants you to have them."

"For free? Oh . . . okay. And I'd love to go out Saturday night if you want to go."

"That'd be great. I should have thought of it earlier."

I thought I knew most everything about Laughlin, but "Mr. McClatchy" was new. The whole romance was bold. Laughlin never traveled in public circles, keeping his gay identity private, especially in the practice of law, where being gay could threaten his position. That was the difference between arts and business, even in New York City. He may have been "out" to me, but no one else in my family knew he was gay; I wasn't sure John had even figured it out, though Laughlin had discussed it with his ex-wife, Carrie.

Julia arrived with the hair comb just as Perry asked, "So are we on for Saturday night?"

"Yes. Laughlin said yes."

"Oh good. Now that we've figured everything out, let's have tea. I always have afternoon tea."

"So do I. Ever since I worked in London."

"I love London. Tell me about the London you know."

"A ghost that smells of lavender lives at the Drury Lane."

"A ghost?"

"A real one."

The tea, arriving on a tray, was served in white china cups, the cream in a porcelain pitcher.

"So, what was it like growing up with your brother?"

"Terrible."

"What?"

"Terrible." I explained how Laughlin tortured me, putting small crabs on my doll's eyes to make me scream; how he once put a lizard in my bed that crawled up my leg in the middle of the night.

"How awful." Perry laughed and offered me a cookie, which I declined, watching as he studied the plate, trying to decide between the buttery shortbread and the chocolate sprinkled crescent. Now that we were together, without the racks of clothes between us, with only the alabaster air of the showroom and what felt to be a huge space between his knees and mine, I could see him fully, and thought he might be a man my brother could love with all his heart, so I relaxed, knowing it was my turn to be in control.

"You know he was never called Laughlin, right? His name was Chico. He was always and everywhere Chico, even in his high school yearbook."

"I don't know about Chico."

So, I told him, starting with the story of Laughlin's adventures on the Super Chief when we were living in Washington and Daddy was stationed at the Pentagon. "Chico was about eleven and traveling by himself for the thirty-six-hour trip to visit our grandmother in Santa Fe. My mother was afraid he'd lose his ticket, so she sewed it into his shirt pocket with brown running stitches. The conductor only had to pull the thread.

"Anyway, the day he came back, a month later, we met him at Union Station, all dressed in Sunday clothes and waving like lunatics at every passenger car until the train stopped, and popping up right behind the porter was Chico, lit like a headlight. Boy, we knew that meant mischief. He struggled with a heavy black bag, something he hadn't had when leaving, and my mother said the bag belonged to my step-grandfather, Dr. Sandy. We hoped it was filled with presents; John wanted a bow and arrow, Suzanne and I turquoise bracelets. We begged to open the case on the platform, but our mother said we had to wait." I took a sip of my tea at that point in the story, noting that Perry had finished all the cookies.

"Surprise! No bracelets and no bow and arrow. Not even close. From the back seat of our Chevy station wagon, he unbuckled the top strap to the bag, and inside was a big fat black snake—a slithery, stinky snake that he'd caught in the arroyo near my grandmother's house."

"Oh my." Perry was now spreading a thick wedge of brie across a baguette.

"The snake was supposed to have stayed in the bottom compartment, where Chico'd constructed a net barrier to separate it from the boxes that held *mice*. He caught those, too, in special homemade traps built out of shoeboxes. Somehow the snake wound itself up, slithered through the net, got into the higher compartment, and ate the mice. So in the morning, when the train was speeding though South Bend, Chico opened the bag to check on his traveling food chain, and the snake LEAPED. Did you know that snakes can leap?"

"No. I didn't know that." Perry poured more tea. I handed him the cream.

"Well, they can. Snakes can leap. Chico scurried on his hands and knees, hopping over and under and around the seats, trying to catch the thing."

"Oh my God. Did he?"

"Just as it curled in a warm spot between a sleeping lady's swollen feet. He snatched it with ONE HAND! Next time he's negotiating one of your contracts and wildly gesticulating in Italian with the fabric makers, just relax. It will all work out. He's quite capable, my brother."

Perry was somewhat speechless, so I added, "You know he had a chipped front tooth?"

"He had a chipped front tooth?"

"Right in front, a regular hypotenuse cutting across his smile."

"Want to know something else?" I added.

He nodded.

"He HATES sweet potatoes, and I know you're Southern, but don't ever serve them, especially the kind with marshmallows, or he might throw up right on the plate." Perry burst with a roiling laugh and almost fell over backward. "I'm glad we're going out Saturday night because on Monday, I'm going to the White House. We're doing a shortened, laundered version of *A Chorus Line* for the National Governor's Dinner."

"No."

"I think Joe Papp wants to talk to Ronald Reagan about the cuts to the National Endowment for the Arts. I'm not sure Michael Bennett is excited, though. We've had to cut all vocabulary considered "lewd," plus entire scenes, which is totally ridiculous. You'd think a Pulitzer Prize–winning, sold-out

Broadway show wouldn't have to be censored for a bunch of politicians, but welcome to the Moral Majority."

"I was invited to the White House once, too."

"Really?"

"I was in the Coast Guard and escorted Jackie Kennedy."

"Jackie Kennedy!" I didn't know the Jackie Kennedy story, although Laughlin had told me that Perry had dressed Ron Reagan, Jr., and his wife, Doria, at President Reagan's inaugural, which had seemed strange to me, Reagan being the most unpopular politician ever, especially among my gay friends.

All afternoon, I felt close to the shimmer of a new possibility, the room increasingly soaked in the brandy-colored afternoon sun. Then, Saturday night, I was introduced to another new world. The fashion crowd was less segregated, populated with more women and more straight people. The girls were stunningly chic and beautiful, though I was sure they paid a steep price to look as they did. I recognized some from magazine ads. They and their entourages floated between tables and booths, draping themselves over one another in poses perfect for the camera. Dorine's rocked, not quite with the rowdiness or campy flamboyance typical in a crowd of theater folk, but still, it rocked.

Seeing them side by side as a couple, Laughlin and Perry were true head turners. Each, on his own, was someone special, but together, they were extraordinary. I had the feeling that I was witnessing the launch of a new trend: the gay man or gay couple who comfortably fit a mainstream social sensibility. *That* was new; the usual depiction of gay men was as morally depraved or swishy queens, a homophobic concept fed to the public because gay men threatened a binary social order. But here was what I had imagined the night in Georgetown when

Laughlin told me he was gay, and I said not to worry, that he was perfect just the way he was—that society was changing. I'd said it without evidence, only instinctually believing that it would be true. And finally, here it was. Laughlin had stepped into a revolutionary, transformative space, and I felt that vestigial childhood bond enabling me to revel in his triumph, just as he'd reveled in my triumph when I was hired for *A Chorus Line*. It was *his* turn to feel legitimate and whole. The fullness of such satisfaction gave me momentary rest; I wasn't convinced, as Perry suggested, that phrasing everything about my career in the positive would miraculously catapult me to the next step, but still, I had envisioned this night for my brother, and traveling in his wake could provide a new vantage point from which to view my bungled marriage, and how eight shows a week were my salvation, even as I knew I couldn't do it forever.

Chariots of Fire

—

1981–1982

With Chad away, I noticed all the little things: how I didn't grip my toothbrush with a fist, how each day was packed with so many commitments that I ran from classes to an audition or the theater and kept up the pace even when arriving home—going from the elevator to the closet, the washing machine, the ironing board I hadn't put away. I was locked into a pattern of urgency, as if my overly ambitious calendar confirmed that my life was full.

When Chad returned home in early March, I walked on eggshells, hoping he would feel better about work and his future. He'd been vague when we talked on the phone, but now he flatly claimed he didn't like company management work and didn't intend to pursue it. When I tried to get specifics, he abruptly dismissed my questions, saying, "Gary is an asshole, and I told him as much."

Good God. Gary was the producer, the one who'd given him the job in the first place and who could help him transition to the production side of the business. "The job was mostly just messenger work or doing accounts," he said.

"Did something go wrong with that?"

"Nah, mostly Lyn did them." And when he said her name, the other assistant company manager, I knew. She did the bookkeeping, and he'd slept with her.

"Lyn?" I pressed, feeling sick, and he looked at his feet. "What about Lyn?"

I'd been compassionate, knowing full well how the insecurity in our business thinned our bones, our self-worth completely tied to our work, but his behavior and attitude doomed him. He'd made himself luckless, and as for Lyn, well, loyalty was just another thing I couldn't depend on.

A few days later, Laughlin called from the Helsinki airport. He and Perry were enroute to Russia.

"This is costing a fortune. Everything okay?" I asked.

"Yes, but Perry says I have to talk to you. That it's clear how unhappy you are."

I sat on the floor and held the phone, not answering.

"He's right, isn't he? Maybe you feel like you can't talk to me."

"I can't live like this."

"Okay. Okay. We'll talk when I get back from Russia."

"I love you."

"I love you, too."

"Watch out for the KGB."

It was easy to say "I can't live like this," even though I didn't have a clue about how to untangle the mess I'd made of my life. I spent the early spring living in two worlds. On the outside, I followed through with "life"—dancing in the show eight times a week, going through the motions with Chad, getting auditions. But on the inside, I took cold-blooded inventory.

Clearly, we didn't know each other well enough when we married. Looking back, I realized I'd made a significant life decision when depressed and desperate, trying to fill up what had become empty and small in my life when my profession gave me my truest sense of self even as the business of it diminished me. Also, I naively believed we had similar ambitions about work and personal life. I had no regrets about buying the loft. I wanted a home, was passionate about that, too, which was why I was willing to take a huge financial risk. *No one* seemed to have anticipated Reaganomics and interest rates doubling, but they had, and rather than being a partner in problem-solving and/or accepting responsibility for his ownership share, Chad was going around naked. He'd done that when it was steaming hot last August, and we didn't have air conditioning. But now he'd take a shower and not get dressed, whatever the temperature. Once I arrived home with Kate. She was visiting Laughlin, and we'd had lunch together because Laughlin had to see a client. When we walked into the loft, there was Chad, naked.

"Oh," Kate said.

I was mortified. "Get dressed. What've you been doing all day?" I supported us: mortgage, maintenance, utilities. More and more, I spent my free time with Diane, a friend I'd originally met at the end of my road tour and who'd recently joined the Broadway cast; or Tom, if he were in town; or Laughlin, whom I saw on Sundays because he worked office hours during the week. On matinee days, I turned off the lights and rolled myself in a blanket, sleeping on the floor of my dressing room, which was better than going home to a man I didn't know.

Then, out of the blue, I had an audition for a role in a six-week summer tour, a four-character comedy starring Jane Powell. It was a chance to do a play, my agent pulling through with what felt like a gift. Chad was excited, too, for better or worse, our enthusiasm enabling us to drop everything that distracted from the thrill of some new potential opportunity. We were like gamblers in that way, falling back into an old pattern as he coached my audition. I made it to a callback, a second callback, then miraculously, got the part, even though when it came to accepting the job, I couldn't do it unless Chad secured some paid work or Michael was willing to give me a leave of absence. I couldn't afford to give up my Broadway contract for a six-week gig in summer stock, even though it was a *play*, a professional leap. I braced myself, calling Michael to explain that I'd been offered a part in a play—*for only six weeks, summer stock*—and said I'd accept whatever he felt was best because I owed him and would always honor my debt to him. He didn't pause, just answered, "Okay, arrange it with the office."

I sank to my knees, then got out my sewing machine, bought handkerchief linen from a fabric store recommended by Perry, and spent every second making Michael a beautiful shirt, wrapping it and hand-delivering it to his office with a note. A week later, I found a signed, one-sentence thank-you note in my mailbox, which I placed in my special box of most-important papers.

I was thrilled to leave my problems behind and luxuriate in the total absorption of learning my part, but as we got close to opening, I was scared, afraid of forgetting my lines, forgetting where I was on the stage, recognizing that for most of my professional life, I'd relied on a different part of my brain, the nonverbal realm of a dancer who knows time and space through her body and choreography. Using only words to convey each beat of a story was a different kind of sustained mental processing, so I taped my vulnerable areas in the script to different wooden posts in the backstage wings.

Katrin Sveg was a caricature of a Swedish bombshell. I wore a poufy blond wig and a big push-up bra, worked on my nonexistent Swedish accent with a dialect coach, and strove to make her real, finding moments of authenticity in the script, as my London teachers taught me to do. I kept to a ballet barre routine each night to sort out my nerves before going onstage and continued to search for pockets where Katrin lived sincerely. I wished I'd had more than six weeks to fully be at home in my first ever straight play, but I grew to love the girl I played, plus the challenge of it all. And on top of all that, I received some good reviews.

Outside work, I spent time alone, aimlessly exploring the summer towns and barnlike theaters, flimsy with age and mold but revered by throngs of summer visitors. In Ogunquit, Maine, I was drawn to the granite cliffs, the color of Puritan gray, feeling as if everything about the world and my place in it was on the verge of some great cleaving.

When I arrived home at the end of the summer, it appeared that Chad had never found any kind of paying work as he'd promised to do. I knew Suzanne would soon be coming to the city for a visit. She planned to stay with Laughlin, and after she arrived, I confided in her. She and Laughlin arranged for me to meet with a divorce attorney in Laughlin's office. A couple of weeks later, I prepared to tell Chad after the show on a Sunday afternoon.

I was calm and just said it: "I want a divorce."

"You're kidding me."

"No. I'm not."

"Really? I can't believe you're saying that. You can't mean it."

"I do mean it. We have completely different ideas about marriage, let alone who and what we want to be in life; I've supported you for over a year and a half, and you—"

"But I was thinking we should have a baby," he interrupted.

"What?"

"I was thinking we should have a baby."

"A baby? You need to get a job and a lawyer."

Over the next few days and weeks, he'd bellow, "Why are you doing this? Some evil has come over you!"

"Evil? It's called reality, real life. Interest rates are nearly 18 percent." I waved the mortgage and maintenance bills.

By October, he had a lawyer of his own, and he moved onto the couch as we staked out separate territories, the two of us coming and going as if the other wasn't there, which was impossible, but was what we did.

We couldn't get divorced until we had a separation agreement, and significantly, by law, I couldn't get a divorce unless he agreed—there was no no-fault divorce. It had never, ever occurred to me when I got married that marriage was covered by laws unfavorable to women, but at the time, it was. Chad refused to agree to divorce, telling his lawyer on the phone, when I was within earshot, "I don't want a divorce. She's my *wife*," and I heard the bitter irony, how he was empowered by the fact that I needed his permission to claim my own life and future. That hardened me and shaped my increased sensitivity to all women and gay individuals who *legally* did not have full control over their own destinies.

Every hour of every day, I forced one foot in front of the other, feeling like I was fighting for my life. At one point, the stage manager called me into his office to ask if I'd received his message.

"I left it with your husband, who was so rude and hostile that I won't ever call you at home again." He went on to say

167

that he was aware my personal life was a mess, and he hoped I was okay, but that I could not bring one bit of drama into the theater. I had to leave it at the stage door.

"Okay."

"Remember you're here to do the show."

I had the warm-up area, my dressing room, and the familiar sound of "Places!" eight times a week, and I used my trust in my work to pull me through. By the new year, I'd survived three months, the stress of Chad living a few feet away from me less paralyzing because outside of the loft, he did not exist. He was not working or pursuing jobs in show business, and we shared no friends, not even a gym membership. We only crossed paths at the loft, and when we did, I looked through him as if he were invisible.

I declined an audition for *Cats*, which was coming to Broadway from London and promised to be the next big thing. There wasn't a part for me, and truthfully, I didn't have the wherewithal to prepare appropriately; given my living circumstances, it was enough to keep up with eight shows a week and my commercial auditions. Tom, meanwhile, confided that he was being considered for a production/dance captain position. He'd gone as far as he could with *A Chorus Line*, but we both knew that his leaving would be considered a defection; Michael's top lieutenants did not leave to work for another director or show.

Diane's situation was different. Michael would never make her more than an understudy in *A Chorus Line*, so *Cats* was the perfect opportunity.

Meanwhile, Perry invited me to my first ever fashion show—his spring/summer 1982 Collection—held at his studio. Laughlin met me outside on the street, then squeezed me into the second row next to Winnie and Alma, Perry's mother and aunt. The standing-room-only audience was packed so tightly that we had to sit sideways on our folding chairs.

In front of me were VIPs from the *New York Times*, *Women's Wear Daily*, and *Vogue*, all with their notepads and pencils, some with cameras strung like medallions around their necks. They were not at all like an opening-night theater crowd, which would be giddy with anticipation; these people were serious, their faces like hatchets. Winnie, Alma, and I were flipping through our printed programs when suddenly, a deep reverberating hum bounced off the walls and engulfed the space. The sound was overwhelming, the vibrations shimmying between your ears. Everyone stopped talking and taking notes.

At the top of the runway, one butterfly of a girl appeared, lingered, and was followed by another, then another. Equally gorgeous men, with hands in their pockets, sauntered after them, languidly secure with the confidence reserved for the extraordinarily beautiful. They looked like modern-day Olympian Graces. Perry had been among the first designers to introduce music into fashion shows, and here, like in theater, it set the tempo and ambience. With another great trembling—the recently released "Chariots of Fire" by Vangelis—models took their cues, and, one by one, started down the runway.

Fashion was an *experience*, which, of course, was Perry's point, and with his spring/summer 1982 Collection, the world burst open. Even though we were looking at volumes of pleated linen and deep V-necked cotton knits, the clothes transcended themselves, the whole hopeful tone echoing what I saw when Laughlin and Perry were together, which, in just a few months, had become *all the time.*

Perry, already successful, became an overnight superstar, the hottest ticket on Seventh Avenue. To those in the inner circle,

Laughlin was an acknowledged part of that accomplishment, some saying that Laughlin gave Perry a new level of personal confidence, Laughlin stressing the difference between gloss and authenticity, and that trusting the latter was ultimately more resonant. He and Perry chose to celebrate by inviting two friends—Lynn and JC—and me to join them in Mexico, where they'd rented a house. The trip, including a first-class ticket (I'd never flown first class in my life!), was a gift, something special, they said, because I had to have a break, Perry adding, "He's still living on the couch?! How can you even function?" then, turning to Laughlin, "Get her another lawyer, someone tough—"

"She won't win that way," Laughlin broke in. "She has to plant her feet, every single day. Her strength will win out." Then he whispered, "I know how divorce forces you to look at yourself, see where you failed. But I also know you can and will come out on the other side to a better place. Pack sunscreen."

The house they rented clung to the side of a steep yellow cliff outside Puerto Vallarta. Running along the edge was a type of Moorish porch, and behind that a living area. Laughlin and Perry, and Lynn and JC had bedrooms there, but I was given my own abode: a miniature fairy-tale Taj Mahal, a single room pavilion, separated from the main house and suitable for a contemplative saint or a concubine. The ceiling ballooned in a blue dome, the big bed lying directly below the center of its peak. I kept the doors to the garden open as nights descended like envoys from another universe. I'd never done psychedelic drugs, but the experience was the very best of what a mind-blowing trip was meant to be, which is what I think Laughlin and Perry's intention had been. Leaving Mexico, I stopped using my brain to reargue all the arguments that had gone wrong, and instead, chose to think about wonder. I'd been hopeful when I got the play and had moved one foot into a professional transition that I wanted to expand upon. I hadn't anticipated how the mess of my personal life would sap my momentum, but still, my struggles were not defeat. I would get back to the "Use what you have" creative mindset, reminding myself that everything, absolutely *everything* was relevant. Even if I had no idea what I was going to make out of my experiences, I believed that magic came from what you chose to do with what you had. I bought a composition notebook at an airport stall and began to write.

With Laughlin and Perry, I had *experiences*, tagging along to the Westminster Kennel Club Dog Show at Madison Square Garden, where they stood in line for hot dogs, then realized they had no money. Luckily, I had twenty dollars in my fanny pack, and we laughed about their absentmindedness, which was either distractedness or the cavalier attitude of extremely successful people who only did BIG things, like creating new companies and signing their names to multimillion dollar deals but who never had to buy a roll of toilet paper at the grocery store. *That* separated us, but I was grateful and indebted to them for pulling me through a horrific time in my life, Chad still living on the couch as spring arrived.

In May, both Diane and Tom had jobs with *Cats*. Tom called Michael to tell him he was leaving, to which Michael expressed disappointed dismay. Soon afterward, our stage manager said Michael would be visiting backstage for a send-off of Tom on his last night. When we'd all gathered in the warm-up area, Michael made a grand entrance, with a bizarre-looking, exotic long-haired cat draped in his arms, something a Russian oligarch might have kept in his private zoo. Handing it to

Tom, he said, "I love you," in a quintessential Michael gesture of outlandish spectacle laced with ambiguity. Later, Tom confided that if his longtime companion who was allergic to cats couldn't live with the creature, he was giving her to me.

By June, my lawyer had wrested a signature out of Chad for our separation and financial agreement. It had taken almost nine months, but a date was set on the calendar. I paid Chad for his share of the loft and a fee for his construction work. When he moved his furniture out, we still did not speak, but later that day, he called to say he'd left some nut oil in the refrigerator and that he wanted to come get it. I left it in a bag in the vestibule of our building and never saw him again.

Later that same month, Laughlin cemented his relationship with Perry by becoming president and legal counsel of Perry Ellis International (PEI), the company Perry owned and controlled, which licensed products in any category that didn't compete with Manhattan Industries, the publicly traded company that bankrolled his clothing collections and the PERRY ELLIS brand. Perry's dream was to be a designer with international reach, and the plan was for Laughlin to reorganize PEI by initiating an expansion of licensing agreements. With Laughlin handling the business side, Perry would spend more time designing.

After Laughlin told my parents about his decision to leave the law firm and take the new offer, my father asked me about it: "Do you think he's making a million dollars a year?"

"I have no idea." But I detected competition in his voice.

I didn't know if my parents suspected that Laughlin and Perry were lovers; without a doubt, *that* would be a problem.

Home and Family
—
Fall 1982

The thrill of Laughlin's life absorbed me, offering respite and keeping me buoyant when *Cats* opened to raves and quickly reduced all of us in *A Chorus Line* to has-been status. Agents, commercial directors, LA scouts, and even friends wanted access to *those* dancers, spooking me with the fickleness of a business that was always on the lookout for the next best thing. My success in commercials had helped me sign with a new, more powerful group, but when one of those agents tried to get me seen by an equally powerful legit agent, I may as well have been dipped in acid. "I wouldn't know what to do with you. You're just another pretty face." She looked straight through me, peeling off my skin with the calm, sure demeanor of an executioner.

I refused to believe that I'd become uninteresting, but I heard her, loud and clear. The trouble was, I didn't know what to do. I loved what I did, even as I was stuck in the in-between: too old but too young, experienced in musicals but not legit work, legit directors not taking commercial work seriously even as commercials (for me) paid bills. It was a lot to process when I still had to do eight shows a week. Within that context, Laughlin gave me solace and hope. He'd made a leap for love and to claim his true identity, his professional move from law to the fashion business a bold and overt signal that he was no longer willing to hide, like so many others who came out because of the sanctuary offered by the art, fashion, dance, music, and theater worlds in New York City. Anywhere else—banking, finance, law— would have fired him for being gay, and many of his friends in those professions remained closeted to keep their jobs.

The lack of tolerance extended to my parents, but luckily, there was little chance that they and their friends in Santa Fe would know much about Laughlin's relationship with Perry, other than that Laughlin was now the president of a growing fashion business. Without the Internet or social media, and because of the reluctance of newspapers or magazines to report on homosexuality or any such libelous personal information, gay men could and did live double lives in plain sight. If my parents wondered about Laughlin's sexual identity, they kept it to themselves. Suzanne, on the other hand, asked. "Laughlin talks about Perry so much. I'm just wondering, are they in a relationship?"

"I'm sure he'd want to tell you himself," I said, and so she asked him, and when he confided in her, they became closer than ever. Suzanne and Laughlin were only thirteen months apart, and even as Laughlin was the leader of the pack of siblings, Suzanne was the consigliere. Every one of us, including Laughlin, relied on her for her fair and infallible judgement. With Suzanne now at his side, Laughlin had all the acceptance he needed. John knew that Laughlin was gay, not because they'd had a conversation, but because John had eyes and navigated the downtown art world.

For all our optimism about the changing status of gay men, though, the election of Ronald Reagan in 1980 and the rise of the Christian Right, represented by powerful organizations such as Focus on the Family and Family Research Council, proved a formidable challenge. These groups engaged in a network of campaigns which claimed gay people were anti-family and undermined "family values" at the core of our country. Such religious organizations spread propaganda, disinformation, and lies that discredited gays and fueled homophobic sentiments. As a gay, family man, Laughlin (and many others) was a threat to the conservative movement and Ronald Reagan. But Laughlin had always been a family man, close to his siblings and the proud father of Kate. His "family-ness" was striking, according to some businessmen who worked with Perry, namely because Laughlin's family-oriented nature was just as upfront and obvious as that of a straight, married father.

Perry's gayness was an open secret in the fashion world; yet, unlike many gay men who were estranged from their families or parents, Perry was close to his, often seeking their advice, and the impact of his father's recent death had been substantial. When Perry met Laughlin, his priorities changed. He left behind a circle of gay friends who could be a bit campy, rather preppy and elite. He no longer wore his hair in a long shag and grew out of his early Fire Island days, becoming more serious both in his professional and personal life.

To the relationship, Laughlin brought a more tempered, Madison Avenue sensibility with his Georgetown law degree and extensive experience living and working in Europe. Perry was a master of promotion, well-mannered like a Southern aristocrat, but with a shyness that masked coldness and rigidity. Laughlin was the opposite. He was charismatic and warm. He could endear himself to the cleaning staff as easily as Georgia O'Keeffe, which he once did at a museum opening, when, after being introduced, she ignored the press and walked around the exhibit of her paintings with Laughlin. Then there was Kate, his heart's greatest treasure. At Laughlin's apartment, his and Kate's bicycles often blocked the front door, and stuffed animals, books, and toys were kept in a corner at his new office.

Laughlin's influence on Perry and the business was demonstrated when one of PEI's first ventures was a line of children's clothes. It marked the first time a well-known fashion designer added children's wear to a portfolio. Perry placed Kate in full-page ads in *The New York Times*, where she appeared as a tartan-clad *Petite Danseuse* (Edgar Degas, 1881), her hands clasped behind her back, her feet in an extended fourth position. The pictures were a sensation, everyone remarking that the pert model was Laughlin's daughter. Family soon became manifest in other new business ventures, too. Suzanne was an expert knitter, always traveling with a project; a knitting company, Burren, was born, so women could knit their own PERRY ELLIS sweaters, the kits packaged in handsome bags that included a pattern, skeins of wool, and wooden (as opposed to plastic) knitting needles, since Perry balked when the prototype appeared with plastic ones: "Absolutely not! NO plastic knitting needles. They have to be wood; it's about the feel of wood and wool." Perry was unyielding when it came to his aesthetic, which sometimes drove those who were charged with containing costs, like Laughlin, crazy. *Vogue* and Butterick Patterns published PERRY ELLIS dress patterns for do-it-yourself seamstresses. And by the time Laughlin negotiated a deal with Levi Strauss, Perry had hired Bruce Weber to shoot models wearing PERRY ELLIS America sportswear in warm and fuzzy family-like gatherings, a distinct change from the solitary, more emotive marketing of his Collection line.

As the business expanded, Perry and Laughlin's personal life became more private, the circle of friends smaller. Laughlin taught Perry to play squash, and they spent most weekends out at Water Island, Perry's retreat located on a skinny stretch of Long Island dunes without ferry access, shops, or restaurants. When Kate arrived for long weekends or summer break, the trio spent most of their time at the beach, Perry and Kate wearing sunbonnets and teasing each other, or Laughlin and Kate plotting pranks to play on Perry. Sometimes, I went out on Sundays, staying until Monday, crossing paths with the rotation of only a few close friends. Lynn, from the Mexico trip, told me that Perry had a whole new life, having discarded some old friends whom she described as "Opportunists. The kind of people who might be fun for an afternoon or might share some business but couldn't be counted on to be *real* friends because they were untrustworthy."

In the fall of 1982, Laughlin and Perry bought a brownstone on West 70th Street, going under contract as partners, each contributing half of the down payment and committing to half the cost of remodeling, legally demonstrating their intent to jointly own and live together in the house. The Upper West Side neighborhood was going through renewal; the house had been in the same family for three generations of doctors, who'd had offices on the parlor level and ground floor, the family living upstairs. The family was now reduced to two ancient daughters, one of whom, Miss

B, answered the front door located on the parlor level when Laughlin took me to see it.

"Well, hello there, Miss B." Laughlin smiled. "Thank you for letting me bring my sister to see the house."

"Well, watch your step." She had a face of cement and blue fingers that grasped the frame of the front door. A small puddle, remnants of last night's rain, pooled on the floor. She switched on a floor lamp strategically placed just inside, exactly where I thought it didn't make sense to have a floor lamp, until she closed the door and I realized there was no other light in the entryway. Laughlin said that much of the wiring was extinct and only a few overhead fixtures worked.

"I hope we're not inconveniencing you," Laughlin said.

"How long are you going to be?"

"Twenty minutes?"

"I'm not climbing the stairs."

"Of course not. How is your arthritis?"

"The cold makes it worse."

"I'm sorry. But soon you'll be in sunny Florida."

"Not soon enough. Well, go ahead, take her through." She waved us away and hobbled into a darkened room that may have once been the parlor. Heavy damask curtains covered the windows, and a recliner sat in a half halo of light coming from another single floor lamp. Beyond that were stacks of crates, boxes, and newspapers, a creepy scene of midnight obsessions.

"Dickens," Laughlin whispered.

We ventured to the ground floor, where an enormous open kitchen, complete with a working hearth, conjured the bustle of a British period drama, a specter that upstaged the miniature Frigidaire huddled in the corner next to a small two-burner gas stove.

As we ascended the stairs, going back up to the parlor level and beyond that to the floors above, the moldings fattened into elaborate patterns, and the doors grew to a stunning height. No one had lived on the upper floors for years, and the rooms were empty.

Yet, despite peeling walls, spattering mold, and air dense with silence and dust, a vitality lurked, almost as if the space were inhabited by a lively set of ghosts. "Don't hold the banister, it's loose," Laughlin cautioned, taking me up and through each room, the echoes of our footfalls rising. He described the construction plans, the gatherings he and Perry would hold, the overnight guests nestled in the rooms on the top floor. He showed me what would be Kate's room, and I heard in his voice the deep conviction of *home*, how he'd finally found a way inside that possibility, the two of us hovering in the shambles of the present even as the vision of what the house would become was more tangible. It was easy to swoon with what more and more was his transformation—the hugely reverberating fact of how he had finally become his whole self. Witnessing it, and being close to the exponential energy it created, inspired me to trust that I could conquer what made me feel stuck; I only had to keep digging. Laughlin always took me back to the highway connecting Santa Fe to the Albuquerque airport, where I dreamed my dreams in proportion to the grandness of the landscape that surrounded me.

The evening after the closing, Laughlin and Perry hosted a small dinner party at the brownstone. At first, Perry was resistant, saying it would be better to celebrate at a restaurant, with beautiful flowers and champagne, rather than in the basement of a creepy wreck. But Laughlin was enthralled by the ruined grandeur and convinced Perry that the whole point was to have dinner at the house precisely *because* of its condition. It would be a waste to ignore the state of their majestically falling down brownstone because that was what they would start with and what they would transform. The debate clarified the difference between them. For all Perry's design success, Laughlin was the more imaginative of the two. Laughlin had a way of being free that Perry was too self-conscious to outwardly express, unless, of course, he was with Laughlin in their private domain, and then he was thrilled to be Laughlin's sidekick.

Six close friends in total—one from Perry's previous life and the others from Laughlin's—three men and three women, were invited for nine p.m. I was the youngest, the little sister, and likely invited because of that. I knew Lynn best, from the Mexico trip and weekends at Water Island. She was one of Perry's muses, a longtime confidante from his early days. She'd been a successful model famous for her Audrey Hepburn, swanlike neck, but in the past several years had been transitioning out of that career—models, like dancers, being pushed to retire when most other professionals their age were essentially at the start of lucrative careers. She knew what it meant to make a living in your tights, so I gravitated toward her, while the others derived their status from family, money, education, or access to business networks.

I arrived late because I'd had a show. At the front door, several broken concrete steps up from the sidewalk, I pounded for a long time before Perry finally arrived holding a tall taper in one hand and a second in the other, which he explained was my light for the night. He escorted me down the back stairway to the ground floor kitchen, where a tangerine fire crackled in the enormous hearth. The little Frigidaire and stove had been removed, the old terra-cotta floor scrubbed, and running down the center of the expanse sat a long table covered in white linen and laid with silver. The room quivered; tall candlesticks and candelabras were everywhere.

"Well. Look who's here."

"With feathers in her hair."

Perry laughed. "Look what you've done."

"Do you recognize it?"

"Of course."

"Is that Perry's?"

"It's his fabric."

"*That* was a scrap on the floor of the showroom, headed for the trash, and look—she took out her sewing machine and made a dress!"

I twirled so they could see the blue tulle I'd sewn beneath Perry's Italian paisley print.

"I paid full price for a dress made out of that fabric," one woman said, pouting. She had an entire wardrobe of Perry's clothes, even a fur coat that was dyed blue because she didn't want people to think she wore real fur.

Quips and bits of conversations ricocheted as Perry hugged me and whispered, "You look right off the stage of the Moulin Rouge."

Lynn greeted me with kisses on both cheeks. "She even smells like a French whore."

"It's Kiehl's."

"I take it back. You smell lovely, and I'm going to call you Lulu."

"And I'm going to call you *Mother*." I underscored the word, eliciting collective whoops and hollers, and was thrilled to have countered her comments with something funny and biting that earned me some respect.

There was caviar and pink Cristal champagne, a Gruaud Larose '61, wild porcini mushrooms, baby zucchini, a Puligny-Montrachet served with swordfish—the caterers discreetly using the former pantry as a staging station. I ate and drank everything in sight.

The men spoke in kinetic bursts, ideas exploding like Christmas crackers, arguing law and civil rights, business deals, and art. They'd seen every exhibit, read every bestseller, traveled to every island you'd never heard of, and finished the Sunday *New York Times* crossword on Saturday night. In my mind, they were changemakers, business and social entrepreneurs, determined to mold the future.

"Yes, but once women are over thirty-five," Lynn, with an oracle's edge, claimed, "especially those who have established themselves professionally, it's as if they are suspended in time, unable to go back to who they were before they were financially independent—and *independent* of the need to be identified by a husband. Men don't want challenge; they want convenience: someone who's willing to devote her life to her husband's ambitions. There is no 'having it all,' and there certainly aren't any men."

Try being gay, someone quipped as another bottle of champagne was opened.

I hoped Lynn was wrong. I still smarted from the debacle of my marriage, not to mention the unexpected debt I now faced, all of which left me feeling spent, like anything plucky had been bled out of me. Despite the fact I danced on Broadway and owned a downtown loft, I was playing catch-up. I saw what little exposure I'd had to the professional world outside the bubble of New York theater and felt I lacked the savviness that defined the dinner guests. They seemed inured to the depths of self-doubt that left me sleepless. I didn't care about power or fame; I wanted to be like Martin and Tom—very good at what I did, respected and secure in my artistic field because I was highly skilled. And I also wanted a personal life that would allow space for me to balance my two loves: work and home. But was that the "having it all" that Lynn dismissed as impossible for women? Seeing my brother and Perry together—acting in concert as they poured the wine, fed the fire—was an inspiring symbiosis even as I believed Lynn's point that the world could discard women like her and me. And what happens to a woman's passion then? What does she do?

When I had to go to the bathroom, Laughlin handed me another candle, saying the bathroom on the second floor was fixed for the girls. "Go to the first floor, turn right and climb the second flight, walk through the room toward the back of the house, and find the door."

"I'll use the boys'. Where's the boys'?"

"It's just an old commode, really just a hole in the floor."

"Like in India?"

"Yes. Go upstairs. Does anyone want some Calvados, or shall we stick to champagne?"

I started up the stairs, holding the taper in one hand and my tulle skirt in the other. Laughlin didn't say whether the exterminators had come, and I prayed there weren't mice, or worse, rats. By the second flight, the eerie emptiness of the house had seeped into my skin. I felt the fine powder of dust on my shoulder and wanted to turn around and just use the boys' hole, whatever, but after all that champagne, I really had *to go*. I hummed a little tune to warn away anything that might come out of the walls, and when I reached the bathroom door, I quickly shoved it open. A gust of freezing air from the open window immediately extinguished my light. Thankfully, one votive candle sat on the floor and guided me to the stall, which must have been part of the bathroom used for the doctors' patients. The doorknob was stiff, barely turnable, but mercifully, the door opened. I grabbed my petticoats, stepped backward to the toilet, and was reaching for relief with my bare bottom when something horrid and furry leaped onto my shoulder and scrambled through my hair. "EEEIIIII!" I exploded out of the stall, dashing down the stairs to the next landing, where in the column of light, I heard their roar: howls of laughter and Laughlin's booming peal.

"It wasn't me. It wasn't me," begged Perry. "I promise. Laughlin did it. It was all his idea. He's awful."

"You're such a *girl*."

"I bet she peed in her pants."

"It wasn't me. Promise you won't be mad," Perry crooned.

"What do you mean, it wasn't you?" Laughlin said with mock exasperation. "Of course, it was. It was both of us. Who got the fur? And sewed it?" Laughlin swatted Perry. Then turned to me. "Do you want me to go back up there with you?"

"No. Thank you. I'll use the boys'."

"How are you going to do that?" someone asked, wanting to know.

"Second position."

"Second position?"

"Second position." I held the tulle and demonstrated a dancer's wide plié.

The boys continued to laugh, and the girls were grateful it had been me, not them. The conversation had turned toward restoring the marble fireplaces, and I thought about how, after signing the papers, opening the floodgates to their bank accounts, and checking on the caterers, Laughlin and Perry had spent the first hours in their new house concocting a prank: gathering hammer and nails, a ladder, and fishing line; rigging an elaborate pulley system over the bathroom door; stuffing the ghastly "bat" with fur scraps swept off the showroom floor; threading the needle and fastening the creature to the ceiling where it was perched and ready to swoop. They struck me as such *boys*, so happy and confident together, Laughlin's love humanizing Perry, while Perry's love gave Laughlin the courage to live openly. Their life together had become such an adventure.

Half Hour
—
1983

The Shubert was always home base—weeks, months, nearly a year going by but always with the reliable voice of our stage manager blaring through the intercom in the voice of God, "Half hour, ladies and gentlemen. It's half hour."

Half hour is the kinetic thirty minutes between real time and showtime. By Actors' Equity rules, it's the time by which every performer must be signed in and physically at the theater. At half hour, if you sliced off the tops of the back-to-back, side-by-side theaters lining 44th and 45th Streets between Broadway and Eighth Avenue, you'd see a throbbing warren: metronomes ticking, trumpets scaling, dressers carrying costumes. With each half-hour call, the time-sensitive ritual of transformation and magic began. We sat at our dressing tables, peering into our mirrors.

I'd become a redhead, Michael asking me to color my hair when a new cast member—a blonde—joined the company and stood near me on the line. I darkened my eyebrows, the way Perry suggested the day he saw my red hair and gasped. "That's it. Change your name to Christine McClatchy. You're an Irish girl!" he'd said, proposing that a new physical identity would spark new professional interest. I was still booking commercials, hoping for some other miraculous professional breakthrough, working harder than ever, thinking if only I could continue to push through, something would eventually give, the way it always had in the past.

Lydia sat next to me. She was back in the cast, having replaced Nicky, who'd been unable to keep up with eight shows a week. Lydia rolled her hair around foam-coated hot rollers, the way she'd always done, but now, she had a two-year-old son—a rarity among dancers—and a house in Queens. We'd become veterans, along with others who floated in and out of the Broadway cast.

Our other roommate was Annie, a translucent Asian beauty who'd come from the West Coast and often brought news of the world into the dressing room. "Did you hear about that friend of Russ's? Daniel? Remember, Russ"—our dance captain—"brought him by before Christmas?"

"Oh. Sure."

"He died."

"What?"

"He went home for Christmas, got pneumonia, and died."

"Oh my God. I once had pneumonia, and a couple of weeks on antibiotics took care of it."

"Don't bring bad luck in here." Lydia made the sign of the cross. "I've got a baby at home."

"Still, it's weird and awful to think about," Annie said with a shrug.

"So, Barker." Lydia was determined to change the vibe and follow up on her fixation that I find a boyfriend. "What does he do? The one here tonight?"

"He's a lawyer."

"A law-yer?" She thoroughly separated the syllables.

"A lawyer? Like a *realperson*?" Annie asked.

"Yep."

They were both quiet, absorbing the news. It was unusual for someone to try to bridge the divide considered to separate us from *realpeople*, the rest of civilization. It wasn't just that we made a living using our creative mindsets and physical skills; it also had to do with the structure of daily life. We worked a six-day week, four of those days revolving around a three-to-four-hour window of intensity; the other two days, matinee days, were twelve-hour marathons. A *realperson* had to adapt to the commitment of time, energy, and focus we gave to our work, which was ever present, even without a Broadway contract.

"A law-yer. Okay. Where's he sitting?"

"Fifth row."

"Fifteen minutes, ladies and gentlemen. It's fifteen," squawked the intercom.

"Let's go look."

"No!"

But Lydia and Annie ran down the stairs, so I followed behind, chasing them through the basement beneath the stage and up the other side, into the wings, where the black velvet drop reached the floor and we could peer out at the audience without being seen.

"Is he there?"

"I'm not looking. You look."

"Fifth row?"

"Yes. Eight seats in."

"I don't see him."

"Neither do I."

"He's in the center seat."

"That's him?"

"*Him?*"

"He wears—"

"GLASSES?"

"Yep."

"What are you doing?" Russ appeared, wearing his head-set.

"Nothing."

"There's a guy in the fifth row who came to see Barker."

"Oh?"

"He wears glasses."

"He's a *realperson*."

"Really?"

"Really."

"Get out of here. It's almost time for 'Places.'"

We scurried back to our room to get our shoes. I'd raised eyebrows dating a *realperson* because joining the ranks of *realpeople* was a stigmatized default position, something that signaled you were moving away from the business, when everyone knew that once you left, you were gone for good. I had no intention of leaving—I was trying to transition—but flip-flopping in my head was my discussion with Martin seven years earlier. What had become weighted was the way I'd yelled, "I'm a girl!" after he'd tried to pimp me out during the cocaine/Michael Bennett opening-night fiasco in London. Here's what was missing in the *realpeople* debate: A female's life is much too complicated and nuanced to be divided in such a binary way. We survive by making compromises, blending who we are professionally with parents, boyfriends, husbands, and children because for us, all life is a constant negotiation and a feat of logistics. We are keenly aware of the finesse and grit required to balance jobs that we do for love with *real* life.

Dancers aren't a rare breed of female; they're just like every other professional female who's looking in the mirror. Most all

189

women who invite others into their lives are acrobats flying from one platform to another. It's just the gooey power of being female that makes it look natural when it's NOT natural at all. It is not natural for us to be asked to live in the world as *halfpeople*, often having to put the many authentic aspects of our selves aside.

A Singular Sensational Night

1983

By July, Michael prepared to make history: On September 29, 1983, *A Chorus Line* would become the longest running show in the history of Broadway. Michael planned a black-tie, invitation-only celebration, flying—at his expense—every dancer who'd ever been in the show to New York to participate. With his assistants, he spent three months mapping out a show within the show, stitching together the script and musical numbers with different dancers who had been in different casts over the years, so the plotline and music continued even as cast members switched off, like one big revolving door. Then, in three manic September days, carpenters hammered sixty-four 4x4 beams under the stage to support the weight of three hundred dancers, and the Shubert rocked with the same glorious insanity that Lydia and I had experienced at City Center years earlier. During the grand finale, dancers flooded the stage, entering in line after line, some even rushing down the aisles into the orchestra and balcony, all of us kicking our legs and singing with bursting hearts.

The audience was on its feet....The theater seemed to shake. The cast and audience had become one, united in the at least momentary conviction that *A Chorus Line* was the best thing that had ever happened to any of us. People were

screaming and, when the lights slowly dimmed to black, they were sobbing....Like those first performances down at the Public, the 3,389th performance of *A Chorus Line* can never be recaptured....A night in the theater that its witnesses will remember for the rest of their lives.

    Frank Rich, "Critic's Notebook; The Magic of 'Chorus Line' No. 3,389,"

    New York Times, October 1, 1983

I'd invited Laughlin and Perry, but they couldn't come because they had to be in Texas for business, and I'd only gone out a couple of times with the "law-yer" and wasn't sure about inviting him, so I planned to tag along with Lydia and her husband at the party afterward.

Michael's reconstruction of the special show called for our cast to perform the opening number, after which, other casts rotated in and out to deliver the characters' lines and songs. After Lydia and I danced the opening number, we snuck out the stage door and entered the back of the house, where we could watch the ongoing show. The girl playing my part, KC, was spontaneous and shimmering—absolutely wonderful, a realization that landed like a stone in my gut, some sense of my own worth suddenly leaking away. Later, I couldn't shake the feeling and was glad to be alone at the party. By the time I got home to the loft, the wound consumed me. I had once been perfect in the part of an effervescent dewy girl, but I felt increasingly burned out. I'd been waiting to feel the pull of the "right time" to make a pivot, but it hadn't come. The vision of KC spooked me, and I knew I would never again feel a hundred percent right about doing the part if I couldn't conjure the blithe spirit I'd lost.

Do-Si-Do

Early Spring–Summer 1984

My agent suggested I go to LA, where there was much more film work and my commercials would count, but leaving New York scared me. I *knew* New York and had a support system here; I would have to rent out the loft; did I have enough money in the bank to sustain a possible long period of unemployment and transition? Such details could seemingly be sorted out, but I heard snippets of Lynn's warnings that women over thiry-five and under fifty were rendered invisible. I still had several years according to her calculations, but I felt weak-kneed and claustrophobic squaring off against a reality beyond my control, not just for dancers, but for lots of women being sidelined as they reached career junctures. On top of it all, *everyone* I knew was also increasingly edgy, a kind of underlying angst percolating in the streets.

The new Reaganomics, extraordinary inflation, and cultural politics pushed against us in ways we couldn't ignore. Martin was explosively livid about Pat Buchanan, the White House communications director, who spewed antigay venom from his official dais, creating an uptick in violence against gays when the community previously had had a few years of silent acceptance. Lynn was struggling to land in another area of the fashion business and nearing forty. She was panicked that she'd never meet a man, let alone have a child, keeping a daily tally of every single expense in a small spiral notebook, afraid she was running out of money and time. Looking at her, I was keenly aware of how difficult the timing was for women who hoped to balance careers with having children. Even things with Laughlin and Perry—who I thought of as indomitable—were off. I'd tried calling the house on 70th Street at least eight times with no answer, then tried Julia at the office, who casually said, "Oh, they must have forgotten to tell you. They changed the number." When I reached Laughlin at last, he spoke in sober tones about challenges with the business. There was a catch in his voice that made him sound distant, which I didn't really get because by the end of 1983, Perry had won three Coty Awards and the Cutty Sark Men's Fashion Award for Most Outstanding American Designer, the fashion equivalent of a Grand Slam. A day after Laughlin's thirty-sixth birthday in January, he and Perry were on the first page of *The New York Times* business section with the announcement of PERRY ELLIS AMERICA, the joint venture between PERRY ELLIS and Levi Strauss.

Media called it the "go-go eighties," hyping with spin the glossy side of New York. For my friends and me in our late twenties and early thirties, though, the years of Reagan's administration had trapped us in a vise of economic circumstances that I would see later repeated with college kids graduating during the 2008 economic crisis. It was a kind of squeezing that at a young age prevented you from advancing, even as other groups raced ahead. We were basically working-class people, most without college degrees but with lots of talent in the arts—skills not easily translatable to steady, higher-paying jobs. Unemployment had always been part of showbiz life, but now it was much worse, with fewer jobs than ever, the smaller professional and regional theaters closing in the unsustainable climate of Reaganomics. Even if we were prepared to pivot, there was nowhere to pivot to, a sense of strangulation pervading our lives and dooming our futures.

The suffering extended well beyond Broadway. In the group beneath the working-class were the barely working, many of whom had become homeless when rents skyrocketed in proportion to interest rates. Crime was out of control, my neighborhood suddenly overrun when the city crammed entire families into single rooms, filling the old, five-hundred-room hotels beyond capacity. Those who didn't qualify lived in boxes on the sidewalk. I'd invested every cent in the loft, trusting that after its bankruptcy in the seventies, NYC was on the mend—our co-op even getting a ten-year tax abatement as an incentive to help revitalize the area. But the city was poorly managed, and now new federal government's policies were draining its budget. My investment in the loft was declining in value, while my salary stayed the same and my mortgage doubled. People like me were clinging precariously to lives that had made sense just four years ago, but we had neither the clout nor salaries that would allow us to transition or invest in the stock market—the only place now to make money. Real money, the "green stuff" as my father called it, shrank. I was a girl dancing on Broadway, the epitome of success by some standards, but my future was dim because I made a living earning a wage, the all-American way, which was slowly devolving in the new economy. What gnawed at me was not that I hadn't worked hard or that I'd been stupid—if so, I was willing to accept the consequences—it was that the changing government policies skewed my fate by deciding who would be rewarded and who would fall behind. Like in the system of no-fault divorce, laws had deep personal consequences, and it seemed politicians either forgot that or didn't care.

When I called to talk about Easter, Laughlin let loose, one of the few times I'd heard him so angry, saying the house's architect, JT, had arrived in a limo when doors hadn't been hung on the upper floors. "Sorry, but his work doesn't warrant his pomp. I want a cigarette"—he'd recently quit—"and I'm sending you and Kate a picture!" Later, we each got snapshots of Laughlin sitting at his desk, his hair ratted into an electrified-Einstein style, ten cigarettes hanging like loose teeth from his mouth. He'd laughed when he'd said he was sending it, but in a half-hearted way when half-heartedness was not his style.

Landing in the existential angst was Perry's voice on my answering machine toward the end of April, calling me himself, not having his secretary do it, and asking that I call back on his private line. Another new home number and a private line I didn't know existed. On the phone, he was his usual ambrosial self, commenting on spring daffodils in Central Park, before taking aim. "Are you a good actress?"

"I hope so."

"Because your brother has something to tell you, and he's being very stubborn about it. I think his not talking to you is standing in the way of his getting better. So, I want you to find a way to spend time with him and make it easier for him to talk to you."

"He has a hard time talking to me?"

"Can you do that for me?"

"Sure. Of course." The conversation was completely convoluted. I thought they'd been avoiding me. And what did he mean by "getting better"? I didn't ask for clarification because I got flustered when he implied that I wasn't easy to talk to, making it my fault they'd changed the phone number multiple times. I racked my brain for something I must have missed. The children's clothing line had failed, something Laughlin took personally, even as Perry took it in stride. But the "getting better" reference recalled something I'd read a year earlier in a 1983 *New York Times* article about a new disease called AIDS, which was formerly called GRID, something I knew only a little bit about from my gay friends. On the one hand, it seemed very serious, though, according to the article, limited to a small, specific group. Besides that, the lack of scientific facts supported accusations by gay men I knew that the situation was being completely blown out of proportion by the new wave of homophobia and a government that seemed bent on delegitimizing gay life. After reading the article, I concluded that Laughlin, Perry, and probably Tom didn't fit the profile—"Sexually promiscuous . . . frequented homosexual bars and bathhouses"—even if others, like Martin, may have.

As I continued reading and trying not to worry, the bagel I was chewing turned to glue. I had to spit it out. After that, I scanned the papers daily, looking for more articles. I eventually found only one—about the French discovering a virus called LAV the year before that likely was the cause of AIDS. For unknown reasons, the article said, researchers at the Centers for Disease Control and Prevention (CDC) and a prominent researcher, Dr. Robert Gallo of the National

Cancer Institute (NCI), hadn't paid much attention. Now, it appeared that maybe Gallo's discovery of a virus called HTLV-III was the same thing as LAV, which meant important research may have been unnecessarily delayed. The article went on reassuringly, though, saying the research would help create a diagnostic test for AIDS, and once that was done, a vaccine could be developed. For now, doctors didn't really know how many people had AIDS; the lack of urgency and collection of scientific data was largely due to the fact that the victims were gay men, the very people pilloried by the Reagan administration, *politicians who didn't care.*

I didn't know how to weigh the limited facts available in mainstream newspapers with the resentments of my gay friends over the antigay political climate. When I checked in with Martin, who had just opened *Brighton Beach Memoirs* on Broadway, he said, in an accusatory tone, "Pay attention."

"But how?"

"Read the *Advocate* or *Native.*"

"Really? You think I should make a trip downtown every week to Christopher Street, making my way past the studded dog collars and leather jockstraps to ask, 'Where do you keep the newspapers?' I don't live downtown; I'm not in on the gossip; there isn't a newspaper kiosk that carries the *Advocate* or *Native* at the subway station, and I can't exactly go to the card catalog at the library, can I?"

"Okay, sweetness."

"I'm dancing fast as I can, Martin. I really am, but I can't be in all places at once. The lack of information or access is a real problem. Tell me what to do and I'll do it." But he didn't say anything more, which sent my guts to my knees. I loved Martin, but we stood in the swamp of an awkward fact:

Girls didn't have access. It was too mean to say, so I didn't, that Christopher Street COULD BE JUST AS EXCLUSIVE as the Harvard Club! I was concerned, but I didn't know how involved to be when everyday life was already a combat zone: aggressive conservative politics, the immediate threat of rising interest rates and economic stagnation, and my career hitting a wall. The men I trusted for feedback and advice—Martin, Laughlin, and Perry—were all unavailable or distracted by whatever occupied their lives that I was shut out of. And meanwhile, my ENT had asked me about the relentlessness of my schedule. I'd had two strep throats in a row and couldn't seem to fully recover.

I hung up the phone with Martin, not having time to process any of it, which was another problem—the way life was like living through an avalanche, pressing issues constantly piling up without any way to separate them or properly evaluate their significance. Just then, I was rushing to 890 Broadway, where I was part of a group hired to help Michael Bennett with a new workshop he was starting.

Michael had bought and renovated 890 to create an arts and dance center. Now its nine floors housed dance studios, rehearsal spaces, and offices. The new show was called *Scandal*; the script had been written by a screenwriter and Michael was "developing" it for the stage. It was about a woman, Claudia, who leaves her husband after discovering he's been unfaithful; she embarks on a wild sexual awakening to find her true self, leading to a happily-ever-after marital reconciliation. A few days into the workshop, I sat on the sidelines during a dance break, watching a jury scene unfold in a disjointed, hyperbolic nightmare where Claudia dreams she is being judged for having had a lesbian fantasy.

Everyone around me and at the production table was howling with laughter, so I feigned a big toothpaste smile and forced an uneasy laugh. It *was* funny, but three days in, I hadn't grasped why anyone thought a project about blatant female sexual adventuring, including the occasional *ménage à trois*, was viable in either the current unease about a new STD or the pervasive religiosity of the patriarchal Reagan/Evangelical conservatism.

When Reagan was newly elected in 1981, we'd performed at the White House, doing a laundered version of *A Chorus Line*, Michael fulfilling the request to eliminate all four-letter words, the "tits and ass" number, AND the Paul monologue about homosexuality. For three years, we'd lived under a cloud of Evangelical Christian dogma and Jerry Falwell broadcasting how "sinful behavior" was "destroying the nation." People like Falwell, who'd never been taken seriously in New York, now had a microphone and a president supporting them. I didn't understand what Michael was thinking with *Scandal*. I would have welcomed some new, funny, authentic female voice talking about sex and fantasy, but this wasn't it, and this wasn't the time.

Meanwhile, the rustlings in the wings at the Shubert were getting louder. As we waited in the dark after "Places" had been called, the boys whispered about friends in the hospital or discussed whether certain clubs or bathhouses were going to be closed. Preparing our stage entrances, the boys talked about not knowing what "safe sex" was, until one of the girls dryly whispered back: "Guess what? Girls get pregnant, so sex has never been safe for us! Get used to it!"

Which started a series of back-and-forth retorts: "I'm

not about to let the sex police tell me what I can and cannot do."

"What do you think the abortion argument is about?"

"Abortion? I just want to know where we're going to go if the baths are closed!"

"It's all connected. Don't you see?"

Later, we got in trouble for talking in the wings.

These conversations played in my head as the *Scandal* rehearsals continued to unfold, the assembled group of dancers from the show rocking with laughter, and Michael Bennett, the designers, composer, and producers investing millions of dollars to keep the project afloat. I felt completely alienated in a room full of some of the most talented Broadway professionals, people I admired who now seemed blind both to the power of growing societal backlash and, more particularly, to what really was a woman's life. The only consolation was the ballet, an extraordinary piece, maybe the best Michael ever choreographed: As Claudia ventures to Europe and is drawn into an enthralling sexual encounter at a *pensione*, the ceiling fresco comes alive with writhing bodies, a leap of imagination that was so very Michael.

The other saving grace was Victor G, one of the co-stars, who played multiple roles. *He* was hysterical, and a good friend of my brother's, Laughlin having friends in both the fashion and theater worlds. After *Scandal* rehearsal that first week, I dropped by Laughlin's office, thinking I'd tell him about Victor and try to get to the bottom of whatever Perry was talking about. But when I arrived and described the *Scandal* plot, Laughlin frowned. "It's about *what?*" All around us, the showroom was frantic, getting ready to launch the women's wear Collection on the heels of Portfolio, a less expensive "young professional" line. The schedule was overly ambitious, plus potentially confusing to consumers—two different lines with two different price points. Patterns and fabrics littered the floor, while Perry's assistants, Patricia and Jed, looked exhausted and exasperated. The business had exploded with still more categories of products. The stress was palpable, and Laughlin couldn't talk, so I left 575 Seventh Avenue and headed to the Shubert, flummoxed: Why had Perry and Laughlin crammed so much into so little time? Why the hurry, and what did "getting better" mean?

In a span of twenty quick blocks along Broadway, I went from one New York City god, Michael Bennett, to another, Perry Ellis. Ahead, the marquee lights twinkled in the theater district, but when I crossed 42nd Street to the triangle of pavement where the subway entrance stood like a tower above a mine shaft, a dark figure huddled in a bivouac of cardboard. He looked like an emaciated ghost, some part of him lingering while life had been stolen from him. I felt dwarfed suddenly, wondering if any of us were truly immune to downturn, failure, whatever it was that had so reduced this man. Did Laughlin, Perry, or Michael remember what it was like to be nobody? I walked quickly then, reaching for the handle of the stage door and the relief of "half hour."

My participation in the *Scandal* workshop lasted only a week. I worried that I'd exhausted my place in Michael's universe, but he let a whole group of us go. With time on my hands, I tried again with Laughlin, dropping by his office after a commercial audition for Scope mouthwash. In the script, a wife and husband wake up with dragon breath. The casting director had ignored the actor playing

the role of the husband and asked me if I had claustrophobia: "Whoever is cast in the commercial will be fitted with
a dragon mask created by a special-effects artist. A mold
of your entire face and head—including your eyes, ears,
mouth, and nose—takes about thirty minutes to harden
and during that time, you must breathe through two thin
straws pushed up your nose. You might not be able to hear.
So, I like you, Christine, but do you get claustrophobic?
Do you have any breathing or sinus trouble? Because that's
really the most important consideration."

"NO. Nothing. No problem with claustrophobia," I
lied, knowing that a national network television spot for
Scope, would pay the loan on the loft for six months, maybe
giving me a chance at LA or some other pivot in my career.

Laughlin sighed when I told him the Scope story, then
genuinely laughed when I showed up at his office a week
later and told him I got the spot. "Let's go for a walk," he
offered, as if by way of celebration, and he called Raymond
the chauffeur to take us to 70th Street, where he leashed
up Josh, his and Perry's springer spaniel. As we headed
to Central Park, I couldn't help but think that maybe I'd
finally have some good news for Perry, who hadn't stopped
pestering me about talking to Laughlin.

My brother wore a heavy sweater and walked briskly;
I had to take two steps to every one of his strides. Josh was
thrilled at the sudden outing, wagging his tail with such
ardor that his behind wiggled, too. Laughlin grabbed a stick
and arced it high.

"I can't see the stick."

"Neither can I. The glare is blinding."

Josh rushed back and forth looking for the stick, the sun

shimmering like a gigantic brass gong as he put his nose down at one spot, rustled the leaves, then ran to another spot and put his nose down there, too. We walked more, but soon the lavender sky darkened, and Josh couldn't find the stick, so Laughlin said, "Let's go home."

I beeped my answering machine from the phone in the 70th Street kitchen, while Laughlin retreated to the library upstairs. There was a message from Perry to call him. "Hi, Perry. I'm at your house. I got your message."

"Where did you go?"

"To the park. With Josh."

"Well, it certainly has been a beautiful day." His voice, like helium, rising with weightlessness. "So, did you have a talk with your brother?"

"Yes, but not about anything in particular."

Just then, Laughlin walked into the kitchen, mouthing, *Who are you talking to?* I couldn't say it was Perry, so I mouthed back, *Bill, the law-yer*, as Lydia called him, who was slowly becoming my boyfriend.

"How's *your* day?" I asked, miserably pretending Perry was Bill and hoping that Perry would sense the change in my voice and understand that Laughlin was there.

"Fine. It's fine." Perry was oblivious. "He has to talk to you. YOU need to make this happen."

"Well, maybe in time."

"Time? I'm going to tell him tonight that if he doesn't tell you, I'm telling you myself."

"Oh— My brother Laughlin says hi."

"He's there? Tell him I say hi, too."

"He says hi, too." Only Laughlin thought it was "the lawyer."

The caginess between them was new. Never, ever had there been anything that looked or felt like a deception. I could only think that they were frustrated with the slow progress of home renovations, or that the business was too highly leveraged. Even Joe Papp was talking about money all the time because of the cuts to the National Endowment for the Arts. Plus, the Collection, which just launched, had received some bad press in *Women's Wear Daily*, which was *very* disheartening, especially because the editor was an old friend of Laughlin's. Still, how bad could things be? Martex now made PERRY ELLIS sheets and towels that were sold at Macy's. You couldn't go anywhere without seeing the label.

The essential thing about Laughlin and Perry was that, even though you might be with them, spending the night, spending the weekend, borrowing their robes, rummaging through their drawers for change, holding their credit cards, or tasting their wine, and as much as you were their family and they put an arm around you when you were blue, you always had the feeling that they really lived in a place separate from you and from everyone else. On the outside, they were generous and gregarious, but they took themselves and each other *inside* to some deep place of privacy. And that was where they *really* lived, that was what fed and sustained them.

I had seen this before in my own parents, who had the same kind of mysterious intimacy. Their bedroom and part of the house, no matter where we lived, was removed from the center of activity and the mayhem of our childhoods. Laughlin and Perry were a bit like that. Out of everyone I knew, the thing between them was the truest depiction of what I thought love must be.

Soon after our walk in the park, Laughlin had a bout of shingles, something I'd never heard of but others explained was mostly related to older people or stress. Laughlin was taking an afternoon off, so I stopped by for tea after one of my lessons.

When he answered the door, he looked fine; the only change was that he didn't have his shirt tucked into his trousers because the shingles hugged his waistline. I wondered if they were painful, but I didn't ask and he didn't say; instead, he cheerfully asked me to follow him up the stairs that he took two at a time, broadcasting confidence and health. Laughlin handed me a stack of clean laundry, and together we put it away. I started, "So how do you know when you've found the right person?"

"You're thinking *that* about Bill?"

His tone upended everything. I wondered if he thought I was about to make another mistake, so I tried to reorient the conversation. "How did you know that Perry was right for you? Was there some sign, when you really and truly knew that he was the one?"

"I think it was that I was comfortable."

"What?"

"I was comfortable." He continued putting away his clean socks.

"*Comfortable*? You speak about the man you love like he's a pair of old slippers!"

He shrugged.

"So . . . what? I'm supposed to go looking for love in the shoe department at Penny's. Is that it?"

I made him laugh, but he continued opening and closing drawers, stacking socks, repeating "comfortable" on his way to the undershirts. How could it be that love, this epic emotion, this thing that changed lives, that had so changed *his* life, was recognizable by its very banality? But Laughlin was checking the orchid on top of the dresser to see if the bark was dry.

"Did you hear back about the commercial audition? What was it?"

"Goodyear."

"Tires? Did you get it?"

"No. Guess it wasn't meant to be."

"It's alright to be frustrated and unhappy."

"What?"

"About things that aren't working out."

"What?"

"How can you change anything if you don't acknowledge that things aren't right? If you don't say to yourself that this isn't working? You need to try a different approach or come to some acceptance."

"Acceptance?" He'd suddenly shifted the conversation to me, which was infuriating. The Scope commercial had not made it out of the test market, so it hadn't been the windfall I'd hoped for. I hadn't had an audition for anything exciting in months.

"You're frustrated. That's a good source of energy. Use it." Laughlin walked from his room through the dressing room to the front parlor. "If you don't acknowledge that you're going through a hard time, you're denying it."

Was I *denying* something? He sat down in his oversized chair and flatly concluded, "You're going through a hard time. It doesn't seem realistic to have a complacent attitude about your failures."

"I'm not complacent," I insisted, choosing to repeat the less painful of the two words.

"Then what?"

"Trying to figure it out." Language left me then. I got a thousand silent messages a day basically telling me that I wasn't "right." I didn't need my own brother to drive it home. Of course, I wanted to be farther along. I didn't know if the problem was the *business* or *me*, while Laughlin seemed to have forgotten what it was like to pray that your checkbook balanced at the end of the month. If he thought I should just walk away from the show, he didn't get it—that I loved my job and career; it was impossible to be happy about accepting unemployment and not belonging to something bigger than me. He knew about burnout. Hadn't he, too, at one time felt exhausted by perpetual dead ends? Maybe it wasn't fair to equate his situation with mine, but I'd hoped for a bit more understanding, and certainly hadn't expected him to turn the tables, making this all about me. "Look, I do eight shows a week and audition for every single opportunity that comes my way." Then I reminded him that I was alone. I shared my life at the loft with my books and my writing journals; I memorized lines for new scenes in my acting class, and often prayed for wisdom, or, like a few days ago, learned how to tar the leak in my roof near the skylight. "Did you know that tar spreads just like thick chocolate frosting?"

He laughed then, but his face froze midway, something essential having been erased. I could feel a monster lurking, even if I didn't know if it was coming for Laughlin or for me. The director of the Goodyear spot thought I didn't "exhibit enough authority." What did they want, these men who controlled my future? A girl with *authority*? A pretty girl? Someone new—a redheaded Irish girl with strong eyebrows? The key word being "girl." And here I was, sitting with Laughlin, who no longer seemed to see me as anything more than a *little sister* when all along I thought he was different from the other men who determined my value.

"So does Bill pick you up from the theater after the show?"

"Yeah."

"That's nice."

Then, suddenly—maybe it was the word "nice," which wasn't really in Laughlin's vernacular—I sensed that the flicker in his face I hadn't recognized before was fear, and I wasn't angry anymore.

What's in a Name?
—
Summer 1984

I was no longer willing to be a pawn in Perry's conniving scheme, and I stopped trying to arrange get-togethers with Laughlin. He would do what he would do. Then I got another strep throat, but Laughlin surprised me, inviting me to the house on Water Island. I had a week's vacation coming, so I arranged to take time off, thinking the sun, beach, and being together would be the perfect remedy, until I arrived, and Perry and Laughlin had to leave because of some unexpected business issues. I spent the week alone.

Walking through the empty house one afternoon, I found a life-sized drawing taped to the full-length mirror in Laughlin and Perry's bedroom. Kate and her friend Jessie, who accompanied Kate on some vacations, had expertly duplicated the blue-and-white kimono Perry often wore and drawn a caricature of a pig's face, writing "FAT Perry" across the top. It was exactly the kind of teasing game Perry loved, and I laughed out loud imagining the girls' delight. I also found a book of baby names, with columns of those that were popular in different eras.

Laughlin called midweek to check in, asking me to collect the trash and put out the garbage because they might not get back out until the following week.

"Do you want me to do a big clean, throwing out things

like the book of names I found, or was that something of Kate's
to keep?"

"Oh, no. Actually, that's something I've wanted to discuss
with you."

"Oh?"

"Yeah. Perry and Barbara are having a baby." Barbara, a
former writer who now lived in LA and worked as a television
producer, was a good friend of Perry's.

"A baby?"

"Yeah. Perry has always wanted a child, especially since
he and Kate have grown so close, and Barbara was reaching
the point where she wasn't meeting anyone, and she wanted a
child . . ."

"Oh." I had friends, including a commercial agent, who
had begun to talk about similar arrangements. They were part
of the group of independent, professional women whom Lynn
had described at the long-ago dinner party—women with in-
comes and property but no partners, who now wanted children
and were initiating arrangements with friends, sperm donors,
or adoption agencies.

"Perry told Kate the news, and they looked through that
book to see if they could find any names they liked."

"Oh."

"Kate is thrilled. She'll have a little sister. The baby is a
girl."

"You know already?"

"The baby is due in November."

"This didn't just happen?"

"No. I didn't tell you until now, in case things didn't work
out."

"Oh. Sure." Maybe this was what Perry wanted Laughlin to

discuss with me, even though it didn't seem related to "getting better"—unless they had some difference of opinion, which I could imagine may have been the case. Still, I felt worse than miserable, trying to express genuine happiness even as I swallowed the hurt at having been left out of the loop, especially about something as important as a *baby*. I was genuinely happy for Barbara. But as for Laughlin, Perry, and me, I didn't know why there was such a gulf between us.

Tea
Early September 1984

"**C**an you come to tea? Be ready in about ten minutes? Raymond will come get you."

"Yikes. Okay, yes."

"Good. I'll tell him you'll be downstairs and will call Angela to tell her to set the tea tray."

"Okay. Good."

I ran from the phone to my bedroom, the tone of Laughlin's voice landing in my gut and signaling that he was finally ready to have a heart-to-heart talk. Luckily, I'd just showered, so I loaded my knapsack and ran out the building, saying "Hi" to the guy who lived in a cardboard box at the foot of the stairs, just as Raymond pulled up in the green Jaguar. The homeless guy gave me a salute when he saw that the car had come for me. I jumped in, and Raymond circled back toward 40th Street and radioed Laughlin, who appeared on the corner.

"You just get out of the pool?" He looked disappointed, getting into the seat next to me.

"Shower. I swim on Fridays."

"Didn't you want to dry your hair and get dressed?"

"You said ten minutes, so I just packed my knapsack and ran out the door." I was wearing what I thought was a real find: a fleecy red sweat suit from the boys' department of A&S on 34th Street.

"You could have said you needed to dry your hair and get dressed." He didn't even try to smile.

I pulled the hood around my throat, saying nothing, though we both knew he was angry. I knew if I'd asked for a few extra minutes, he might have postponed this meeting, again, for the gazillionth time, so I'd risked what he thought was part of my job—to present an image in public. I was sure he was thinking that I could have dressed in something new from PERRY ELLIS AMERICA. I had clothes—he'd made sure of that—but I hated feeling like a paper doll, and I thought today was about *us*, not appearances.

"I brought you something." He pulled out three slippery silk scarves. "I like the blue one, but you take your choice."

"Oh, Laughlin." That he moved so quickly from criticism to appeasement was also distressing. "They're gorgeous. I like the blue one, too, thank you."

He turned his head to the window, seemingly absorbed in the parade of rushing cars, his disappointment still hanging between us.

Meanwhile, he was impeccably dressed in a caramel colored cashmere coat, looking like a statesman dipped in gold, more beautiful and handsome than ever. I didn't believe he was so superficial. Deep down, like me, he didn't fully trust appearances and beauty, so with the silk scarf on my lap and his profile pressed to his window, I wondered what I'd missed, why he was harsh and rigid. Maybe he thought he could rely on beauty to mitigate a blow because I'd begun to seriously worry that whatever he said, *it would be a blow*. Maybe it was easier to say something awful when the person you were confiding in had something to immunize them, like a red, spangled PERRY ELLIS AMERICA sweater, some radiance to distract from the ugliness. I thought all that, even though it was convoluted bunk.

"*1984?*" Laughlin lifted the book from the open pocket of my knapsack.

"Everyone wants to reread it now that it's actually 1984."

"God, I remember it from high school and how creepy it was. That and getting under our desks. Remember the Saturday morning black-and-white commercials in Arlington? The bomb shelter stacked with canned goods, the kids smiling as they huddled underground?"

"I was too young and too in love with Gene Autry and Sky King. Besides, I used the commercials to go into the kitchen and get another bowl of Cheerios."

"Well, I remember. What was it called? The language?"

"Newspeak."

"Right. Newspeak. And the rats, those rats. Did you go to ballet this morning?"

"Eleven thirty. Then I had an audition for Os-Cal, a calcium supplement. If I get it, they're going to age me with prosthetics. I start out with a youthful, perky posture, then slowly collapse into myself." I hunched my shoulders and rounded my back, pretending I was Quasimodo.

His face flattened. "Anything else going on? No new plays, films?"

"No. Nothing." Laughlin didn't laugh at Quasimodo, and I was haunted by the feeling that he was relying, just as much as I was, on my ability to catch some new opportunity—a part in a soap opera or play, something with bright lights and me at the center, where he liked me best. If I were suddenly to pull that off, I might change the downward momentum that was consuming us. I'd done it before, when I got *A Chorus Line*, stunning everybody and proving that dreams could come true. Laughlin had had his turn when he found Perry and created his fabulous new life. Now it was my turn again, an invisible rope tying us together: Whoever was in front moved forward, but not without pulling along the one languishing behind.

"Why don't you try going up Eighth Avenue?" We were stuck in traffic, behind a bus that had just stopped to pick up a whole line of passengers. "Geez," Laughlin muttered. "Just our luck."

In the theater, we never used the word "luck." Instead, we said, "Break a leg!" out of fear of waking a monster. To us, luck was a charlatan, and we didn't invite his presence, knowing it was just as easy to be in the wrong place at the wrong time as in the right place at the right time.

"Oh, wait. I forgot! I brought something for you, too."

"What?" Laughlin tried to read the label of the package I handed him, but it was written in the swirly curlicues of an Eastern language. When he finally found the English wording, the Chico of my childhood joined us in the car. "Fried grasshoppers and BUGS! They're perfect. Where did you find them?"

"At the Little India store around the corner from the loft."

"Can you get me a case? I'll pay for it."

"A whole case? Wow, a regular infestation."

He laughed. "I don't care. The more the better. You just don't know how perfect these are!"

The tea table was set when we arrived, the silver so perfectly polished it reflected our faces. "Pour the tea," Laughlin said, bending to light the fire in the parlor fireplace. He struck the match with a broad sweeping gesture, like that of a conductor calling to order all the discordant elements in front of him.

"There are two things I need to tell you." He used the bellows then; the fire reaching with red fingers. "I want mine with milk, too. There are two things I need to tell you, and they're both kinda sad."

When Laughlin talked to Kate, he used "kinda sad" as a preface before explaining something disturbing. But he didn't seem disturbed, and I wasn't Kate. He was smiling, unfolding his large linen napkin carefully before laying it across his knees.

"The first thing is that Suzanne and Jeffrey have separated. He's moved out, and she wanted me to tell you because it's too hard to go through the whole thing over and over, telling everyone in the family. But she wants you to know."

"What?"

"He moved out over the weekend."

"Two days ago?"

"He's been unhappy for a long time, and Suzanne has had it. She told him that if he was so unhappy, then he should leave."

"I can't believe it. What about the children? She must be devastated. Why wouldn't she have said something?"

"Well, you know, your life is . . . different."

"What?"

"She has a hard time imagining what you do. Anyway, I think it's better that he moved out. Here, take a sandwich."

"Wait. What do you mean she has a hard time imagining what I do?"

"You know, what you do."

"What I *do*? I do eight shows a week! I'm out of the house by ten a.m. every morning, auditioning for commercials. It takes an average of sixty auditions to get a single booking. I have a mortgage, for God's sake. I *qualified* for one, a single female, even with interest rates at sixteen percent. How is my life *different*?"

"It's just—" He shrugged, like I was being melodramatic. "She doesn't know what you do all day. It's hard for her to relate."

"I *work*, all day, every day."

I was sorry for what was happening to her, but I was insulted, and belittled by the "kinda sad" reference. Even so, I swallowed what felt like betrayal—he and Suzanne forming a secret alliance—knowing full well that I'd have to match his dispassion in order to find out the rest of what he intended to tell me. Sipping my (now) cold tea and straightening my back, I asked, "Is there something I can do?"

"Do? No. Suzanne is going to be fine. She's a well-respected attorney with her own client base. Albuquerque is a good place for her. In the long run, she'll be better off. The second thing I have to tell you is that I have AIDS." He said it casually, tacking it onto the list about Suzanne, and as much as I had imagined in late night fits of terror that he might one day say those words, I never anticipated the horror of hearing them spoken with such banality. I was stunned, and his eyes were stones.

"Do you want to know the whole story from the beginning?"

I nodded, so he proceeded to tell me that the reason he and Perry couldn't come to the 3,389th performance of *A Chorus Line* was not "business," as they'd said, but that they'd traveled to Houston, where Laughlin participated in an experimental program at MD Anderson Cancer Center.

"And remember when I was in the hospital last fall?" In October, after the gala performance, Laughlin had been in the hospital because he had mononucleosis and was put on a course of antibiotics that needed to be administered through an IV. At the time, it never occurred to me that it might have something to do with AIDS, even when I visited at the hospital and there was a yellow paper caution sign taped to his door. Instead, I'd been struck by his VIP suite, which looked less like a hospital room than a Hilton hotel, with dark wood floors, brass knobs, and heavy floral drapes. Laughlin, still bronzed from summer, was standing by the window in his plaid boxer shorts, tracking the steady stream of boat traffic up and down the East River through his binoculars. When I teased him about putting on weight since he'd quit smoking, he whipped his hand in the air and said, "Welcome to the most expensive East Side hotel and spa. This is more expensive than Claridge's, if you can believe it!"

The atmosphere was lighthearted; nothing in his attitude or appearance made me suspect something serious, though he did mention that I should keep the fact that he was in the hospital secret because he was in the middle of some very big deals, and he couldn't afford to let anyone think he was sick. "Especially the Japanese," he teased.

The Japanese were the only businessmen Laughlin had trouble reading. He understood the Irish—their whiskey, linen, poetry, and souls. And with the lavish, emotional

Italian textile manufacturers, he arranged meetings around pasta and wine and spoke to them in their own language about art and opera, then sent gifts home to their wives, and more importantly, to their mothers. But the Japanese didn't eat and do business at the same time. They wore impassive expressions and sharkskin suits, held calculators in their hands, and Laughlin often complained that he couldn't find the right environment to spin the air into something warm, comfortable, and persuasive. His charm and magical gifts as a negotiator were lost on them.

Now, with the tea tray in front of me, I couldn't help but notice that for this meeting with me, he had most definitely orchestrated an environment: The tray was layered with cucumber-and-watercress sandwiches, miniature cakes iced with a thin vanilla icing, and truffles dusted with chocolate. The tablecloth was embroidered in high relief. There were violets.

"That's all you're eating?"

"I don't like to eat too much before the show."

"I would think that's when you really should eat, so you have enough energy to get through it."

"If I didn't have a show, I'd eat all these cakes. Every single one of them, but Michael Bennett is not very nice about reminding us that he doesn't pay us to be fat. Sometimes we have to stand on a chair while the dance captain measures our thighs by putting his hands around them. He's supposed to be able to get his fingers all the way around."

"Oh."

Cake and my weight were the most stupid topics in the world, but there was no other way to wiggle through the unbearable tension.

Laughlin went on to describe his AIDS diagnosis: He was aware of health problems going back to January 1983, when a blood test showed impaired immunity. Since then, he'd had three opportunistic infections—Pneumocystis, Kaposi's sarcoma, and shingles—the combination of the three necessary to meet the CDC's determination that he had AIDS. Even though the medical community had isolated the virus in April, they had yet to develop a test to produce a scientifically accurate diagnosis. Consequently, some very sick men may have AIDS, but if they didn't have the combination of those specific three infections, the CDC didn't give them an AIDS diagnosis. Not that there was a vaccine or a specific medication to treat it, anyway. Patients were given medications that treated the illnesses arising from immunodeficiency, though such drugs were not always effective. Some other drugs, available only in Canada and Mexico, showed promise, so a Canadian friend of Perry's brought the drugs with him when he visited New York

"Look," Laughlin continued. "AIDS is like polio. I know you read that article in the *New York Times*, and there are a lot of rumors going around, but what isn't being said is that many doctors are likening AIDS to polio. Polio was terrible. Some people died, some were paralyzed, but then, when we were kids, we ate the pink Sabin sugar cubes. Remember?"

"Yes."

"Well, AIDS is going to be just like polio. Polio was eradicated and the same thing is going to happen to AIDS."

I stumbled then, trying to verify his bubble of optimism when I couldn't square what he had said with the horrors I'd been hearing, though I was afraid to ask a question that might sound doubtful. "What is the Canadian drug?"

"Ribavirin. It's tightly controlled because it's part of an FDA study that isn't yet approved."

"He smuggles drugs across the border? That's scary."

"I don't want you to tell anyone."

"I'm not going to tell, Jesus. You don't have to worry about that."

"I don't want you to tell *anyone.* Not even John."

"Not *John?* He's your brother . . ."

"No one can know right now. Look what's happening. New York's too small." There was too much at stake. Laughlin was a clever lawyer turned businessman, who in a little more than three years had expanded the Perry Ellis business into close to a $750 million enterprise, all of which depended upon Perry's name and designs. "We could go down in a day. Contracts can be canceled. Hundreds could lose their jobs. This isn't just about me. It's much bigger than that. It's everything I've built. You have to swear."

"I swear."

The environment *was* changing rapidly, and without a doubt, the fear of AIDS was as threatening to businesses as AIDS itself, especially to those businesses run or populated by gay men. One hundred thousand had shown up over the summer for a keynote speech at the Democratic National Convention in San Francisco drawing attention to a looming crisis and demanding government action. Fear fueled discrimination and discrimination was becoming rampant. Little was published by the medical community because they still lacked scientific understanding, while newspapers were inhibited about publishing stories that invariably mentioned gay sex. On the other side of the fence was a divided gay community, some groups publishing safe-sex pamphlets, while others insisted the crisis was exaggerated by Reagan "hate-mongers," who were using the disease to discredit the gay community. Indeed, the Reagan administration labeled AIDS the "gay disease," conveniently distracting from the notion that it could spread to other populations, and even worse, using the label to stigmatize the afflicted, a condemnation that would reach past the grave, demeaning lives even after men were dead. Outside the gay community, people either ignored the situation because they thought it had nothing to do with them or became paranoid, demanding to know if they needed to wear rubber gloves when riding a public bus. Social media, the internet, didn't exist. Truthfully, there was nowhere my brother or the men I knew could turn. And now Laughlin was saying it was like polio.

"You can trust me. I won't tell. But not *John?*" Because Laughlin was so emphatic, I didn't dare mention David and Patrick. *They're your brothers*, I wanted to say. The age gap between them was substantial, but from my place in the middle, the sibling group was sacrosanct.

Then he uttered something inaudible. "What?" And in the repeat, I heard "stigma."

"Did you say 'stigma'? Jesus, Laughlin, don't waste your energy."

"What do you mean?"

"I mean stigma is grotesque. It's real, but you've never let it into your life before, so don't let it in now. Stigma is toxic. You know that. It's an enemy. And I refuse to let it be stronger than us." I let loose now that the conversation had turned toward something safe to rail about. I wanted to protect him, say something powerful that would prove I could share this burden. I ached that he'd kept me out of the loop, but it was more important to reassure him, the way I'd told him he'd be fine nine years ago, when I sat on his Turkish carpet in Georgetown and he told me he was gay. That night, I had reassured him that things were changing, and look! He'd become an enormously successful businessman in a committed relationship, with a full, happy family life. "One of the things I've always admired about you is that you've always been unafraid in the world, an adventurous—"

"Oh my God!" He spit the words at me.

"What? No, listen." I waved my hands to clarify. "Listen . . ." I thought I was saying something about how he seized opportunities in life.

"Forget it. It's okay. Just forget it. It's been a long day. I'm tired."

"No. Please. Laughlin. I was saying—"

"It's late, and you need to get to the theater."

"But I—"

He called Angela on the intercom and asked her to take away the tea tray. I shrank, completely dwarfed by the severity of his dismissal and my apparent failure. I didn't understand how our conversation had gone wrong but remembered that he hadn't fully understood what I'd said that night in Georgetown, either. Today, I was trying to say that I admired him; all my life I had believed that he was boundless, brave, and I still felt that way. But he heard the word "adventurous" and must have thought that I was speaking of sex, when *sex* was the furthest thing from my mind. I was talking about being adventurous in life, taking risks while reaching for dreams. Because life was a risk. AIDS wasn't about character or even sex, really; he wasn't to blame. But

Laughlin wouldn't meet my eyes as he moved to the stack of mail on his desk.

Angela entered. "Was everything all right?"

"It was wonderful, Angela. Thank you."

"But there are so many sandwiches left."

"I just can't eat much before the show."

"Why don't you pack a bag for her? Christine will take them to the theater. She's leaving."

"Of course. I'll have them by the front door."

With Angela out of the room, Laughlin said, "Why don't you try calling Suzanne later in the week? I'll talk to her tonight and tell her I told you." He went to the windows and closed the wooden shutters. "I don't want anyone to know. Promise me."

"I promise. And I'll do anything, just tell me how to help. Something with Kate? Mom and Dad?"

"I don't think they need to know yet. Suzanne's divorce has rattled them, not to mention the whole thing last summer when Perry and I wanted to rent a house in Santa Fe for the opening of *Blithe Spirit*." Perry had designed the costumes for a Santa Fe Festival Theatre production. "Remember Mom thought it would be better if I stayed at home with them, and Perry stayed at a hotel?"

The fact remained that Laughlin could never be who he was in our hometown or with my parents, who were kind to Perry but who weren't comfortable with any sort of public acknowledgement that the relationship existed.

Laughlin was looking out the window, anywhere but at me, and I so wanted a chance to explain that I wasn't saying what he thought I was.

"What's your schedule? I still have Raymond on, but I think Perry needs to be picked up."

"I was planning to take the bus to the theater, anyway."

"Which bus do you take from here?"

"The number 7. It stops right at the corner of 68th and Columbus. I have to be there soon," I lied. "Some friends of friends are coming tonight, and I've got to check on their tickets."

"Okay then. Well, you better go for the bus."

I tried to gather my things, but everything was in the wrong place. My wallet was buried at the bottom of my knapsack, and I couldn't locate my keys. I didn't have a bus token, so I counted out change as Laughlin sat at the mahogany secretary, sorting his mail, opening the envelopes with one long slice from his sterling silver letter opener.

"Do you have any change?" I was afraid to ask, but I was stuck. "I have a single, but I need coins for the bus."

"I don't keep money in my pockets. Go look in the top drawer of my bureau."

I pushed open the enormous doors that led to his dressing room—part of the nineteenth-century design—a room with drawers and closets, a marble sink and shaving mirror, a stool to sit on while tying your shoes. In the top drawer of the bureau was a wooden bowl filled with dimes, nickels, pennies, lire, shillings, pesetas, and some hammered copper from Senegal. Bizarrely, I remembered that Perry had been sick when they came back from Senegal, and he had talked about camels and blood. I wondered if he had AIDS, too, but didn't yet meet the criteria so couldn't be diagnosed.

"Okay. I'm off."

"Did you get the change?"

"Yes. Thanks. Well. Good night. I'm sor—"

"Have a good show."

"I love you, Laughlin."

"I love you, too." He didn't get up to kiss me, only looked at me blankly, then went back to reading his letter.

I took the bag Angela had prepared and let myself out. On the street, a woman smiled as she hoisted a dress covered with plastic from the dry cleaner's. A man exited a hardware store and unlocked the metal grate that unfolded in clankety-clanks on its way down. It was closing time, the gray flux before night and after day, when planets shift, and the world is unplumbed.

AIDS is like polio.

There were one, two, four other people at the bus stop, a fifth coming from the opposite direction. I took my place at the end of the queue. A sixth person arrived. One bus passed, not a number 7. Then another approached. *AIDS is like polio.* I opened my palm, counting the coins again —twenty cents, thirty, fifty—just to make sure they were still there.

Red Soybeans and the Front Line

—

November 1984–July 1985

I kept my mouth shut, the circumstances of Laughlin's life a profound darkness that I carried to the Shubert, the place where I was practiced in separating out fear and confusion, channeling those emotions in an inward process alongside bodies I knew and trusted to work in synchronization, which eventually landed us in pools of light. Laughlin's AIDS lived in the ethers of subtext in a musical about hope, dreams shared, and standing on the line—life in real time. But in the fall/ early winter of 1984, apparently others, too, made their performances fresh by bringing to them the truth of their lives or what they knew of the coming epidemic. A scourge of Mo-Mo Mouth spread, and every time we thought it was better, it got worse. Cloistered in our private silences, we buried secrets and fear, and relentlessly fell on our asses, dropped our lines, or rasped through songs. Other things fell apart, too.

Scandal, the show Michael still had in workshops, was abruptly canceled, leaving dancer friends unemployed and coping with the depression that accompanies the loss of a future they'd hoped for. Lydia and a few others gave their notices and left the cast of *A Chorus Line*—not to new jobs, but also to unemployment—saying they needed a break, acknowledging that the scars from the Mo-Mo Mouth debacle ran deep; they'd experienced a full-scale dismantling of faith, a kind of sobriety that there was no turning back from. Their departures signaled how battered they'd become. You didn't just walk away from a Broadway contract, because you only had a slim chance at replacing the job or starting again. Still—even given all that— no one admitted or talked about AIDS.

Tom brought in fresh recruits—all well qualified, but strangers to me. I worked hard, harder than I ever had, to be present during the show, but I couldn't staunch the flood of a strange conscientiousness, a sudden objective distance from everyone and everything, exactly the wrong kind of emotion to feel when performing, even as it was the one thing that pulled me through the two hours and two minutes on a fast night, or the two hours and three and a half minutes on a slow night. When you're trying to transition yourself to some new place at the same time the world as you know it is collapsing and possibly taking with it the lives of people you love, you can't concentrate. Every minute of the day trembles with unpredictability. You learn that you're never going to be bigger than that level of need, sadness, or fear, no matter how heroic you dream yourself being. And no matter how fiercely you hold on to the belief that you'll eventually come back to yourself, you also have no assurance of that possibility when the crisis is over.

As per their arrangement, Suzanne told my parents that Laughlin had AIDS. They immediately wrote to him. They didn't call, they wrote, maybe believing writing was better, a way to keep communication in a format through which the reach and impact of words could be controlled. They were of a generation that continued to rely on postage stamps, even though long-distance telephone rates were increasingly dropping. Their letter offered love and support, and Laughlin returned the sentiments, explaining in his reply the original discovery in 1983 of an imbalance in his white blood cell count and the treatments he'd received. He described AIDS as a "problem" but said he was "enormously positive" and "convinced that he would get better."

Both Suzanne and Laughlin stressed the importance of not telling or talking to anyone in order to protect the business and maintain privacy, my parents fully agreeing but upping the ante on their side because the tight circle of secrecy meant they wouldn't have to tell relatives, including my younger brothers. They made plans to spend a few days in New York at Christmas, staying with John and me at the loft.

Meanwhile, I told John the truth about Laughlin's health, knowing with all certainty that he was trustworthy and believing that it was not right to keep him uninformed. Once in New York, my parents never discussed AIDS with any of us—not Laughlin, John, or me—even though on the first morning after they arrived for Christmas, my father found me crying. I'd given my parents my bedroom and was sleeping on a cot in an upstairs nook adjacent to the skylight.

"What's wrong?" he asked, and when I told him a friend of a friend had died of AIDS, he patted my leg, saying, "I'm sorry." But he asked no questions and expressed no curiosity about what I may have learned about the disease, instead reconfirming the schedule for opening presents and having dinner, which was complicated because we had to work the celebrations around my performance schedule. Presents would happen at the loft on Christmas morning, Laughlin and Perry joining us, and later that night, we'd have dinner together at the house on 70th Street, even though the dining room was unfinished.

Around the tree—fatter than the one four years ago, when I'd untied the silky ribbon that had begun the great unfolding of Laughlin's life—Laughlin appeared thinner, a bit less vibrant. Still, from the look of him, AIDS appeared no worse than a terrible bout of the flu. In fact, Laughlin's appearance supported another claim in his letters: that the "virus affects people in individual ways—some have no symptoms, others mild ones, and others a full-blown case." He seemed to be falling in between not mild and not full-blown, which was false hope because every day, I stood in the theater wings *listening*—and now a friend of a friend had died. Plus, if you looked under his corduroy pants just above Laughlin's ankles, you'd see toasted skin flaking like phyllo dough, the result of recent radiation treatments.

Still, Christmas dinner was lovely, Perry and Laughlin serving a pink Gruaud Larose champagne, my parents exclaiming over the pudding how lovely the house looked even as we sat in the unpainted dining room, even as they never traveled farther than the distance from the front door to that room. They never ventured to the upstairs bedrooms, either out of respect for privacy or their incapacity to imagine Laughlin and Perry as a legitimate couple who shared a bedroom. They gave no indication that they saw the house as Laughlin and Perry's *home*.

Soon after the holiday, Laughlin developed Kaposi's sarcoma lesions in his lungs and began receiving more radiation treatments that completely drained him of energy. His situation was worse than a brick on my chest; I couldn't keep powering through show after show and admitted to myself that if the right professional move hadn't presented itself, the right personal choice *had*. I told him in early February that I thought I'd leave the show to spend more time with him. He only looked at me with a long stare, so I repeated myself a couple of weeks later, when he nodded, saying, "That'd be nice. I'd like that." I'd hoped for more, but he had no strength, having just come from another radiation treatment that reduced him to a lump. I wanted to know if the treatments were working because I'd recently discovered that he'd previously been treated at Memorial Sloan Kettering with interferon, a cancer drug that hadn't been effective. But Laughlin staggered into bed, so I asked Perry, who only replied, "Laughlin's getting better. He just needs to make it through this round," normalizing the situation and adding that they had "the best care in the country and were working with doctors who had access to researchers all over the world." He had every reason to believe Laughlin would be cured, and I wanted badly to believe him, even as the two versions of "truth" to which I had access—the doom in the wings and Perry's optimism—were contradictory.

By mid-March I told the stage manager I'd like to give my notice but would leave when best for the show. I even asked if KC could replace me, and by late April, she did. On my last night, I was numb, neither sad nor excited—just stuck in a dissociative fog because it truly is impossible to process the reductive quality of a *last* show. When the cast sang "What I Did for Love," I felt the measure of my life, the authentic self I'd gained from my spot on the stage, a spot I always thought would propel me to another beam of light, but here I was—leaving to spend time with my brother, whom I loved and feared may be dying. No question it was the right choice; it was a family emergency, and I was passionate about protecting Laughlin, even as I didn't fully imagine other people and friends who also might be infected. To protect themselves, everyone was secretive, and the world was without multiple media platforms that may have revealed the scope of the epidemic. I only had my intuition and observation to rely upon. The show ended, and I headed into the wilderness.

On the first weeknight without a show to do, I noted that I hadn't seen dusk on a Tuesday night in years. I moved a chair under the skylight of the loft and waited for Venus, then broke down and sobbed. I didn't know how to keep myself tethered to the life I thought was mine when all the events of late had crept out of some dark, forbidding corner that kept me floating above a war-soaked trench, not close enough to be infected even as I could smell fear and disease.

Then Martin called. After *The Real Thing* closed, he'd been in and out of town directing in regional theaters. He was the one person who understood the loss of a show. "What do you miss?"

"Being on the inside of a story. And the story being enough."

"Yeah."

"It was enough once, but—"

"You need a new one."

"Yes, I do. *A Chorus Line* spoiled me. Why would I ever bust my ass eight times a week for something less? *Dancin'* and the other shows available aren't worth it. I'm making money doing commercials; and they give me some film exposure that'll maybe help if I go to LA. But really, it's this claustrophobic sense of being boxed in where I'm not sure I really belong. At the same time, it's nearly impossible for me to get a chance at the important stories, like what you do."

"Well . . . listen, I'll be in New York for a quick weekend at the end of June. Will you go to *The Normal Heart* with me?" The play had just opened, and, like *A Chorus Line*, was another Public Theater triumph.

Christine Barker

"It's sold out."

"I'll have tickets. Don't worry."

The Normal Heart was a New York sensation because playwright Larry Kramer was the public voice on AIDS, portraying in his play all the known facts, including the political and medical negligence that was contributing to the epidemic. That *the theater* was the only public arena providing such comprehensive information—not newspapers, nor nightly news broadcasts, nor reports from the CDC—illustrated how polarized the world had become in the summer of 1985: two nations living side by side in two separate universes, divided by completely different realities.

Two months later and halfway through the first act, I began to sweat with the extreme effort it took to stay in my seat. The actors with their scarred and emaciated bodies provided a front-row illustration of everything I didn't want to see, not to mention the grotesque trickery of the word "normal" on the playbill, which sat like a hot blanket on my lap. "Normal heart" came from a W. H. Auden poem, but "normal" in the context of the play, and by any humane standard, meant that gay men and their yearnings for love were products of their normal hearts. Kramer's play was a window into the real-life consequences for men who had never been considered normal in our society, who could never really belong, and who many believed didn't deserve to belong.

I shrank in my seat when the character Felix, in one of the last lines of the play, said he should be wearing "something Perry Ellis," Perry's name flying to the rafters like a live spark, leaping from the play to my world, connecting Perry and, by extension, Laughlin to the painted walls on the set, where every day the cast and crew erased the current number of

AIDS cases and entered a bigger one; then, in another column, the death toll; then, in yet another column, the government funds appropriated (the only number that was declining); and, in the last, the paltry number of articles published that were providing the public with information. There, on the walls of the theater, was daily reality in plain sight.

Martin hugged me after the standing ovation, and I wanted to spill my guts about Laughlin, but he had to get to the train, so I headed across the street and watched him go, thinking of my other friends finishing their Saturday matinees and worrying about the future for all of us.

In the two months since leaving the show, I'd adapted to a rhythm of isolation. I saw Perry and Laughlin, maintaining the secrecy they insisted on, spent time with Bill on weekends without ever discussing my brother, and instead of my usual voice and dance lessons during the week, joined Laughlin at the house, where we relaxed into the absence of time and people. Diane left me messages, but I didn't call back. She wanted to know what I was planning for my next step: A new agent? Joining a small theater group? Pivoting to another aspect of the business—stage managing? LA? But by then, I was standing on the side of Laughlin's illness (something she didn't even know about) and the growing AIDS crisis, the fault lines separating me from Diane, my friends, my career, my former life. It was as if I now lived on another side of the world. I was terrified that I didn't have a career plan, but how could I? If Kramer were a modern-day Sophocles, using his play as a warning, then I was headed toward the saddest, most gruesome days of my life. Still, Laughlin looking like *that*? *All sores and bones*?

I hurried uptown, numb but trying to process what I knew. The epidemic was of a magnitude requiring institutional help and widespread public awareness—the only things that could make a vaccine or effective treatment possible. Too many people, even in New York, were oblivious; it was a crisis too removed from their lives, like something sad happening in far-off Zanzibar, and something rarely mentioned in the news. Yet, as deaths and the growing number of afflicted men rose in cities like New York and San Francisco, President Reagan and a good portion of Americans continued to look away and accept the deaths of those they believed had brought the problem onto themselves. It was their and the government's way of marginalizing a group, saying gay lives didn't matter. I'd never again be so politically naive. Divisions in the gay community were worse than they'd been a few months ago, some believing Kramer was exaggerating. And beyond that were Laughlin, Perry, and men like them who had enough money and clout to belong to a privileged class, able to navigate the crisis differently than even the professional people below them, like Martin and Tom. As for the class of people below that—dancer friends—I shuddered to think how they would manage, many having lost their health insurance when they became unemployed.

The weekend after *The Normal Heart*, on a hot July night, I returned from a wedding reception to an unfamiliar voice on my answering machine telling me to call Perry back at a number I didn't recognize. He answered with a weak "Hello" then handed the phone to his Canadian friend, who said they were at the hospital; that Laughlin had had a stroke but was okay. Earlier in the day, Laughlin had awakened from a nap and slurred his words, the left side of his face suddenly drooping. I said I was on my way, but the man from Canada said it wasn't necessary; it was already past nine, Laughlin was asleep, and Pat, a private-duty nurse, would be with him all night. But after I hung up, I realized I wanted to be there when Laughlin woke up, so I called back and said I was coming and was given the name of the concierge on the hospital's VIP floor.

I wore my PERRY ELLIS raincoat with the collar turned up and carried a basket of flowers from the wedding reception I'd attended. The elevator ascended, and the doors opened to a dark hallway just as Perry and the friend were pushing the Down button. Both wore sunglasses, afraid of being recognized. The theater and fashion districts were buzzing because suddenly it seemed you couldn't have a conversation without hearing a story or rumor about someone being sick. At the elevator, Perry was too upset to speak—I'd never seen him so distraught—and his friend said to call in the morning.

I'd never met Pat, the private-duty nurse, but she took my cold hands in her warm ones, her voice soothing as she reassured me that Laughlin was going to be okay. I wanted to believe her, but she looked too exhausted to be credible, and I wondered who else she had taken care of recently.

Laughlin was awake, a bit drowsy, but he recognized me, and seemed to rally, speaking enthusiastically, though the words came out backward and upside down. I pretended to understand and matched his energy with animated stories of the wedding. When I showed him the basket of lilies and orchids, he smiled and said, "Red soybeans." I didn't know whether to correct him or to act naturally. I just sat on the bed next to him and told him I'd stay until he fell asleep.

I arrived back early but couldn't go into the room because a team of doctors was examining Laughlin. I waited outside the door; he did not have a fancy VIP suite like last year, but a similar yellow caution sign was taped to the front. This one included a typed list of precautions: Avoid needles, contact with open cuts, and more that I didn't finish reading because a short guy in a white coat scurried toward me. "Who are you?" he asked, pushing as he tried to get inside. He looked to be about my age and spoke in a know-it-all playground voice. "Well, you know his prognosis is very bad," he said, even though he had no idea who I was or how I knew Laughlin, so I leaned my weight into the leg that was preventing him from entering Laughlin's room, and said, "NO, I don't know that. Who are you? And what exactly do you mean?"

"Oh, you must be next of kin," he said, growing smugger and puffing out his chest like a peacock: "He's been diagnosed for over two years. *Two years*. Most others are dead. He has KS, the shingles virus is attacking his nervous system, and now he's had a stroke." He assumed his officious stance, lumping my brother into a statistic that Kramer had reported: 11,010 Americans with AIDS, 5,441 dead. Even though he'd revealed important information about Laughlin's condition, I thought he was a feckless rat, so I blocked the door.

When I finally got into the room, Laughlin was alert and no longer confusing his words. He vaguely remembered my being there last night, and said Pat was going to accompany him for some tests the doctors had ordered, but would I wait for him to come back? "Of course," I said. I'll be here."

I waited for more than an hour, growing antsy in the stillness of the room, so I stood outside the door. Down the hall, the nurses' station buzzed with activity, and when a nurse came out of a room across the hall, I introduced myself and asked if she had any idea about how long Laughlin might be gone.

"Oh—it can take hours. Things are really backed up. We're overburdened with so many patients."

Despite the CDC officially declaring an epidemic, medical

services throughout the city had not been coordinated, and some hospitals, like St. Vincent's and Memorial Sloan Kettering, were turning AIDS patients away, afraid of getting the reputation of being an "AIDS hospital." Mayor Ed Koch, who was rumored and privately reported to be gay, was of no help. Despite being up for reelection, he hadn't even set up a city-wide AIDS plan, when New York was at the epicenter of the epidemic. As a last resort, private physicians who could not get their desperately ill patients admitted to hospitals recommended that their patients go to the emergency room, where, by law, they could not be turned away.

I waited in the room for another two hours. Perry arrived just as Laughlin and Pat returned—they'd been gone more than three hours. Perry was angry, a relief after seeing him so paralyzed the night before, and plans were made for him to wait in the room the following day, when Laughlin would go for a radiation treatment. That turned out to be another three-hour excursion, and by the time I arrived to relieve Perry, he was anxious and exasperated. I told him that I had been alarmed the day before so had asked John to be on standby in case we needed more support at the hospital. Perry agreed that that was a good idea, and later, Laughlin returned completely distraught, describing long hallways of men alone in freezing-cold basement corridors waiting on gurneys. The conditions were appalling.

I asked Pat, "Why can't we go with you when you take him next time?"

"You?"

"Yeah, us. What's to stop us?" Both Laughlin and Perry looked at me, puzzled, but I was adamant. "If it's going to take three hours for a test or a radiation treatment, at least Laughlin won't be alone."

"Well, maybe you're right," Pat said. She had a badge as a private-duty nurse, but I'd observed all sorts of badges, and people with different colored coats. She agreed that the significant number of doctors and nurses mixing in with private doctors and nurses, as well as technicians, cleaning staff, and food-service employees, made it difficult to know who was who. Pat found technician's coats that Perry, John, and I could wear, and the next day, when Laughlin had to go for a CT scan, the four us assembled around the gurney. The confusion in the halls and elevators worked to our advantage. Pat took the lead, adopting a military nurse kind of authority, and people instinctively moved out of the way when we walked by. John and Perry held on to either side of the rails and I pushed from the back, holding a fake chart—another Pat procurement.

We took the patients' elevator, which was manually serviced in case of a power failure, and where only one patient at a time was to be transported. It took twenty-five minutes to arrive, and when it did, the elevator operator wanted to see the chart, but Pat, flashing her badge, intervened, protesting that no one had asked for a chart the day before. The elevator operator agreed that the rules were changing every day. He held the chart she handed him, barely looked at it, nodded, and we got on.

We repeated the process down other hallways and on other elevators, traveling through areas where people with AIDS were herded to avoid exposure to the regular population of patients. I'd seen for myself how hospital staff wouldn't enter Laughlin's room, leaving trays outside his door. Even the cleaning woman arriving with her mop and supplies turned away when she saw the yellow sign. Now, in the bowels of the building, the halls were old and decrepit, rust stains smearing the white tile walls. We walked through basement and subbasement passageways in an underground maze that reminded me of the subway tunnels that connected the rarely used L or Q lines. Above- ground, we would have covered blocks and blocks; in all, it took us over an hour to arrive at the CT area.

Once there, we waited for another hour, freezing and standing. There were no chairs. Instead, the hallway was lined with other gurneys, more men waiting alone, wasted and forlorn. It was so cold I was shivering, but Pat was prepared; she'd stacked extra blankets on the lower shelf of the gurney. Laughlin's mouth was perennially dry, so I'd started carrying Life Savers in my pockets, handing them to him periodically and making sure his blankets were tucked tightly under his body to keep him warm.

In the belly of the hospital was a *Normal Heart* scenario: blatant despair on the faces of people at their most vulnerable. And despite the freezing cold, Pat said I could not share my blanket, so I offered the man lying next to us a Life Saver. Earlier that morning, I'd heard on the news that the Catholic Church had just won its appeal to Executive Order 50, which meant that it could legally discriminate against hiring gay people. Abandoned by the government and now religious institutions, at the mercy of a health system that provided inadequate access to care or insurance, the men I saw had to rely on the kindness of strangers, unless, of course, they were rich like Laughlin and had a private-duty nurse. Grotesquely, that seemed to be the only thing protecting him besides us, his family, who held a tight perimeter around the gurney.

Perry never said a single word, relying mostly on John,

who was a regular chatterbox; John could talk about anything and talked even more when he was nervous. But he never left Laughlin's side, just stood right up next to the gurney, wearing his fake lab coat, talking the whole way and the whole time. Then, I noticed his hand under the sheet. He was holding Laughlin's hand and must have been doing so from the very start.

When we finally got back to the room, we'd been gone almost four hours. We sat in stunned silence, watching the five p.m. news report on the television.

Perry said, "Rock Hudson."

The actor was at the American Hospital of Paris. Right away, I thought of the link between Paris and AIDS treatments and research, and although Perry didn't acknowledge it, I had the feeling that he and Laughlin had visited the hospital on one of their many trips to Paris for work. One reporter said that Hudson possibly had cancer of the liver.

Laughlin was discharged two days later, as the world was learning the truth: that Rock Hudson had AIDS. On Sunday, July 28, 1985, for the first time, network news and most major newspapers ran headline stories on the epidemic. Rock Hudson had broken the fourth wall.

House

August 1985

No one could pretend that Laughlin would be going back to the office anytime soon. As his life grew smaller, so did mine, with one exception: Bill. I told him the truth of what was happening. I wanted him to understand why my life was no longer my own, how I needed his support, and why everything had to be kept secret. "AIDS?" It was a choked sound. "Oh my God," he said, followed by an anguished silence. Then, "Tell me what you need." With those words, he became guardian of the before and after, the world as it had been and what we hoped it would one day be.

Voice lessons became impossible, and I danced alone in the loft or did barre in Laughlin's bedroom, trying to keep in touch with myself—I always knew who I was when in a leotard. One day I auditioned for a commercial director who liked me and had hired me several times for national spots. He was in a bad mood, which I had always handled with aplomb, but on that day, he yelled at me in front of clients, bellowing, "BE FUNNY. Make me laugh. Make the script funny."

"How?" I asked. I felt as if I was drowning. It was impossible to split myself between two realities, taking turns living in each as if the other didn't exist, which was all a form of magical thinking because as much as you chant "The show must go on" mantra—You can do it!—you really can't.

We hired around-the-clock nursing care, and Perry

moved out of their bedroom and into the guest room on the second floor. Margot, the day nurse, was big and strong, lifting Laughlin when he needed assistance. She would be with us until we could find someone who could commit to several months running, or however long it took to get Laughlin back on his feet. When Margot was off, I was in charge for the day.

"Okay, lazy bones." I jiggled his shoulder.

"It's too early."

"It's one o'clock. Time for exercises. I brought the stretchy band." Laughlin's legs were weak due to the shingles virus in his spinal column. He was on acyclovir, plus doing physical therapy exercises with me.

"Later. Please. Not now." He said "please" all the time now.

Meanwhile, Perry was dealing with bouts of thrush and had lost a little weight. One morning, when he and I overlapped before he left for work, I noticed that his gait was uneven. Walking to the car, he looked back over his shoulder, as if he were asking, *Is this where I am supposed to be?* Without Laughlin by his side, he'd lost his bearings. A highly placed business executive once described how Laughlin had provided emotional security that anchored Perry. Still, I expected Perry, who could be a demanding tyrant at times, to take control when the circumstances required it. I hadn't anticipated disorganization at the office that was so bad even I'd been hearing about it, or that he would seem so completely lost at home. Supposedly, he wasn't sick. But I wondered. When he walked in the room, he looked like he'd lost even more weight.

"Laughlin wants a few moments to wake up," I said.

"What? Come on. Your sister is here to help you get better. Don't be a gimp."

"I'm tired." Laughlin almost spit the words, but he didn't open his eyes so didn't see Perry's hurt. Illness had diluted their chemistry, when *absolutely everything*—the house, the business, their life together—was a product of their chemistry.

Perry turned his back and remarked with false assurance, "He did have breakfast this morning: Two eggs, bacon, and toast. And I notice his color is good today." If Perry spoke of Laughlin, he spoke of only "good" things, reminding me of the first time I met him, when he admonished me for saying I was stuck, saying I should speak only in the affirmative, only about what it was I wanted to bring into my life. Clearly, he believed that he could make this thing—AIDS—go away. In the dressing room, he'd tacked up pages from his mother's handwritten letters, line after line of affirmations and prayers. She and I had become friends when we'd met during the *Chariots of Fire*-inspired spring show of 1982, and despite being of the same generation as my parents, Winnie's values were completely different. She believed love was love and was thrilled that Perry and Laughlin had found each other. If Laughlin was Perry's anchor, Winnie was *the* voice inside his head.

Now, as Perry started his distracted fussing again, going to the mantel, rearranging objects in such a way that their best side was forward, I noticed how he'd also changed the position of the chair where I now sat. The chair was angled so that you saw the side of Laughlin that looked like Laughlin, not the side that still drooped slightly due to the stroke. Perry said he was going to the office for a few hours, and asked if I would please be there when he returned? Of course. I did whatever he asked.

A few days later he came home bubbling, seemingly himself again. He'd bought two small, several-hundred-year-old end tables with inlaid designs that cost more than what I paid for my loft, including renovations. I commented on how extraordinary they were, not daring to touch them, knowing that any oil from a fingertip might stain their perfectly preserved surfaces. Purchasing the tables was beyond outrageous, but doing so restored some of Perry's confidence, improving his mood and outlook, just as Laughlin was also improving, his energy and strength returning so that he could get in and out of bed without assistance.

While my role was often blurry, in the long, isolated hours together, Laughlin and I were becoming a team. I took comfort in the fact that he trusted me, describing a flutter in his lungs, and sharing news about his T-cell count (stabilizing but still very low). I offered to give him my blood or bone marrow, but he said it was more complicated than that, and that in any case, my blood or marrow wouldn't help him. Together, we focused on the day-to-day, doing physical therapy and our best to outwit whatever circumstances appeared: currently, three knots of Kaposi's sarcoma in his lungs, another bout of shingles (also called herpes zoster), some diarrhea, but—good news—no residual motor problems from the stroke.

Though sometimes, I observed Laughlin settling into an unusual and deep state of quiet, something in his psyche shifting. The same was happening to me—something I couldn't fully articulate but that was tied to the question, Without the stage, the nightly audience, the thrill of it as well as the labor, who was I? I took Jimmy Kirkwood's long-ago advice and wrote down everything, even using the subway ride to and from Laughlin's, the writing of words becoming part of the daily ritual, along with my hybrid version of a barre in his bedroom. Frequently, I caught him watching me as I enjoyed full use of my body, while his body was at war, every ounce of his energy spent on trying to recuperate and heal, a process so arduous, he had nothing left to feed his imagination or curiosity. Some evenings, I wanted to throw open the window and say, "Laughlin, look! The moon!" I was afraid he was getting too far into a private inwardness and wouldn't find his way back. I watched the moon alone, wondering if the weakening of imagination and curiosity was a benchmark of the downward progression of serious illness; at what point did serious illness become dying? No one ever talked about death or dying as such a process. I feared I was witnessing the beginning of a loss of hope, that hope was a fragile thing entirely dependent on imagination, which in turn, was entirely dependent on health.

I would have liked to have gone downtown to the Gay Men's Health Crisis, an emerging organization started by Larry Kramer, where I might have been able to stand shoulder to shoulder with others facing similar experiences. But I was afraid I'd have to give my name or that I might be recognized. The theater, fashion, and art worlds were closely connected, and I was only separated from Laughlin and Perry by one degree. My showing up might fuel rumors, when Laughlin's absence from the office had already caused twitters. In fact, I'd had a couple of messages from friends of Laughlin's on my answering machine inquiring about his health. I didn't return their calls, afraid I would get trapped into revealing something. I wished I had someone to compare notes with. Oddly, I didn't know anyone else who had been diagnosed. Sometimes friends were sick, but they didn't have a definitive diagnosis of AIDS because their illnesses didn't fit the necessary criteria, which we accepted because (1) we had no choice, and (2) until results were "official," we didn't have to face the demon that was already draining our capacities.

Life in the house was completely isolated from the world, except when John visited, bringing with him funny stories from the outside; and sometimes, Julia, Perry's assistant with the orchid-like face, arrived from the office with paperwork. My parents began calling to "check in," spending a few minutes talking to Laughlin before saying they didn't want to tire him out, then later grilling me about his prognosis. I tried to be upbeat, though I hadn't been a part of any discussion with his private physician; that was Perry's domain. I said the outward signs of improvement were steady but was more honest with Suzanne, admitting that his "improvement" could be temporary. There was no telling. She was on the phone several times a week, talking to both Perry and Laughlin. She told Laughlin that our brother David wanted to come for a visit. Both our younger brothers—David and Patrick—knew about the stroke, but not yet about the AIDS. They thought the stroke was due to stress and were reminded that my mother's father and brother both had heart attacks and died at relatively young ages. The secrecy increased my apprehension, but Laughlin promised he would tell them. Still, I wondered if he'd ultimately have the energy. When I mentioned my concerns to my parents, they were firm: "We cannot tell them because those are Laughlin's wishes." I believed they were shortsighted, ignoring how exclusion creates irreparable divisions, so hoped I could convince Laughlin.

I kept to the routine, every day carrying the weight of unpredictability, arriving at the house to do whatever needed to be done, and sometimes walking through the empty rooms that now breathed with an air of expectancy. The cushions were plumped, the wood at its polished best, the glass dining table rubbed so clean, it disappeared. The "living" room, the "dining" room, and the "drawing" room all strained to live up to their names, as if life began at six, when friends would usually arrive. It was impossible to stand in the rooms without imagining parties, though there hadn't been any since Laughlin got sick. It seemed a waste, so I began encouraging Margot to take her pick of rooms when she took her breaks, so at least *someone* might enjoy them. One afternoon, I served her a cup of tea and cookies in the drawing room.

"Does Laughlin ever talk about the fact that he might not get well?" she asked.

"No, he never does." Looking into her generous face, I wanted to cry, *Help me. I don't know what I'm doing.* I wanted insight, to know what to expect, but after I said that Laughlin doesn't talk about it, she covered her mouth, pretending she'd taken too big a bite out of her ginger biscuit.

Covenant

—

Late August 1985

Margot left and was replaced with Gillian, who was smart, insightful, and plucky. In less than two days, she earned our trust and initiated a playful repartee with Laughlin, who continued to regain some strength. With the sickroom brightening, Perry felt better, too, so plans were made for him to visit Barbara and the baby, who lived in California. His daughter, named Tyler, was now nine months old, and he'd barely seen her because of the distance, his and Laughlin's health, plus the growing complications with their business.

Part of the plan included a visit from my parents, who'd been wanting to come to New York since Laughlin's stroke. I would temporarily move into the house and act as hostess. As it ended up, my father was very involved with a new real estate project, so he decided to visit later in the month, sending my mother on by herself, which I suspected she preferred. Being by herself meant she wouldn't have to divide her attention between Laughlin and my father, a subtle competition that likely began the day Laughlin was born.

Perry left me with a yellow legal pad full of handwritten instructions, including to tell my mother that Laughlin was "looking for TLC that only a mother can do for a son" and that the toilet on the third floor needed to be "flushed and held until the bowl clears." I was to call him twice a day, and then, he'd doubly underlined, <u>DON'T FORGET TO CLOSE THE SHUTTERS IN THE PARLOR AT FIVE</u>, another one of his obsessions. Menus were prepared, groceries ordered, linens ironed, and Maria, the cook, was practically plucking the chickens herself. Then, *poof*! Suddenly, Perry was off to the airport and the thrill of new momentum lifted us off our footings.

Laughlin had a surge of daring energy and demanded that Gillian and I walk him to the park. All summer he had refused to go out, afraid of being recognized, which was a possibility in the neighborhood. But now he was insistent, arguing with Gillian that it was only one block to the park bench "if you include crossing the street," plus he had both of us to accompany him. He would wear a hat. She was gently reluctant, then he teased, and she teased back before shockingly relenting, and suddenly I was looking for his shoes.

Plodding down the sidewalk toward the park, Laughlin leaned so heavily on us that I worried we might buckle under his weight. Gillian asked if I was all right on my side, but I didn't dare answer with the truth and instead kept my eyes focused on our feet. Laughlin forced one leg, then the next, dragging himself forward until finally we reached the green bench at the park's edge. The three of us, with sweat on our faces, sat facing the traffic, and Laughlin sighed. "Heaven. Thank you." There wasn't energy for anything more than that.

We watched as the light turned from green to yellow to red, then back again in a revolving loop. Finally, Gillian whispered that Stephen—Laughlin's private physician, who often made house calls—was stopping by.

"Oh?" Laughlin was surprised. But Gillian said he had called just as we were leaving, saying he was going to be in the neighborhood and would like to drop in. On the way back to the brownstone, Laughlin hoisted his legs beneath him and held onto us as if we were grab bars. At the curb, I saw his right foot curl under, like a dead fish hooked to his trouser leg. He literally walked on the stub of his ankle but didn't seem to notice.

Back in bed, Laughlin told Stephen about a numbness in his legs that moved up toward his abdomen and chest. Stephen, older than Laughlin, wore a white starched shirt and tweed jacket, something proper and formal about him belying his gentle demeanor. As Laughlin explained the lack of feeling, Stephen's face became more tranquil as he absorbed what Laughlin articulated, which gave me confidence that Stephen knew exactly how to treat Laughlin's problem.

"Close your eyes," he said. "Say 'touch' when I touch you." And with that he drew out his handkerchief, sweeping it across Laughlin's hand.

"Touch."

He passed it over Laughlin's right foot.

The left shin.

Laughlin's hand, the other one this time.

"Touch."

"Good."

Stephen took an instrument from his bag and drew it across the sole of Laughlin's foot, scraping the point upward in a line from the heel to the big toe. My foot curled in response, but Laughlin seemed to have momentarily stepped away from his body. His foot was an impassive lump.

My cheeks flushed. It was so hot in the room! Jesus! In a rash of claustrophobic, illogical panic, I was sure I'd forgotten something: Checking the thermostat? Something Perry put on the list that I'd missed? I had a sudden, unbearable urge to rush to the parlor to check the yellow pad, but I couldn't leave the room.

Stephen brushed the handkerchief across the right side of Laughlin's chest.

"Touch."

The left shoulder.

"Touch."

I got up to check the thermostat, then remembered that there wasn't one; the temperature was controlled by a panel in the basement. My heart was pounding, and I hardly knew what I was thinking. I sat back down, rearranging my skirt over my legs, pressing each fold separately and neatly into a series of bladed accordion-pleats. Stephen drew the pointed instrument across Laughlin's other foot. No reaction. He traveled from body part to body part, as if he were looking for the thread to lead him through the maze.

Stephen pressed on Laughlin's right hip with the palm of his hand. "I was thinking about the *Ambience* the other day," he said. The *Ambience* was Laughlin and Perry's sailboat that they kept at the Water Island house. It was teak, small, and beautiful. He ran the instrument along Laughlin's thigh. If it were sharp, it would have sliced Laughlin's pajamas in one fine line.

"Oh yeah." Laughlin laughed. "She's a real beauty." Stephen scraped the point across his belly.

"That was a great afternoon, when I visited, and you took me out into the bay." Stephen brushed the handkerchief across Laughlin's neck.

"Touch. Why don't you go out there and use the boat? We're not using the house much this summer."

"I'd like that. Okay, open your eyes."

Laughlin opened his eyes and looked past Stephen to me. I smiled with my best, most cheerful Crest/McDonalds/Pepsi/Coke smile and refolded my hands, lacing the fingers so the left thumb was on top, the backward way, the wrong way, the way I never, ever fold them.

"I think it's just another reoccurrence of the herpes zoster," Stephen said. In someone with an immune disorder, it wreaked havoc on the nervous system. "The acyclovir seemed to work last time, so let's do it again."

Stephen made notes in the chart and had a brief chat with Gillian in the dressing room area. Laughlin's face relaxed, and I kissed his forehead, keeping my hand on his chest as Stephen walked back into the bedroom. He'd never fully acknowledged me before, except for a sideways nod. Now, he rested his eyes on me like they were a pair of heavy hands. I said I would see him to the door.

Laughlin always said Stephen was a very private man, socially awkward but then capable of the most personal intimacy and connection. He was so zipped up that I assumed he was part of the secret society of closeted men, like the doctors who'd treated Martin in London. I felt nervous as he descended the stairs, the quiet making it even worse. Finally, at the landing, he stopped under the sixteenth-century chandelier: a large, bloated globe. Perry claimed it was bronze, but it was so ancient, it was hard to tell. A separate band of tiny shapes—stars, crosses, and other Coptic symbols—floated around its middle, orbiting above Stephen's head. Surely, they meant something, only I didn't know what.

Stephen looked me straight in the eyes, started to speak, then stopped. I smiled to make it easier for him and thought I should say something about the heat, but then he smiled back at me, harder, and I had to stop smiling because there was something about his smile that felt like too great a burden to bear. The heat made the room feel unstable, with only the grand piano—as glossy and steamy as wet tar—to anchor us, but still Stephen couldn't say whatever it was, and instead asked if I played the piano.

"The piano? Oh, I tried, but I was awful. I hated sitting on the bench and having to be still for so long—I'm not good at sitting still. My fingers would tighten into claws and all I ever really wanted to do was just bang, bang on the keys."

"No one plays it?" he asked.

"No, no one." Then he let out an audible sigh, so big and disappointed that I almost thought to apologize for the waste of it all. He clasped his hands in front of him, and I decided to speak up about the heat, and the possibility of a broken thermostat, but he began first.

"The numbness is the herpes zoster again." He repeated what he explained to Laughlin, then added, "The neurologist who saw Laughlin when he was in the hospital in July thought that Laughlin would have had a heart attack a long time ago. He didn't expect him to survive this long or to rebound the way he has. It's astonishing, really, how he has rebounded. No one expected that. But now, the zoster is spreading through the nervous system. He's losing the ability to use his legs. It's spreading up toward his chest, and while the acyclovir may control it for a while, there is nothing that can stop it or cure what has been damaged." He looked like a schoolboy, with a solemn expression of complete and utter disappointment, his eyes watering as if every one of his hopes had been dashed. "The KS is in his lungs. I think if you can you should schedule your family visits sooner rather than later. No more walking.

He shouldn't even be tempted to try." He pulled out the white linen handkerchief and wiped his eyes. "By the same token, we don't want to alarm Laughlin or do anything to make him feel any trepidation, wondering why everyone is coming."

A thousand particles flew with the shake of his handkerchief, his words like tiny puffs of confetti. I strained to grasp their meaning, but every syllable was a smattering of light that ceased to make sense because of the way he'd scraped at Laughlin's feet and sliced at his thigh. It was obcene, how he poked him, the way we used to poke dead jellyfish on the beach at Pozzuoli near Naples.

"There is something else," he said.

What else could there possibly be?

"I need to know for the nurses what you want me to do—what you want them to do."

"To do?"

"Yes. *To do.*" He looked at me carefully. "In case of emergency."

"An emergency?"

"In case there is an emergency and he needs to be resuscitated."

"Resuscitated?"

"Do you want him resuscitated? I need your permission."

"You need my permission to resuscitate him?"

"To *not* resuscitate him."

"Oh. Are you hot?"

"No."

"I— You're asking *me*? What about Perry?"

"I haven't been able to talk to Perry. Which is okay. Probably it's best in the long run. He's denying it all still, and maybe that's good. It protects him."

Protects him from what? The thrush in Perry's mouth looked like he'd swallowed a handful of cobwebs, but as far as I knew, he still didn't have the "specific opportunistic illnesses" that confirmed AIDS. In any case, I was too flustered to ask if Perry had AIDS. I didn't ask any one of the thousand questions I had about AIDS and Laughlin and Perry because now that the truth had finally been spoken, it was too much to hear, and I felt woozy, like birds were flying in my head. I couldn't think in words, but then some suddenly popped out. "Kate's supposed to be coming. What do you think about that?"

"How old is she now?"

I honestly couldn't remember, but of course I knew how old she was, and besides, maybe they were planning to have parties with music, and that's why they had a piano.

"How old is she?" he repeated.

"Eleven."

"Will you be around?"

"Yes."

"Then I think she should come. He's been talking about her coming. He's looking forward to seeing her, and probably in the long run, it will be better for her to see him. Even looking like he does." Though Laughlin had improved, he looked like an invalid, and we had to keep the sheets pulled up to hide his blistered chest. I decided Perry would have placed the piano at that exact angle so that people sitting in the living room could see and hear the music, while outside from the sidewalk, a passerby could also catch a glimpse of the grandness of life inside.

Stephen waited patiently, but it was an impossible question. In the end, I recited lines that came from outside me. "Laughlin never leaves this house and is to be kept comfort-

able. If that means morphine, whatever, give it to him. He is
to be peaceful, have his dignity, and be here in his home. If he
starts to go, well, then let him. But here at home, in his own
bed. He is never, ever to be taken from his home and to any
hospital, and I will be here. You have my permission. I'll tell
my family about this, but I think they'll agree."

"It's really the best thing."

"Is it?"

"Yes. It would be cruel to try to keep him alive. You've
made the best choice."

"But do you have any way of knowing when?"

"Not really. Maybe three weeks, maybe early this fall."

"My father wants me to ask. It's preposterous now, given
the circumstances, but out of respect."

"Sure."

"He wants to know about rehabilitation. He wants to know
if we can *rehabilitate* Laughlin. I guess he's thinking about how
people recover from a stroke."

"No. There's not going to be any rehabilitation." Then Stephen paused and paused some more. "You're going to have to
figure out a way to talk to them."

"I know."

"Isn't your mother coming?"

"Yes. Today."

"Today?"

Stephen lifted his hand and patted my shoulder in an awkward thump, and I felt grateful for his presence and compas-
sion. He picked up his bag as if it were weighted with stones.
He had rounds at the hospital to make, and I wondered how
many conversations like this he'd had recently. I touched his
hand. "Thank you."

I stared down the length of the front room, which was long and white, eerily quiet and museum-like, with mirrors lining the walls. I headed to the activity of the kitchen, where Josh the dog slurped water from his bowl, Maria was testing the chocolate cake, and Angela arranged summer zinnias. No one noticed me, and from inside my head, I screamed, *A cake? And zinnias?*

I hid in the downstairs bathroom, locking the door. I wanted to throw up or faint, fall flat and split my head, taste the salt of blood on my tongue. At least that would be something, because anything would be better than the slow sensation of leaking away from the world.

I sat, pressing my bare legs against the marble floor. *One, two.* I counted my breaths. Clasped my fingers tight. Drew oxygen in through my nose. I stretched out so every part of me connected to the floor, lengthening my tailbone toward my heels, stapling my wings to my shoulders. *Three, four.* On all fours, I pushed my hands to the ground and split my legs, one straight to the floor, the other rising against the wall. It was the only thing I knew to do: move my bones, align the lines, put my body in different positions so it would speak to me as I tried to name this no-name thing. I pushed back hard. *Five, six.*

I had just turned six when our younger brother David was born in Alameda, California. Like most Navy wives whose husbands were often away on a mission, my mother was alone when she went into labor, so my uncle and grandmother who lived nearby rushed over. The next day, my mother came home with a baby brother in a basket that she placed on the dining room table. He slept all day, no matter how many times I ran the circuit between the table's edge and the packing boxes. We were moving again. Daddy had been gone a very long time—my mother said six months—but as soon as he got home from sea duty, we were taking a train all the way across the United States; then we were sailing on a ship across the ocean, where we wouldn't see land for two weeks, until we arrived in Italy, where everyone ate spaghetti, and some children were raised by wolves.

Because David refused to wake up, I unwrapped the present my mother gave me: a new book, *Dumbo*, about a flying elephant, which my mother started to read aloud, except her mother, Nana Helen, who had stayed with us when my mother went to the hospital to have the baby, kept interrupting to talk about the baptism. By the time the mean boys had teased the baby elephant and the walls of the tent had come crashing down and the police had locked Dumbo's mother in jail, I knew that Suzanne and Chico were going to be David's godparents. "Godparents," another new word. My mother would not cross the ocean unless David was baptized. She spoke like it was a law, even though I knew it wasn't a *real* law. And I didn't think God could be a part of it, either, because a lot of times my mother didn't go to church, which meant that either the Catholic rules didn't apply, or she wasn't afraid to break them.

This, however, was different because the blessing had some magic to it that David needed, and the only way to get it was to have Chico and Suzanne be godparents, which Suzanne, who had entered the room and picked up on the conversation, prattled about in a know-it-all fashion. Her tone revealed that Suzanne had been told earlier about her exalted status, as she repeated words to me that my mother had said to her, "He has to get baptized or else he could go to Limbo!" I flew off the couch and would have smashed her smug face with my fists—and not been sorry—if the vision of Limbo hadn't knocked the breath out of me. The word itself was as alive as a coiled snake; when Sister Mary-Margaret had described Limbo at my nursery Sunday school, her jaw opened wide; I'd had to grab my desk to resist the strength of her pull, that big black sinkhole of a mouth.

Twisting through physical shapes in the brownstone's powder room that day, the words "Limbo" and "Dumbo" intersected in crisscross syllables, cementing themselves in some cerebral hub that remains there still. *Seven, eight.* Threads of memory wove themselves into fragments of meaning. I moved my balance from the left leg to the right—always a challenge, the two sides so different. People think their bodies are symmetrical, but dancers know that each side has its own identity. If I could reel back time, I would scream at all of them, "He's my brother, too!" *My brother.*

The world had blown open, starting the moment Laughlin's foot did not move with the scrape of Stephen's probe, while mine curled in reflexive response. The absolute rigidity between what was possible for me and impossible for him threatened the promise that had always been bigger than the sum of us, our covenant: that we would never abandon each other. Giving my permission to not resuscitate him shifted the alliance and created a no-name space, where he was suspended as I was hurtling forward to somewhere I couldn't yet imagine, except to know that he would not be there with me. I felt guilty, complicit in his being left behind, and angry that the responsibility for his life had been given to me, which was not right. If Laughlin couldn't make the choice, then Perry should. But in all such significant matters, the law made them nothing to each other. Only the contract naming them co-owners of the house was legal. I realized that Stephen had asked me because, by law, I was the only one he could ask. I was next of kin. And then he implied that Perry was incapable of making choices, so it was likely Perry had AIDS and had had it for some time.

Angela knocked on the door. "Christine? Christine? Are you in there? Raymond called. He's at the airport. Your mother is coming."

My Mother

—

Later the same day

Even in August, my mother would be wearing gloves and a hat. I knew that as well as I knew my name, and that she would have started planning her wardrobe well in advance, carefully laying out dresses and skirts, then looking for something else, something that was "good-looking, sophisticated, and versatile" so she didn't over pack. She would think it too extravagant to buy a new outfit; but still, she would have shopped for something, probably a pair of shoes, and once she found them, they would forever be memorialized: "My New York shoes—the shoes I bought for the trip to visit Laughlin." Everything that was hers—in the closet or on the bureau, shelves, or mantel—had a story that served as a place marker mapping the years of her life.

"Oh, darling!" she called from the street, waving her small, white-gloved hand. I waved back from the front stairs as she instructed Raymond about her suitcase, and thanked him.

"Was the flight okay? Meeting up with Raymond?"

"It's sooo good to be here." She threw her arms around me; I smelled *L'Air du Temps*.

"I love your new shoes," I said, and she laughed, looking exactly as she did in the picture on my father's bureau. She was laughing there, too. When she laughed, she looked like she was singing.

"What time is it?

"Almost six thirty."

"Oh—the time change." We walked into the foyer. "The house is lovely. I haven't seen it since—when? When was I here last?"

"Christmas."

"Christmas? No. Daddy and I had Christmas with Suzanne and the children. I'm sure. No, wait a minute. You're right. It was Christmas, and we stayed with you on that makeshift bed in your loft. Oh, darling, you're always so creative." Walking forward to the dining room, she gestured with her arms. "We did have Christmas here. The dining room wasn't finished. Was Laughlin still living in his apartment?"

"No, he and Perry lived here."

"Here? Wait. Yes, we sat at the glass table, and the room was draped with fresh greens and holly; there were candles everywhere. The cook made that delicious pudding." She licked her lips. "We *were* here for Christmas. But it seems so long ago."

"Angela." I waved. She had silently come up the back stairs that led up from the kitchen. "Come meet my mother."

My mother grabbed my arm, surprised, as if she'd forgotten that the housekeeper lived in the house.

"Mrs. Barker." Angela extended her weathered hand. "It is so nice to have you. You must be tired, traveling all day. Let me show you to your room. Raymond, he took your bag up already."

"Let's follow Angela," I directed. At the first-floor landing, we passed Laughlin's room—his door closed—and my mother hesitated, looking back to me, then ahead to Angela, finally cocking her head in the way mothers do when they think they hear their children calling, even as she continued following us up the stairs.

"So, here we are." Angela pushed open the door. The second-floor bedroom was crisp and airy: the pineapple-posted bed fitted with an antique patchwork quilt, the blue porcelain Chinese lamps balancing on mahogany tables, the French doors opening onto a tiny balcony hanging over the garden. "I think you'll be comfortable here." All traces of Perry, who had been living in this room for the past month, had been removed.

"What time shall I have dinner served?"

"Let's see. It's six thirty now, so seven thirty? On trays in Laughlin's room?" Angela and I both knew the dinner plans had already been set. The questions and answers were really a ceremony.

"Yes, of course. Let me know if you need anything, Mrs. Barker. So nice to meet you."

"Thank you so much." My mother took both of Angela's hands. "I appreciate it."

The door closed. "Well. I approve of the help. She's excellent."

"Oh, yes."

"Now." My mother took off her hat. "Tell me, because I am so confused. Isn't this *Laughlin's* room?" As she spoke, she lifted the hem of her dress, revealing a lace petticoat with a zippered pocket hidden in the seam, from which she produced the keys to her suitcase. "Aren't we in Laughlin's room? Remember when he showed us the original drawings of the house, with Perry's bedroom on the first floor and Laughlin's on the second?"

"Laughlin's bedroom is on the first floor. We passed it on the way up here."

"Oh." She pleated her eyebrows. "I guess that's easier."

Her suitcase open, I handed her coat hangers from the closet, but she waved me away. She'd packed her own. They were on top, between the plastic dry-cleaning bags and her clothes. "Where is Perry's room?"

"Perry used to be downstairs, too. That was their bedroom. But now he's mostly here, in this room."

"Here? I'm in *his* room?"

"Well, his temporary room. Angela put his things away."

"Oh. Well. The original plan was different. Perry's room was on the first floor and Laughlin's was on the second; they had separate rooms. It was on the blueprints when they bought the house. Laughlin showed me. Isn't that right? Isn't that the way it was?"

"I think they always planned for their master bedroom to be downstairs and another bedroom suite for guests to be here on the second floor. Perry's only been sleeping here since Laughlin's stroke."

"Oh." The suitcase zipped closed with an angry snap.

Any talk over the blueprints had been limited to how exciting and beautiful the house was going to be. Actual sleeping arrangements had never been discussed, and the lack of curiosity at Christmas had further allowed her to pretend that Laughlin and Perry neither slept in the same bed nor lived openly as a couple.

She straightened, saying, "Now, I'm here to help, so just tell me what the schedule is. But how is he?" Her chin quivered. "The door to the room I thought was Perry's was closed, and I hoped coming up the stairs that we were coming to Laughlin's room, and he'd be waiting here for me. And I didn't want to ask Anita."

"Angela."

"What?"

"Angela."

"Who's Angela?"

"The housekeeper."

"I thought she was Anita."

"No, Angela."

"Angela. Angela. I'll think 'angel' and then I'll remember Angela. Don't you think? Angel, Angela. Don't you think that's a good idea? What is the nurse's name?"

"Gillian."

"And the doctor. What do you call him?"

"Stephen."

"Stephen what?"

"Stephen Hagan."

"You don't call him Dr. Hagan?"

"No."

"Why not?"

"He's always just been Stephen. That's how Laughlin introduced him to me." The phone on the nightstand buzzed.

"Oh!" She jumped. "What's that? Is that the phone?"

"Answer it."

"I'm not going to answer it. This isn't my house. It's probably for Perry."

"Perry's away. Besides, that's the housephone."

"The housephone?"

"For calling inside the house."

She flapped her arms like a duck. "Hell*oooo*." It had to be Laughlin by the way her face suddenly glowed and her voice dropped. "Aren't you sweet. On the mantel? No, dear. I've only just arrived." She flapped her arms again, pointing to the mantel and a small vase of flowers. A tiny card sat off to the side. I handed it to her.

"I'm just opening it now, dear. I'm so touched. I mean, roses, sweet peas, and stargazers in my room. When will you be ready for us? NOW?" She covered the phone with her hand. "He's ready for us now." Then she laughed with that same laughing-song face from the photo on my father's bureau. "Well, I'll be right down."

"I think I'll return some phone calls while you're visiting with Laughlin."

"But Laughlin is ready now. I can't go by myself. I need you to take me."

Laughlin looked great. The yellow parchment quality to his skin had disappeared. Gillian had dressed him in a white shirt, buttoned all the way to the top, and had turned the cuffs at his wrists into perfect origami folds. He was propped up high in the bed; creamy linen pillows were behind him, and a paisley silk duvet was draped down his body in such luscious puddles that it was easy not to wonder about what lay beneath.

"Darling." My mother melted. "You look wonderful."

"Mother, meet Gillian." He waved his hand grandly. "The woman who has moved into my bedroom." Gillian gasped in horror, burned red, rubbed her hands against her nurse's uniform. When she left a few moments later, she would change into the cashmere cardigan and linen skirt that Laughlin had given her, along with several other boxes of clothes, all tied with red satin ribbon and delivered from the showroom.

Gillian sat my mother near the bed, and I took a chair back by the fireplace. Laughlin carried on as if he were the king of England, and I had the sudden awful urge to shake the sheets, disrupting the whole preposterous scene in a surprise attack, just as I would have done at age five to test the speed and strength of my very big, very important brother, who would do whatever it took to never, ever disappoint my mother.

His charade tonight was better than "The Last Days of Pompeii," a favorite childhood game whose name we copied from a movie that had inspired us after visiting the ruins when we lived in Italy. We draped the attic of our Arlington house into a series of exotic Roman tents, then wound our bodies in faded curtains and costume jewelry. All six of us were cast in the re-enactment, from Emperor Chico to baby Eros (Patrick). It was a grand tableau with proclamations made and edicts rendered, when, without warning, just as the orgy reached its height and the dancing girl (me) was about to shimmy through the curtains clanging her cymbals, a loud and sudden crash would stop us. Chico, with outstretched arms, would scream, "Run! The wrath of Vesuvius is upon us!" It was a mad, excited frenzy; we tore at the walls and played at dying over and over again.

It's makeup, I realized. The crispy surface of his skin had been smoothed and blended with a thin bronze putty, he and Gillian doing an excellent job of duplicating his former self. He kept the conversation up, keeping the attention on my mother, saying, "I like your hair."

I had cut Laughlin's hair the day before, cutting it bluntly, straight across the back of his neck while he hummed Simon & Garfunkel's "Scarborough Fair," and I added my voice. We climbed the melody with "*la-la-la*s" when we struggled to remember what came after "parsley, sage, rosemary, and thyme," one voice after the other until we both got it right and, for one brief line, I was sure I was saving him.

"What's going on at home?" he asked.

"I think the Palacio property will be finished soon. Your father is very involved with the remodeling."

"Did he find a restaurant to go in the new space?"

"I'm not getting involved," she said, holding up her hands like stop signs. "It's his *thing*, as you children would say. But I do think the skylight structure is too big.

Dinner had been served, my mother arranging and rearranging her food into tiny pyramids, pushing her fork around every time she took a bite, piling the rice in a mound on one side of the zucchini slices, then narrowing her triangle of fish. Her plate never lost its manicured look. The food shrank in unison.

Laughlin only pretended to eat. It was getting harder for him to keep up an animated conversation but talking about Daddy's business kept him focused. "He doesn't have someone to go into the new space yet?"

"No." She changed the subject then, perhaps sensing a whiff of potential unpleasantness because she began to talk louder, as if volume would fix whatever it was that was starting to feel not right in the room. "David and Lisa put in a little garden at their house and a pond with goldfish that survive every winter; the fish just go to sleep under the cover of ice."

270

"Did Maria bake a cake, Christine?" Laughlin suddenly interrupted.

"Yes." I got out of my chair and walked to his bed, where I put my plate on top of his, hiding the uneaten food. "A chocolate cake, but I ate too much. Maybe we should have it later."

"Later?" my mother lamented.

"Oh, you aren't full? I'm sorry, but I really can't eat any right now." She looked at me with disappointment.

"I'd like to wait, too," Laughlin added.

Just then, Barbara —the night nurse—entered, carrying the pill tray. Barbara reminded Laughlin of a wasp, tiny and always buzzing when you didn't want her around. I was looking for a replacement but finding a night-shift nurse for an AIDS patient was not easy.

"Barbara, this is my mother, Mrs. Barker."

"How do you do?" Barbara's eyes darted, then she handed Laughlin the cup of pills.

"There's more than usual," Laughlin said.

"It's in the chart," Barbara said. "Dr. Hagan added some. The pharmacy delivered them not long ago."

"The doctor was here?" My mother looked at me.

"How many?" Laughlin asked.

"About fifty-six."

My mother straightened and stood. "Well. If you have to swallow all those pills, we'd better let you get started, shouldn't we, *Christine*?" She weighted my name with a sinker.

I brushed my hand across Laughlin's forehead. Little bubbles of makeup were beginning to foam at his temples.

"Love you," he said.

"Love you, too." I left them and thought I would try to call Suzanne from Kate's room, where I often stayed when sleeping at the house. I was headed there when I heard my mother close Laughlin's door and call my name.

"Be there in a minute."

I'd waited until Suzanne would be home from work, not wanting to call when she was at her office. But now that I knew she was home alone with James and Meredith, who were only five and four, maybe now wasn't a good time, either. It wasn't that she didn't know. She had prepared Laughlin's papers. Still, she was alone. I put the phone down.

Back in the guest room, my mother was in the rocking chair, rocking with the unyielding rhythm of a metronome. "I like your hair," I began.

"What do you think about the color?" A sly smile spread across her face.

"That's what it is. Did you have a dandruff treatment before you came?"

"Yesss." She drew out the word, and we laughed. "Dandruff treatment" was code for coloring her hair, a phrase her mother and aunt had adopted rather than admitting they had their hair dyed, all of which was a convoluted scheme. "I told Jacques I wanted that soft color—I can never remember names: African Queen or something."

"African Queen?"

"Something like that."

"I thought you used Clairol products. Born—"

"That's it. Born Free."

"Blonde. Born Blonde."

"Right. I knew it was something African."

"It's cold in here. Doesn't it feel like the air-conditioning is turned up too high?" I asked.

"How can you be cold? I feel perfectly comfortable."

"It's just . . . I don't know. I'm going to get a robe." I suddenly felt encased in ice, when earlier with Stephen the house had felt like an inferno. I returned to Kate's room for the plush terry robe of Laughlin's that I'd borrowed on an earlier occasion and smelled like his shampoo.

"Oh, that's so big. Don't you have a pretty one with a flowered print or something on it?"

"This is Laughlin's. I wear it when I'm here. I like that it's big."

In the seconds it took to say the words, I'd unearthed thousands of childhood battles over my choosing to wear something other than what she wished. Now, in addition to being cold, the room was claustrophobic.

"Are you tired?"

"No, not really. But I don't mind getting into bed. Your father and I are in bed by eight thirty every night. I can't understand how people have trouble sleeping. They must not get enough exercise."

"Well, I went to ballet today and walked through the park. I'm exhausted. It will be good to go to sleep. Shall I tuck you in?"

"You're not sleeping here?"

"Oh. I've been sleeping in Kate's room."

"I thought you were going to stay here with me. The bed is plenty big enough for both of us." She patted the spot next to her.

I was still cold, trembling from the inside out, so I kept the robe wrapped around me.

"You're wearing that robe to bed? It's August, and we're in New York City."

"I know. The heat is awful. I'm not used to air-conditioning. I don't have it in the loft."

"Well, you'll probably be hot in a minute. *Oh.* The sheets feel sooo good."

"They're ironed and changed every day."

"Every day?"

"Yep."

"What did the doctor say?"

"Oh." For a minute I couldn't remember. I thought we were talking about sheets. Besides, I didn't know how to start. I stalled, tracing the patchwork squares on the quilt, thinking that however I said it, it had to come out *nicely.* "He thinks we should schedule our family visits sooner rather than later; he said that Laughlin is dying; the Kaposi's sarcoma is in his lungs. Stephen doesn't know when or how long, he just said maybe sometime this fall." I strung the words in one long thread, keeping my voice steady in a silky vocal tone, looking up from the quilt every second or so to peek at her, sitting so close to me yet with a distance that had taken a lifetime to create.

Her face was blank, and I saw in her what I had felt when I first heard the words: nothing, as if I were caught between hearing and understanding, the words passing through me in some unrecognizable form. I considered repeating, "Laughlin is dying," to make sure she got it.

But then she changed, moving beyond herself and hardening off the way I'd seen her do all my life. "Do you have a calendar?"

I stared at her, not wanting to follow her cue and ignore

the racking pain of having said the words aloud. But I knew my mother, so I struggled for my datebook, saying, "Kate is supposed to be coming next week."

"Oh my God. Can you be here with her? She's old enough to ask questions. Maybe she shouldn't come, or if she does, only for a few days."

"We're—Laughlin, Kate, and I—supposed to go out to Water Island next week."

"Well, you take Kate straight out to Water Island from the airport and don't even stop here. Go for two days, then come back here for just an overnight. Maybe your father can come to help make things easier."

"But Kate is coming to see Laughlin, not me, and not Daddy."

"Chris-tine," she hammered. The cold was eating my bones but listening to her made me sweat. "After Kate...we can't have everyone suddenly appearing and making Laughlin think—"

Her sentence broke, and I thought, *Say them. The words: that Laughlin's dying*, but she fixated on what to do, which was for her the priority, and a buffer. But she had mentioned Daddy, so I probed, "What does Daddy think about this?"

"Your father?"

"Yeah. What does he think?"

"He just can't believe it." She splintered with the admission, and I heard her desperation. I believed deep in my gut that she was divided, and that if my father were somehow out of the picture, she might be different. But she only stiffened, saying, "I think it's just stuck inside, and he can't let it out. Laughlin is his son, and he loves him, but he can't stop thinking that his son, this fine, bright young man got himself into this. *And you know how*."

Those last words were hard and blunt, reminding me why I couldn't trust her. She fingered the pages, turned to September, counting the weeks. Finally, she banged the book shut and the words poured out. "I just don't understand it. The doctors keep saying it is a venereal disease, transferred through blood. But I just don't understand it. I mean, there isn't any blood in intercourse."

She didn't look at me; she looked everywhere else, imploring the curtains, the walls, even the floor, as if they held the answers. I'd never heard my mother say "intercourse." Who ever said "intercourse?" We said "making love," "fooling around," "having sex." What an odd word. You would never know what it meant by the sound of it. My mother looked at the walls, and I clung to the dull thud of "intercourse" because I wished I'd never heard her say, "And you know how."

"I'm cold." I began rummaging in my bag, putting sweatpants on under my nightie.

"We are not to tell anyone," she asserted.

"But the boys need to know—they're *family*."

"Those are Laughlin's wishes. We do not have permission to tell."

I felt my ears lie back. Laughlin had asked for secrecy, but things were different now. Her refusal to tell even my brothers was a corrupt form of self-preservation. To admit *to anyone* that Laughlin was dying of AIDS, a gay disease, would erase her version of him forever. The disease would kill Laughlin, but she would protect her version—as imperfect and unfair as it was even to him—since that was all that she would have to keep him close to her. And he was the child she most needed to keep.

"Maybe Suzanne can come." It was pointless to argue.

"Yes, of course. She'll have to plan for the children, but there's her housekeeper, Mary, and Dad and I can help, too. But yes, she should come as soon as she can. What are the plans for tomorrow?"

"I have an audition for a television commercial in the morning, so you can spend some time with Laughlin while I'm gone. I'll be home for lunch, and afterward, I'll take you out. Would you like to go to the Metropolitan Museum of Art? A movie?" I didn't know how I'd have the strength to go to an audition, but I was more afraid of not going—the mere act of showing up had become my one, tenuous hold on my professional life.

"Of course. I'm in New York: Fifth Avenue, Tiffany's. Are there matinees on Thursdays?" She spoke without attachment to either the question or the answer, and I softened, understanding that the grief was too big to digest and likely had to be worked out alone. It made sense to find some full expression of something somewhere that could hold you for a few lovely moments, displacing all that was permanently broken. The one thing my mother and I did share was faith in the redemptive nature of art.

She turned her back to me and turned out the light. "Would you scratch under my shoulder blades? Oh, your feet are like ice."

I turned the scratches into rubs, pushing the muscles in her back up toward her shoulders. When we were little, my siblings and I took turns sleeping with her during the long months Daddy was away on sea duty. She surely must have felt lonely, and for us, the proximity to her meant knowing we were *of her*, some part always attached, even though her love mostly played out in day-to-day expectations that we would work hard and be involved in something important. All I ever wanted was to be important enough to be recognized, which for the most part, was determined by the public; when the public noticed me, so did she. And yet, now, she wanted me to be near her, so I figured we had that, this night together.

She slept, but the day had been too much. I couldn't relax, and I couldn't get out of bed without waking her. Still, I knew where to go, the place most true, where I was never a stranger, never ordinary, my lower spine dropping, my shoulders relaxing into place, breathing into the port de bras and feeling relief in the long stretch without so much as moving a muscle, my head carrying me through the barre to an imaginary center where my right foot swung in rond de jambe and my left leg rooted like a pillar. I was not so good when I changed sides and asked the left to do the filigree work. But I repeated the sequence in my mind until I was dancing in my dream. *Balance- balance-run- run-leap. . . . Step-turn-step-turn.* I repeated the combination, going back to where I started, this time with the left foot in front, and on the third round, at the height of the grand jeté, the world stuttered in a broken frame of time; I stayed suspended in the air, flying. "Do it again," I said. "Fly." So, I repeated the steps, and for a second time, I was up, this time high above the ground, banking over patchwork squares of green backyards, my mother below me, shielding her eyes from the glare of the sun. She stood in the middle of the street, the traffic lines solid, then breaking into yellow dashes, white shoulders sloping off to the side. And I was waving, calling to her, "Here I am. Look up, Mommy. It's me. *Look up!*"

City of the Dead
—
August–December 1985

We shortened Kate's visit, which made her and her mother angry, but when Kate saw that Laughlin couldn't get out of bed, she softened. Carrie, Kate's mother, asked me point-blank if Laughlin had AIDS, and I point-blank lied, saying again that he was recuperating from a stroke, repeating the story of family heart conditions, every word carving a hole in my soul.

Suzanne arrived shortly after, following up on some personal papers that Laughlin had long ago asked her to review. She mentioned that David wanted to come for a visit, and I hoped Laughlin would see to telling him—and later, Patrick—the truth about his illness.

Bill sublet his apartment and moved in with me. He'd mentioned marriage more than once, but I'd made a mistake already and had learned that making significant life-altering decisions at the same time I was drowning in overwhelming circumstances was not an effective strategy: good judgement depended on timing and having a clear head. I had Laughlin's impending death from AIDS weighing on me, and I was still weary of the societal pressure placed on women that made them feel that they had to be married to have a fulfilled life. Marriage seemed such an enterprise, fraught with expectations of male dominance and female domesticity; I hoped for what I'd observed in some (not all) gay relationships where commitment, equitability, and power were a shared flow, like a tidal current, reliably advancing forward, then retreating before advancing again. Still, I completely trusted Bill and didn't want to be with anyone else, so we agreed to live together.

My father came in on a Thursday for a long weekend. He stayed at a hotel because Perry was back, and it was awkward for him to stay at the loft now that Bill was living with me. Visits with Laughlin would be short, his energy waning, so I arranged tickets for a baseball game with John and Bill, and planned time at the gym for my father to run on a treadmill and swim. I escorted him to and from the hotel and the house. I couldn't remember when I'd last seen my brother and father alone in a room. They shared light talk about the construction on the Palacio property, the baseball game, how Laughlin was feeling, but mostly, in the moments between, they shared a palpable silence, a thing of brokenness between them that was theirs and theirs alone.

The break had happened long ago. My father had taken Laughlin to the mountains when he was a teenager and had beaten him up after finding out about some inappropriate "boy games." Suzanne told me about it, Laughlin confiding the whole story on the day three years ago when he finally told her he was gay. When Suzanne told me later that very same day, I collapsed; it was so horrible. She said Laughlin had only ever told her, Perry, and Carrie. I'd never in my life known my father to be violent or hit anyone, and as much as I couldn't imagine it, I believed it because there had always been something dark between them.

Years later, when I confronted my mother, she explained, "That's how homosexuality was dealt with back then." My father had sought advice from a "highly respected, renowned doctor," who'd advised him to "scare the living daylights out of his son, because it cannot be."

Sitting in Laughlin's room that weekend with my father, I didn't have the information about the "advice" my father had acted on, not that it would have changed anything. Death wouldn't be a great reconciler, and from my spot where I sat at the back of the room, their meeting appeared harder on my father than it was on Laughlin. My father sat at the bedside. He knew Laughlin was dying, while Laughlin seemed convinced that he wasn't. My father spoke in fits and starts, seemingly unprepared—when he was never unprepared—his posture stooped, not straight-backed as he demanded of us our entire lives, having us sit on benches at the dinner table rather than on chairs. I thought about that night when my mother was visiting, and she said, "It's just stuck inside," and I tried to imagine how he might feel—how the "it cannot be" advice from the doctor had trapped him into acting with violence against his son, which on some level must have destroyed him. I'd always known my father to be relatively invulnerable, but he was different during the face-to-face in the bedroom, reeking of something desperate that may have been regret, holding Laughlin's hand, saying, I think, "I love you." But then, I heard my mother's voice, saying more words: "He loves him, but he can't stop thinking that his son . . . got himself into this. *And you know how.*" Hearing her, hearing him, their words and actions seemed a grotesque muddle, a distortion of love, so sick and stinking that I covered my nose and mouth to keep from puking because I thought, for sure, I was going to puke right there in the room. When I took my father to the airport, I was enormously relieved to say goodbye.

A few days later, Gillian told us her mother was sick, and she had to go home to Ireland. I believed she was lying but couldn't blame her; she'd been in the room with me when Stephen did his probe. She handpicked her replacement, Catherine: an angel with dark hair and sapphire eyes.

We weren't crazy people, but the next part seemed insane: My parents, Bill, and I had tickets for a trip to Egypt that had been planned well before I left *A Chorus Line* and Laughlin's health became the center of my life. By the first of October, I couldn't fathom traveling halfway across the world for several weeks. I told my parents I was anxious about the timing, but they were stuck in their peculiar form of denial, answering, "Let's see," and changing the subject. I thought the world stopped when someone was dying, but they seemed convinced that we should stick to our plans because we had no control over Laughlin's health.

Then, on October 7, 1985, armed PLO terrorists hijacked the *Achille Lauro*, a cruise ship docked in the Mediterranean Sea off the coast of Egypt. The hijackers took crew members and tourists hostage before killing an American Jewish passenger, sixty-nine-year-old Leon Klinghoffer, whom they shot and pushed over the side of the ship and into the sea. With shameful and exhausted relief, I was sure we would now stay home, Mr. Klinghoffer having paid my ransom with his life.

I said we had to reschedule. My father disagreed, claiming security would be tight. Then Laughlin said, "You should go."

"I feel unsafe."

"Egypt depends on tourism." He shrugged. "The State Department hasn't issued a travel ban. My God, the pyramids, Cheops." He exercised the upper half of his body, using the new triangle bar hanging over his bed to do pull-ups, defying the fact that his lower body had stopped functioning. He argued briefly, then told me that the blisters from the herpes zoster were itching and burning and asked if I would run my fingers lightly over them, which I did until one spot grew too sensitive, and he screamed.

Every day was a battle of will, with me feeling the increasing horror of my own powerlessness. The words "death" or "dying" were never spoken, no matter how many sores appeared on Laughlin's body. I didn't understand, until I finally did. Laughlin pulled on the triangle bar with Perry egging him on, relying on Laughlin's strength to give him the courage he himself lacked. Laughlin was trying to live for them both, while Perry's denial was self-serving, the only way he could cope. His denial left Laughlin alone, without the support of the man he loved when he needed it the most. Because from Laughlin's standpoint, dying of AIDS, a "gay disease," was *failure in excelsis*. It reduced his life to nothingness, harkening back to the "it cannot be" message delivered to him, first by his father and then by the world at large, a negation of who he was endured over the course of his lifetime. AIDS gave society permission to erase him, and he knew they would. I stopped talking about Egypt out of fear my resistance would be interpreted as a vote of no confidence, so I did the only thing I could: stand beside him and blow on blisters.

Suzanne agreed that I had no choice but to go on the trip, and finally, Bill, too, said we had to go.

I held my breath the entire trip, but at night on the Nile, Bill and I shared a paperback, reading silently together until the first of us reached the bottom of the page and whispered, "Beep," so the other would know, and we could turn the page together. He held my hand in the City of the Dead, our tour guide, Ahmed, speaking the words my parents never uttered and that were forbidden in the house: "death" and "dying." They arrived in strangely accented Arab-British-English syllables: "When he died," "death brought him," and "at the funeral," Laughlin slipping through when Ahmed said, "the sun" or "his son."

The afternoon I returned from Egypt, Laughlin was waiting for me, wearing a pressed blue pajama shirt. His bed had been replaced with a hospital bed, Perry apologizing, "It's not pretty," but it made it easier to raise Laughlin's upper body or feet. Laughlin liked my stories, but I only stayed a short while, explaining the time change and that I'd be back the next morning.

When I arrived, Perry had a bandage plastered across his face; he'd had a nosebleed that the nurse had taken care of. I made him tea and an omelet. He was so very thin and fragile, and I suggested he sleep while I took my post in Laughlin's room. I lost track of the hours until much later, when Perry appeared, looking better. His nose had healed, and he'd shaved and dressed.

"Shall I put the kettle on?" Perry asked.

For the first time all afternoon, Laughlin rolled over, Perry's presence rousing him. "It's such a battle." Laughlin said the words as a direct statement of fact, coming out of nowhere.

"I know, baby." And they locked eyes like synchronized swimmers checking on their timing before going off to simultaneously execute the next feat.

Then Perry said, "Stephen will be coming."

And I reassured, "Stephen will be coming."

Perry left, and I climbed onto the bed. "Everything is okay,"

I said. I wanted to add, "I'm sorry," because I was so, so sorry, but everything came out in a smear of syllables. I pressed my body against legs he couldn't feel and placed my hand on his head. He moved toward my touch, emitting a faint wheezing sound. Then I whispered, "It's okay. You can let go, Laughlin, you really can. You're not alone, and it's okay to die."

At some point, the sound of Laughlin's breathing darkened in pitch, like a wail in the far-off distance, something I wasn't completely sure of, but it was eerie, with a dense and foggy texture. When Stephen came that night, I asked about it, and he said it was air passing through the larynx, but I wasn't talking about the whoosh, I was talking about the other thing—the pitch. But Stephen didn't hear it.

Rage

January 2, 1986

As soon as I unlocked the downstairs door and entered the hallway, I could hear Laughlin.

Angela stuck her head out of her basement room. Her eyes were black circles. With one hand she held the door, and with the other, a pillow. She said to call her on the intercom if I wanted something to eat. She closed the door and stuffed the pillow under it, part of it coming out near my feet, like a roll of white foam seeping into the hallway. In the kitchen and going up the back stairs, Laughlin's screeching inhabited the air.

"Thank God you're here," said Robert, Perry's friend from Canada—the only friend Perry had confided in—had come.

"The subway is on a holiday schedule."

"I was wondering what took you so long. Perry's upstairs in the room where I'm staying, with the air conditioner turned on high. It drowns out the sound. We can't take it and haven't been in Laughlin's room since last night."

"Okay."

"I'll tell Perry you're here." He disappeared, and I started up the stairs, the walls crawling with the sound of Laughlin dying.

"He's been like this on and off since I got here this morning," Catherine said. "Anne, the night nurse, reported it was the same all night." Laughlin was thrashing about on the bed, a delirious madman, his tongue swollen, the color of red-currant jelly. I put my hands on his shoulders, forcing my face inches away from his.

"It's all right, Laughlin. Laughlin, can you hear me?" He quieted. "It's me," I said, climbing onto the bed next to him. "It's me. You're safe. Feel my hands? See, I'm here." He fell back then, into the bed pillows, and I heard a whoosh of breathing.

"He's out now," Catherine said. "You can tell by the change in the sound."

Stephen's explanation the night before—that it was air flowing through his larynx—was ludicrous. Laughlin was screaming; he had to be hallucinating.

Catherine took out a handkerchief and wiped her forehead.

"Would you like a cup of tea?" I asked.

"Do you think you can be in here alone?"

I nodded.

"Well, in that case, yes. I would like to go down to the kitchen. I won't stay long."

Just then, Laughlin jerked and squealed. "Laughlin. Laughlin." I grabbed his shoulders, but he bucked with such ferocity I could barely hold him.

"Keep talking to him. He recognizes the sound of your voice. He knows you're here."

"Laughlin," I called. "It's okay. Are you in pain?" I asked. He looked at me, his eyes focusing, and suddenly his old self appeared on the surface of his face. It looked like he was trying to smile or answer, but his mouth couldn't coordinate itself and all that came out was a nasal "Oh."

"He can't speak," I said to Catherine, but she stood with her hand on the doorknob, the door halfway open, her body halfway out of the room.

"There's nothing you can do, really. I do notice, though, that you bring him back to us. Keep talking so he knows you're here."

"But is he in pain?"

"I don't think so. I've watched him throw these fits on and off all morning. The morphine is taking care of the pain."

Alone with him, I had no idea what to do, only that it was less frightening to lie on the bed, my body alongside his so, when he started warring, I could push myself against him and hold on through the bucking. "Laughlin, you're here. You're home! You're safe." Sometimes I yelled over his screams. I'd never been in a birthing room, but my friends who had started having babies told me about their coaches, so I tried to think of dying as being born in reverse. "Come on, Laughlin, breathe with me. I'm here. You're not alone. You're home. You're okay. I promise. *One, two.*"

At one point, we were breathing together, and after a few synchronized moments, he became completely still, in a stillness that carried the force of its own vitality. He didn't move, though I sensed an inward withdrawal, like an undertow pulling him toward a depth that was inaccessible to me. It unnerved me, so I got off the bed and started jumping. I jumped haphazardly, ordering my legs to obey: *changement*, right, left, faster. The warring frightened me, but the feeling of his complete removal was worse—at least when he was fighting, I knew where he was, and I could fight and scream along with him. I climbed back onto the bed, shaking.

"I heard something. Is everything okay?" Catherine came back in.

"I think he's finally asleep. Or is it that he is unconscious?"

"Both."

Immediately, Laughlin started up again. My jumping didn't disturb him, but he noticed the change when Catherine entered, and this time he came back braying, with chilling violence. I pressed on him, laying my chest on top of his, holding his hand in mine.

The pattern continued, erasing time. At some point, the light outside the window turned pulpy and gray, and Stephen arrived. He asked to see Perry, but only Robert came down, just long enough to tell Stephen that Perry wasn't coming.

Once we were alone, Stephen said, "It may be tonight. Thank you for being so loving and so strong." But his words had little meaning. He was speaking sideways in an upside-down world, and I'd stepped outside of myself a long time ago.

Anne arrived to relieve Catherine, and when Catherine left, she advised me: "The hearing is the last to go. Even after the heart and the breathing stop, the hearing is still there." Then she took Anne aside, their heads bobbing like chickens.

John called, having just returned from visiting our family in Santa Fe for the holidays. I told him what Stephen had said, so John took a cab, arriving quickly. He gasped when he saw Laughlin, then recovered and put his face right up to Laughlin's as if it were the most normal thing in the world, and said, "Hey, Laughlin, it's me, John. Hey, are you awake?"

Amazingly, Laughlin focused, and it sounded like he said, "Hey, buddy."

John started to talk, telling Laughlin about reading Hunter S. Thompson and describing a scene with Richard Nixon, how they'd talked about football. "Can you believe it? They hated each other." John carried on, and it was a good idea because Laughlin caught something, maybe the inflection of John's voice, speeding up and slowing down as he exaggerated stories. Thank God for John, who brought us back to ourselves. Laughlin tried to say something that sounded like, "Where's Perry?"

I asked him if he wanted Perry, and it seemed that he did, so I said, "I'll go get him," and took the stairs two at a time.

Perry sat in a chair in the far corner of the room where Robert was staying. "He asked for you," I said, and when Perry expressed disbelief, I insisted. "He did. Please, please come down."

Finally, he agreed. When he arrived, he was dressed in a crisp, fresh shirt and khakis, taking Laughlin's hand and saying, "Hi there." Laughlin stared intently, as if he were memorizing every detail of Perry's face, but he didn't talk or couldn't talk, so Perry looked across the room at me, raising an eyebrow as if to say: *See?* Then he put his hands into his pockets, looking past Laughlin and across the bed to John.

John and Perry talked about the holidays and football, the game between Pittsburgh and Denver. John was a Cowboys fan and Perry loved the Redskins, but neither team was having a good season. They stood on either side of the bed, with the wide stretch of the pillows and Laughlin dying between them, their sentences going back and forth as if they themselves were tossing short passes, Perry predicting the outcome of the playoffs and likely preparing to leave as soon as John finished some comment about the Patriots. Laughlin gave no indication that he was conscious, but I believed he did know we were all in the room; after all, he was quiet, maybe even comfortable. I considered excusing myself and taking John with me so Perry could be alone with Laughlin. Intruding on their intimate space felt wrong, but Perry hadn't been in the room all day, nor the day before, and had refused to come down even when Stephen asked.

Soon Perry excused himself and told me to come get him if I needed him, which were merely polite, meaningless words. He mounted the stairs, and I followed him. I wanted to thank him for coming down, and to say that I was sorry, but Laughlin *had* asked for him. I was sure of it. When he reached the top, he slammed the door to Robert's room. It was a loud crash, so full of rage that it shook the banister I was holding.

With Perry gone, Laughlin started rolling and wheezing, and John quietly said that he was going crazy, so why didn't we take a little break and let Anne take over? I was afraid to be out of the room, but John convinced me.

Angela had put a tray of sandwiches and drinks on the sideboard, but neither of us could eat. Within minutes, we ran out of things to talk about, the tick of the clock on the end table swelling the space, the second hand mimicking the rhythm of Laughlin's breathing, which we could also hear because we'd kept the door to his room open. After about ten, twelve, or maybe thirty minutes, John said, "He sounds different. Listen."

We went into the room, and John bent toward Laughlin. "Do you want a sip of water?" Turning to me, John said, "I think he wants us to raise him up." But in the second it took to say the words, John was already tracking something else. In a burst, he grabbed Laughlin as if Laughlin were falling, pulling him to his chest and calling into his face, "Laughlin, I love you. I love you." The lines around Laughlin's eyes crinkled the way they used to when he smiled. I moved quickly then, joining them on the bed and saying, "And I love you, too. And Perry loves you, and Kate. Suzanne, Daddy and Mom, they love you. David and Patrick. Talk to him, John. Say everyone's name. He hears you." And so we repeated names: the names of Perry and Kate, everyone in our family, friends, Lynn, the names of everyone we could think of. John and I sandwiched Laughlin between us and clasped each other's arms, so that Laughlin was held securely against our bodies. We spoke slowly because suddenly we had all the time in the world.

Anne appeared at the bedside occasionally, coming and going as freely as vapor. She placed the stethoscope to his heart and at one point said, "His heart has stopped." She may have said it more than once, and then, may have left the room to give us privacy. I don't know. I didn't know anything, only that it was quiet, the quietest it had been in days.

Then John suddenly said, "Close his eyes!" and was off the bed in a skittish leap. "Close his eyes. I can't stand the way he looks."

I reached, running my hands over Laughlin's eyelids, but his eyes stared with cloudy astonishment.

"Close his eyes. I can't stand it." John paced.

I reached out my hand for a second time and felt a dizzying pull, like I was fainting and Laughlin was receding in space, until I was jolted by the sight of what John saw: a frightening corpse. It had never mattered to me what Laughlin looked like, no matter how awful, because he was *sick*. But now, he was dead, and death on him was unimaginably grotesque. I was afraid to touch him, when I'd never, ever been afraid.

"Anne," I called. She was no longer in the room but came immediately. "Please go downstairs and find Angela. Ask her to bring some candles. Long white ones. Lots of them." I climbed onto the bed, not looking at Laughlin's face, and scooped my arms under his in the way I would position myself with a dance partner, then tried to shove his body upward, but he was too heavy.

"John, you have to help me. I can't lift him by myself. Don't look at him. Just come over here on this side and lift him."

Together, we shifted Laughlin's body. "Just hold him up," I said, running to the closet to get as many pillows as were there, then gathering what was on the chairs so I could prop him up on either side. I pulled the covers high up on his chest and tucked the sides in tightly. Gravity worked. His head slumped forward; the lids closed. I opened the night table drawer and reached for his silver comb.

Anne arrived with Angela, who looked at me, looked at Laughlin, and made the sign of the cross. She understood why I asked for the candles and had boxes and boxes. "There are more," she said. "Different kinds in the linen cupboard in the dining room. Shall I get those, too?"

I nodded. Without having discussed it, John and I knew what we would do with the candles. It was instinctual, a remnant of habit or imagination, like lighting the *farolitos* every Christmas in Santa Fe so Santo Niño could find his way to us or repeating what we'd seen as children in tiny Italian hillside churches, watching in awe when the faithful lit their candles and whispered intimate pleadings. It was the flame that got God's attention. *Dona nobis pacem. Dear God, hear my prayer. Bless my brother. A good man whom we love and revere. Give him peace.*

Anne reminded me that I had to speak to Stephen to report the death.

Stephen cried in embarrassed man gulps as I held the phone. Then he asked me about Perry, and I said I wanted to comb Laughlin's hair before I went to get him. It was quiet again, so he said, "There is something I need to know. That the nurse needs to know. Would you be willing to let us do an autopsy? There are things we could learn."

I went mute, silently stumbling through words but coming out with something like, "I'd have to talk to my family," and then Stephen stuttered with the rest of his explanation about blood and medicines and how unusual it was for Laughlin to have lived for so long, that his was a unique case. By then, the sound of his voice had turned to an underwater communication, like exaggerated gestures in a story ballet. When he said, "We have to know tonight," I hung up.

In the mirror above the fireplace, John was a wavy reflection. He looked like he did when he was five, the gloaming candlelight blurring the edges of him, and for a brief, wonderous moment, I remembered who we'd been, Laughlin's death unleashing time, letting it run free so every memory lived all at once and together; every flicker a half-bodied spirit rising, dancing in the light.

One, two, three: Anne, Angela, and John looked toward me. Their heads turned in three-four time, and the next beat was mine. I picked up the comb, ran it through Laughlin's hair, and started up the stairs.

The door was closed, but I could hear the roar of the air conditioner. I knocked. There was no answer, so I knocked again and called their names. "Perry? Robert?" I waited, and finally opened the door to blackness.

"Perry?"

"Who is it? What do you want?"

"It's me. I'm sorry. I'm so sorry," I said. "Laughlin went. A few minutes ago." *Why did I say "went"?* I had no idea where that word came from, but I'd told him, so I walked downstairs, where John, Anne, and Angela were still waiting in the same exact spots where I'd left them, as if no time had passed. They could have been standing on their little *x*'s, the spots the stage manager places on the floor so actors know where to stand when the play begins.

Perry entered, ashen, gaunt, and fully dressed. He screamed, "Get out! All of you! Get out!"

We scurried, couldn't move fast enough. Anne and Angela fled toward the kitchen. John and I retreated to the sitting room, where from the sofa we could hear Perry sobbing, crying out, "My baby, my baby." I winced hearing him use the kind of endearment I imagined Perry saying to Laughlin when they were engaged in intimacy, and I felt I'd trespassed somewhere I had no right to be. Yet at the same time, I was happy, thinking that at some exquisite moment in his lifetime, Laughlin knew what it was to be someone's "baby."

John's hands were rubbing up and down his thighs when Perry's sobbing stopped, and all turned quiet. I looked behind me. Jesus! I'd forgotten to close the shutters at five. They were open, so I started for the back of the room just as the bedroom door swung open. Perry stood in a harsh circle of light. I looked to the shutters, then back to him, meeting his face and his screaming, a scream that burst with such force, I thought the window had exploded in its frame behind me, the sound incomprehensibly violent, like a rock being hurled through the glass, until his words caught up to my ears: "I hate the candles! I hate the candles!"

I was stunned, confused, my hands reaching to catch what I imagined was shattering glass as Perry moved toward the hall, a dead man walking.

John paced, and I wanted to fill the room with some other sound or words, but I couldn't think, so I closed the shutters, letting the locks slide into place with a click.

Once the shutters sealed us in, I whispered, "Stephen asked me something."

"What?"

"He wanted to know about an autopsy. If they could do an autopsy."

John wheeled. "You tell them to keep their fucking hands off my brother. No one is touching my brother." He raged until the roar of his fury obliterated Perry's words, and the air felt clean again.

In the bedroom, Perry had blown out all the candles and turned on all the lights. It was bright and harsh, so John walked around, pounding each switch with his fist into the "off" position, except for the lamp on the night table. Then he sat on the edge of the bed, a sentry carved in stone.

"Promise me. I'm not leaving here until you promise me. No one is touching my brother. No one."

"I promise. No one's touching him." John and I would protect the sanctity of Laughlin, and we would have our secret.

"Okay," he said. "Okay."

Anne appeared. She had prepared all the reports and charts, going over them with me, telling me what I must fill out and sign. I asked her to report our decision back to Stephen, and John offered to walk her to a cab.

A Brown Paper Shopping Bag
—
Two days later, a no-date day

The message on my answering machine said, "Your package is ready."

The funeral home awning was burgundy and gold; the doorman wore a matching burgundy coat with gold braids on the sleeves and gold buttons down the front. Inside, it was all marble, like a boutique European hotel, with one person at the reception desk.

Suzanne had told me to remember to get eight copies of the death certificate, so I counted them as the clerk handed them to me.

"Sign here, miss."

I signed, and he reached underneath the counter, producing a brown paper shopping bag. I froze.

He pushed the bag toward me.

I refused to touch it.

The clerk nudged the bag again, and I almost grabbed his skinny, arrogant neck. *I gave you my brother. And you dare to give him back to me in a brown paper shopping bag?* I snatched the bag and ran.

The doorman was blowing his whistle, raising his gloved hand in the air for a cab, but I ran past him and continued running to the end of the block, and then the next and the next, running until I was out of breath and could no longer see the funeral home. Then, I hailed a cab.

Bill drove John and me to the airport the next day. He would not be coming, my family situation too fraught and complicated by my parents' need for absolute control and privacy. Despite traveling through Egypt with him, in this situation, and particularly on their turf, Bill was a stranger. I still did not even know if they'd told David and Patrick the truth.

John had the window seat because his legs were longer, and I took the middle. "Do you have it?" he asked, when he had not asked anything about it beforehand. I nodded and squeezed my ankles together. The bag holding the box of Laughlin's cremated remains sat between my feet, and even when the stewardess said to push everything under the seat in front of me, I kept it where I could feel it the whole way home.

The Funeral
—
January 1986

Although my parents had never been practicing Catholics, they organized a memorial service at Loretto Chapel, to be held the day before the private family burial. Father Bruneau officiated, someone my mother called for Suzanne's wedding and now Laughlin's memorial and funeral. He spoke in religious garble about death, all of which had nothing to do with Laughlin and his life. The ceremony was not punctuated with music or other speakers; it lacked any sense of the personal, so Laughlin was not only dead, but absent. My family and I stood in a line afterward as people came forward to tell us how sorry they were and how they remembered Laughlin. Lung cancer was reported as the cause of death. I do not believe AIDS ever crossed anyone's mind.

Early the next morning, my mother woke me up. "I just want to make sure that you remember that you're to take all the children's baskets don't forget they're on the dining room table I've labeled all of them." Her words were strung together without periods or commas. She stood in the doorway, in a blaze of winter sunlight, wearing a white slip, nylon stockings, ankle boots, and an imposing black hat. She was ready for the funeral. She only needed to put on her dress.

"I'll remember." The words were sand in my mouth,

but I repeated: "I'll bring the baskets. They're on the dining room table, and I'll bring all of them." Everything had to be exactly as she envisioned. Our tasks were merely to assume our positions. "Anything else you want me to do?"

"What are you going to wear?"

"I don't know."

"I hope you're going to wear your black hat."

"Sure, that's a good idea. I'll wear my black hat. That will look nice."

Outside the window, the yard was covered in snow. I wanted a low ceiling, dark clouds, but instead the view was immaculately beautiful, not a wrinkle in the air. I put on my hat and hoped that when we gathered around the grave, she would notice, and remember that she had a daughter, who, just like her, was wearing a black hat.

Fairview Cemetery was established in 1884, but control over operations was passed in 1892 to a civic group, the Women's Board of Trade, of which my great-grandmother was a founding member. It is a private cemetery and, at the time, an alternative to the Catholic cemetery, which was the only other burial ground in Santa Fe. Fairview is where some original New Mexico politicos, Jewish merchants, an early African American family, artists, journalists, and my family are buried.

My father organized who would drive with whom, who was to lead, who was to follow on the route along Paseo de Peralta, the road leading to the cemetery. It was just us Barkers, Perry, Robert (who'd accompanied him), Carrie, Kate, my aunt, and cousin in attendance. Father Bruneau, who had served at the memorial the day before, stood on the gravel path close to the family plot. His once gaunt aestheticism, part of what had drawn our family to his folk masses in the sixties despite our lapsed faith, was now buried in the folds of fleshy cheeks and puffy eyes. His beard spilled like ropy seaweed over his black muslin robes. He called out, embraced me, said how happy he was to see me after all these years. "You made it to Broadway." I smelled the oil in his hair and wondered about his fingernails. He did not wear gloves. Thank God he hadn't brought his guitar. My mother thought a funeral required a man with a collar who would impose a higher authority. But Father Bruneau had no real authority; he was nothing to us. "Isn't it nice that Father will be there?" she'd asked yesterday, her mouth shriveling like a dried apple. "He knew Laughlin."

Of course, he didn't *know* Laughlin, and now my mother looked at Father's feet, likely wondering about his socks. There were patches of snow on the ground, yet he wore monkish leather sandals with straps that wrapped around several layers of tattered wool stockings. He patted her hand, saying, "We do not say he has died. Rather, we say he has *changed*." I choked, felt my throat flood, wanting to remind him that *Laughlin was dead*, then ask, *And where were you and your church when my brother died of AIDS?*

Daddy introduced Kate to Father. The priest hugged her as Carrie stood by, twisting and retwisting a single glove. She stood in a deep pool of isolation: Laughlin's former wife, the mother of his only child, who now had no clear place in the family.

Kate and I wandered off through the tombstones as the others were arriving. "I didn't know what to wear," she said. "I only brought my ski parka and didn't think I should wear that. I borrowed this coat from Sheila Hart." Sheila was a family friend.

"It's pretty. I like the red."

"Yeah, I like it, too. I wanted to be more dressed up. I think my dad would've wanted that. Like when we used to go places and he'd tell me if it was dressy, and whether to wear a dress."

"I always have a hard time deciding what to wear."

"I like your hat."

"Thanks. I wore it for my mother."

"Well, you know Nana. She always wears a hat. What did he look like?"

"What?"

"My dad. What did he look like?"

"You mean— Oh. Like he was sleeping," I lied. "He looked just like he was asleep."

"You mean he looked like he was asleep when he died, or he died and closed his eyes and then looked like he was asleep?"

"He closed his eyes, died, and then looked like he was asleep."

"I still can't believe I wasn't there." She glared at me, then said, "Don't tell that I asked. I just wanted to know, you know, what he looked like. What a dead person looks like."

"Of course. If I hadn't been there, I'd want to know, too. I'd want to know everything."

The last car—Suzanne's—arrived, bringing Perry and Robert, who we'd booked into a suite at La Fonda, an old, historic Western hotel. With everyone present, we took our places. My father was at the helm, Father Bruneau stood next to him, and the rest of us circled in a perimeter around the gravesite, the hole having been dug earlier by the cemetery staff. We huddled close, coat collars drawn, shoulders pulled to our ears. David stamped his feet, his wife, Lisa, leaning against him; Perry and Robert stood next to Suzanne, while on the other side, Suzanne held my mother's hand. Her children, James and Meredith, stayed close to their cousin Bobby, who stood alongside his parents, Patrick and Robyn. Carrie, Kate, my cousin, aunt, John, and I connected the frame. All of us corralled in the bloated, dark shadows of the cottonwoods.

Father Bruneau raised his arms and voice, "*In the name of the Father.*" Our voices repeated, "*In the Name of the Father, and of the Son, and of the Holy Spirit.*" He blessed the grave, then lifted a silver wand high in the air, sending sprinkles of holy water that caught the light like flying crystals. Then, he pitched his voice higher. "*I am the resurrection and the life. . . . Whoever believes in me will not die forever.*"

We were a painting—distilled in dark swirls of heavy coats, our faces shrunk to a high finish of pink cheeks and sapphire eyes. Some held the baskets Mom had made from bundles of flowers she'd brought home the day before, trimming stems, picking off leaves, arranging blossoms. She decided whose basket was whose and who would share, labeling everything, coordinating colors. I asked if I could help and she said no. She worked late into the night, sitting in the quiet at the kitchen table, her shears and water spritzer at her side, her apron tied at her waist, her back to the world.

"*I have called you by name; you are mine.*" On the ground was the box—small, square, wrapped in white linen and knotted awkwardly at the top. It looked, to me, like a mistake, a cumbersome prop, out of place when we and everything else fit the scene in some beautiful tableau. I'd heard my mother say to my father, "It's nice, dear, what you have done. It was a good way to do it." I'd had no idea what she was talking about, until now. My father had covered the box of Laughlin's remains with one of my great-grandmother's hand-embroidered linens, which my mother kept in the dining room buffet. Maybe he was thinking of burials at sea, when men were wrapped in linen before being released. Maybe that's why he put Laughlin in the family linen. Maybe I should be thinking of John Paul Jones and sea heroes instead of how appallingly stupid the box looked.

Father Bruneau nodded to my father, who took a ceremonial step forward, bent down, and raised the box of Laughlin in his hands, like an offering. During a mass, the priest presents the chalice with similar choreography as the first of three bells rings, alerting the worshipers to bear witness to the promise of life transcendent in communion with God. But today, the priest was nothing; it was our father who had authority, so we looked to him and waited for his—not the priest's—blessing that would forever tie us to Laughlin and this day. My father had only a makeshift altar, the plateau of shrub and sky, so he continued to hold out the box that contained the bits and pieces of his namesake, while somewhere in the world, a mass continued with bells ringing and the priest saying, *Do this in memory of me.* Yet my father said nothing. He was quiet, his pause growing to awkwardness, as if he'd momentarily forgotten his role, even the trees leaning in for the redeeming words of a father's blessing, until finally, his silence gave way to a sigh, and that—the sound of my father sighing—was what accompanied Laughlin to his grave, my father placing the box in the waiting hole.

My back arched with blinding rage. He'd asked me and Suzanne yesterday if there was anything we thought he should do during the funeral. I'd never been to a funeral and felt traumatized by Laughlin's death, and though I appreciated his asking, I couldn't fully explain that there should be some words or a symbol to link Laughlin's life to ours. But my father looked at me puzzled, so I half-heartedly suggested a poem, maybe Robert Frost's "The Road Less Traveled By." But Suzanne said, "That's so depressing, and besides, that isn't the right title. Isn't it named something else?" which was thick smoke billowing, the title not being the point, the point being that *Laughlin screamed his way out of this world, and I just brought home what remained of him in a brown paper bag!* I couldn't breathe, so left the room as quickly as possible, glaring at my father, wishing I could say: *Don't ask what we should do—ask yourself.*

How could my father have possibly thought this ceremony would be enough, when it was *so pathetically not enough* for who Laughlin was to us? There were no gravediggers present; my father had told them we'd do the burying ourselves, so the shovel sliced; the dirt fell. I watched with fury and bitter disappointment.

My father worked as if he were alone in the world, every once in a while looking well beyond us to study the western horizon. Whatever he saw, down toward the flat basin of Agua Fria and the Jemez Mountains, it washed over his face with deep resolve. And I thought, *This must be who he was when he was Lt. Barker, standing on deck of the* Preble, *scanning waves across the Pacific Ocean, binoculars in hand, searching for mines or enemy ships—twenty-four years old, with a crew of men whose lives were dependent on his judgment.* My father had been trained to resolve a dangerous situation, but we were not a cohort of soldiers in enemy waters; we were his family, Laughlin was my *brother*, his *son*.

When he finished burying, my father patted the top of the grave mound with the back of the shovel in the way some people might give others a reassuring pat on the back. If there were words, which there weren't, his gesture might have been accompanied with something like, *"There now, it's done. It's over."*

But it wasn't over and could never be over because the silence, the thing between them—visible even on that day my father stood by Laughlin's bedside—had grown: It was now a summary of waste and regret. *"Forever and ever, Amen."* Father Bruneau finished the prayers to mark the finality of it all.

"Children," my mother said, taking her cue now and enunciating as if no one spoke English, and began to tell the little ones what to do with their flowers. But they looked at her with crumbling dismay; James clutched his basket, and just as he moved forward in obeisance, she reversed herself, saying, "Wait," and, deferring to Perry, "Go on, dear. You go first." She offered her basket, and Perry chose a single white gardenia, as pale and as fragile as his hand, and tossed it to the grave. Trembling, he pulled his coat tighter, and Robert led him away to the car. We heard the door when it closed shut.

Like a tollgate, my mother's arm swung back, releasing the children to their assignment. But they had become afraid of her, so James and Bobby remained stapled to the ground.

But not Meredith. Meredith, *the brave*, in white tights and Sunday best, pointed her patent-leather Mary Janes forward, setting her face and her intention. Alone, she began, taking one rose and tenderly placing it upon the earth. Then she took another and another. From behind her, a bud was tossed, then two more. She turned patiently, gazing at the tall figures behind her, then went from person to person, taking their baskets. And we accepted her grace because, in our hands, we could not hold both the baskets and the weight of Laughlin's death. His death had brought us to nothingness, when we were not nothing, when *he* was not nothing. James and Bobby followed Meredith's lead, taking baskets from yielding hands before sitting down next to her at the edge of Laughlin's grave. And so it was through the indefatigable strength of four-year-old Meredith that we began the task of saying goodbye.

When the circle broke, there were hugs all around. My father faced me and held out his arms, the way he had every time he came home alive after nine months of deployment. With perfected strength, he stood like a pillar, pulling me to his chest, and I couldn't resist. I was too weakened by grief and rage to forego the deep security of his embrace—my one protective, sure anchor to the world—because there was no doubt, he loved me more than he loved himself. *I knew that even as I knew he did not feel that way about my brother*, and the discrepancy broke me with racking sobs. He held me tighter then, whispering firmly in my ear, "Don't cry. Be brave now. Be brave and be an example to the children."

He may as well have driven a sword straight through me; such ruinous words, spoken with blithe oblivion. I backed away from him toward the deep shadows of a nearby mausoleum, where drifts of snow and leaves had gathered. I was totally defeated. I was a girl who wanted to be more than she was in that moment. I wanted to have been able to stand up to my father and tell him to his face that he was wrong, that *I am an example, a brave warrior. When the crisis arose, I did not blink; I faced it straight on and did what needed to be done. I loved Laughlin. And I also love you, Daddy, but these new, fresh tears are for you, because you are stuck. When you had a choice, you chose what would make you small.*

A Private Thing
—
January–May 1986

John and I flew back to New York a day after the funeral, and Bill was at the gate waiting. A week later, Suzanne arrived because Perry had asked her to be his date at the Council of Fashion Designers of America Awards (CFDA) at the New York Public Library, which was scheduled for January 19. I wished he'd asked both of us, but he only asked her. He was serving his second term as president of the CFDA and had been instrumental in building the organization over the years. Despite looking aged and withered, he was determined to attend because the previous summer, before Laughlin's health declined, he had arranged for Katharine Hepburn to be the guest of honor, an amazing feat as she did not make many public appearances. The gala, a big, New York City celebrity–type affair, now loomed like a zeppelin.

Suzanne spent a couple of days with all of us at the loft. We were soaked in grief, and I was glad to have her, especially because January 16 would have been Laughlin's thirty-eighth birthday. We'd shared a room growing up, and no matter how many times we'd pulled string down the center of the room to mark off our separate territories, we still came back to each other, knowing that what bound us was stronger than whatever separated us. The day before the gala, she moved to the house on 70th Street. Perry had said he would dress her and picked out a white-collared navy blue dress, a knockout from his recent Collection. When they arrived in a limo at the gala, a rush of "organizers" separated them. Perry had asserted that Suzanne would sit next to him, but she was led to a table in the back as Perry, befuddled, was whisked forward to the front. Suzanne, from her discarded place, watched as Perry stumbled through his opening remarks, worse than we ever imagined. She flew home the next morning.

I crawled into a quiet place, hoping the world would shrink into something manageable. A memorial for Laughlin—something I barely remember—was organized, the room filled with New York friends and colleagues who described the influence he'd had on their lives, and who'd been included in the halcyon years of his life. After that, I saw Perry only once. He'd retreated from the world. Most of my phone calls were not returned, except early in March, when his assistant, Julia, called, saying he wanted to see me.

He was propped up in his and Laughlin's old bed, in the same position that Laughlin had once been in, lying among manicured ruins, still so many beautiful things, but he was as alone as the wasted men lying under white sheets in the basement of New York Hospital. I sat on the bed, the whole time praying that he'd go to sleep that very night and never wake up, because he'd already left the world, having died the night Laughlin did. Seeing him was overwhelmingly sad and humbling, leaving no room for anger or resentment about the way he'd treated me. He'd finally received an AIDS diagnosis, having had it all along, the medical community recently catching up to his symptoms, one of which was toxoplasmosis, what the grapevine called "toxio," a brain on fire, which explained Perry's irrational decisions and the neurological problems I'd witnessed for more than a year. Laughlin's demise was an unspeakable cruelty in that Perry had witnessed his own future, which he could not face alone. But alone he was. I held his hand and trembled, weak with the dwarfing of his life.

Another six to eight weeks went by with me trying to persevere through a completely changed landscape, looking for someplace where I might belong, and religiously going to ballet class, not because I considered dancing profession-ally, but more to feel my body and hear the music. I was lost in the murky world of mourning. Then, the week before Memorial Day, when Laughlin and Perry would normally be heading out to Water Island for summer fun with Kate, I learned from television news that Perry was in the hospi-tal. I called my parents, saying that after I spoke to them, I planned to call Carrie and Kate to tell them the truth about Laughlin. They exploded, arguing that, "We promised not to tell. That was Laughlin's wish." But no, I countered—we were to protect Perry and the business, which we had done. Now it was time to protect Kate.

Carrie picked up. We'd spoken frequently since Laughlin died, both she and Kate point-blank asking, "Was it AIDS?" And I always lied. Now, as she got Kate on the phone, I said, "I need to talk to the two of you about what happened with Laughlin."

"Okay." That was Carrie.

"Okay," followed Kate.

"The first is that your dad died of AIDS."

"I knew it! You lied!" Kate screamed.

"I'm sorry. I'm so sorry. Please let me explain." I heard Carrie taking a deep breath, and angry silence on Kate's end.

"Is that okay, Katie?" Carrie asked.

"Yes." Kate spit the word. "I could've helped. I could've been there."

"Your dad didn't want that. He didn't want you to see him dying. He was afraid you'd remember him that way, and he wanted you to remember him differently. He made me promise I wouldn't tell you."

"But why? Why didn't he want me? *You* got to be there," she accused.

Carrie suddenly offered, "But Katie, think about it. Think about what your dad was going through."

"It wasn't that he didn't want you with him. He always wanted you. You were the most important thing in his life."

"Who else knew?"

I told her then that David and Patrick did not know Laughlin had AIDS until Laughlin died, and about the conversation I'd had with my parents that morning, telling Kate they still believed I was betraying Laughlin's wishes by telling her.

"I'm glad you told us," Carrie said.

"I know you might not ever forgive me, and I'm not asking for that. I'm calling because I think you deserve the truth. And to explain that your dad was in a terrible position with the business. If people knew he was sick, they would have believed that Perry was sick, too, which would have threatened the company. It could have closed down, and everybody that worked at PERRY ELLIS would have lost their jobs."

"Perry?"

"Yes. Perry. That's also why I called—he has AIDS, and he's dying."

"But I got a letter from him. He pretended he was Josh, and he wrote to Gibby, my dog, playing games like how we always used to. I have his letter; he can't be dying."

But he was, which was more bitter tragedy: Perry had been been like a stepfather to Kate, a relationship important enough to him that he'd written her from his death bed.

Carrie said, "This is a lot to take in. Why don't we hang up and talk to you later? Is that okay, Katie?"

"Yeah."

"But will you call us, Christine, when you have news about Perry?"

"Yes. I will. I promise." I hung up, terrified I would lose Kate forever.

I went to ballet the next day and the day after that. Then, at the end of the week, I stopped at a pay phone on Ninth Avenue after class to beep my answering machine, and I heard Stephen's voice. I hadn't talked to him or heard from anyone at PERRY ELLIS in several months.

Stephen said, "Winnie wants to know why you aren't here with Perry at the hospital. She wants you here. Please come." I jumped in a cab. Stephen had put my name on a list at the nurses' station, a guard posted outside his room. Despite the news reports, the press didn't know where exactly Perry was, but precautions were being taken.

The room was small, not a VIP suite as I'd expected. I wrapped my arms around Winnie, who sat in a chair near the bed where Perry lay, seemingly unconscious. Robert, whom Winnie knew, was back in town, filling a cup with Diet Pepsi. I hadn't seen or spoken to him since Laughlin's funeral, and now he said, "This is only the tip of the iceberg," and walked out, taking his Diet Pepsi with him.

I tidied up, getting rid of paper cups and half-filled drinks, remembering how careful Perry was with Laughlin, always making the room beautiful, no matter how sick Laughlin was.

"His mind is dis-eased," Winnie said in her thick Virginia drawl. "A mind can have dis-ease. He has been that way for a long time. When Laughlin was so sick, day in and day out, that's all Perry thought about, fretted about. And I just don't know if he's going to come out of it. Miracles do happen, but his mind is not there. I keep thinking that where there's life, there's hope. And Perry's all I really have, except for IW and you." IW was the man she'd married several years after Perry's father died.

"You have Tyler."

"Yes, I have Tyler, but she's only a baby, and I wish she weren't so far away because I don't really know her or Barbara."

"But they will need you."

"I know. I just—I don't know what to do. I was all ready to come, and then when I arrived, everything was so awful. A guard at his door and a guard around the house. Now I feel nauseous, and my voice is going. I'm not sick. I'm perfectly well. But I'm afraid I might not even be able to speak to Perry if he wakes up. I must get my strength back in case he wakes up. I wanted to know where you were and why you weren't here."

Perry didn't regain consciousness by nightfall, and Robert

never returned to the hospital, so I took Winnie home to the house on 70th Street. She asked me to stay, handing me her extra nightie. We slept in the same bed my mother and I had shared, until sometime in the middle of the night, when Robert appeared. "Wake up," he said. He'd spent the night upstairs, in the room where he'd stayed before Laughlin died.

"Robert, is that you?" Winnie asked.

"Perry died, and I'm going to the hospital. Do you want to go?"

I turned on the light. Winnie held the sheet to her chest. Robert was already dressed, so I told him to leave, that if Winnie wanted to go, I'd bring her after she'd had a chance to collect herself. But Winnie didn't want to go. "Perry's not there, and I want to go home," she cried.

The next morning, I took her to the airport. In the car, she said Robert had talked to her about a memorial, but she didn't want to go, and as I was listening, I understood the scale of what was seemingly already being planned to memorialize Perry in New York. It would be too much for her. "But what am I going to do?" she asked.

I shared what my mother had said after Laughlin died, that although people mean well, some forms of public grieving are too much for families to bear. Death is a private thing.

Winnie looked relieved. "Yes. It is private." She squeezed my hand. "I'm not going to go to any memorial, no matter what Robert says. Are you going to go?"

"I don't know. But if you were going, I'd go with you."

"I love you," she said.

"And I love you, too." At the airport, she said, "You take good care now. And write me soon."

Winnie buried Perry privately. I did not go to the memorial. It was by invitation only, and I did not receive one. Neither did Suzanne. But I did do as Winnie asked and wrote to her.

Tom

—

Summer 1986–1987

To keep my health insurance, I began doing extra work on television commercials. Some actors thought extra work was beneath them, but I couldn't be choosy given that my insurance was dependent on the number of weeks I worked in a calendar year, regardless of the job. I had established good relationships with several producers, so I called them, and they kindly gave my name to assistant directors (ADs), who were responsible for filling the "background." Truthfully, I was so emptied out that I didn't mind doing jobs that required little more than showing up and that solved the pressing issue of health insurance.

In August, two months after Perry died, I arrived on the set of a bank commercial. The AD instructed, "On 'Action!' walk into the lobby of the set, sit down, pick up a magazine, and start to page through it. Got it?"

"Yes." On "Action!," I followed through with the instructions, but when I sat, the magazine on top of the pile was the most recent edition of *New York* magazine, with the cover story, "The Death and Life of Perry Ellis." I hid my face inside the pages as the principal actor delivered his lines. No one at PERRY ELLIS had warned me the article was coming out.

"Okay. CUT. Let's do it again." Two minutes later, the AD repeated, "Action!!"

With each successive take, I walked into the frame, sat down, and picked up the magazine, finding something more each time: a picture of Perry at the Council of Fashion Designers awards—the gala he'd invited Suzanne to—and on the seventh page, a picture of Laughlin. Overall, the article was a distortion of the truth. I put the magazine on the bottom of the pile and began to sweat.

It was an outright assault, the hideous and purposeful blurring of Laughlin and Perry's relationship. It had started with the obituaries, where evasiveness and blatant lies were publicly necessary and commonplace for all men dying of AIDS, especially in the early days. Laughlin's obituary in the New York Times in January mentioned his leadership at the company without implying a personal relationship with Perry. At the time, with Perry's acknowledgement, we made that decision for the protection of Perry and the business. On the other hand, Perry's May 31, 1986 obituary in the New York Times, which summarized the growth of his career and business, never once mentioned Laughlin's name, even as it described the very licensing deals Laughlin had initiated and brokered when he became president of Perry Ellis International. It was those deals that quadrupled the value of the PERRY ELLIS label. The omission of Laughlin's role in the succesful expansion of the business seemed intentional, cruel, and unnecessary because both men were now dead.

The long reach of erasure continued through the years as other articles and books obscured Laughlin's role in the company and claimed that Perry owned the house on 70th Street when legal documents provided evidence that it was always owned and paid for equally by both Perry and Laughlin. That fact correctly identified the house as *their* home, dignifying their relationship and illuminating the role they played in giving other gay men confidence to live full lives in familial partnerships. For more than twenty-five years, no reporter or biographer ever contacted anyone in my family to provide information or verification about anything reported on Laughlin's life, or Laughlin and Perry's relationship. The result was that Laughlin and Perry, as the couple they were, don't exist in history, as is true for many gay couples of that era. As Laughlin feared, he'd been erased.

Over the next six months, Tom, Diane, Martin, and I stayed close. The AIDS epidemic was growing exponentially; both Diane and I had agents who were now sick. Tom was busy, supervising casts of *Cats*, and Diane was on the road playing Grizabella, the cat who sings "Memory." Martin went from directing *Brighton Beach Memoirs* in Chicago to being production stage manager of *Long Day's Journey Into Night* on Broadway, and then on to *Broadway Bound*. Miraculously, I rebounded with a couple of good moneymaking commercials, even as I stepped hesitantly into each new day, the membrane of grief hanging like a curtain between me and the present. I enrolled in classes with a new acting teacher, looking for stories and structure to help me identify where I might fit professionally. I approached a commercial director about choreographing commercials, and again wondered about stage management. Always, I went to ballet, and less frequently, a jazz class, all of which felt less like dancing than an effort at self-affirmation.

In the fall, Bill and I went to Tuscany for a vacation. We

were each the opposite of what the other's parents expected when they imagined suitable partners for their children. Bill wasn't an alpha male, and I wasn't Jewish. I was probably the more ambitious risk-taker, while he focused on the small print of insurance policies. We both loved art, theater, and books, even though he mostly read nonfiction tomes. But we'd navigated the trauma of AIDS and the loss of life, which provided a substantial scaffolding to our relationship. When we came home from our trip, we got married, but given the circumstances surrounding my life, I didn't feel like a bride; I was merely trying to walk my life forward in the land of the dying. Bill's father, a judge, officiated, writing us a beautiful speech. My parents, Suzanne, John, and Kate came. Diane sang. I danced with Tom, but Martin was out of town again.

In spring 1987, Tom received a positive AIDS diagnosis around the same time that Michael Bennett withdrew from directing and choreographing the musical *Chess*. Michael was reported to have heart problems, the *New York Times* publishing a long story and interview, full of what everyone knew were blatant lies. We trusted what we saw on death-beds or heard through the grapevine—never the media.

By summer, Michael was dead. At his memorial, the Shubert was packed to the rafters. It was the first time I'd been back to the theater since I'd left *A Chorus Line* two years earlier. I'd never sat in the audience before, and there wasn't an empty seat. Except emptiness was everywhere, the names of those now dead on everyone's lips, Michael's death hastening the avalanche.

A few days later, I was at Lennox Hill Hospital, sitting

with Tom. I held his hand but suddenly grabbed the nearby garbage can and threw up my breakfast.

"Jesus!" Tom looked at me wearily. "You're pregnant."

"Don't tell. I'm not telling anyone."

"But you shouldn't be here."

"I'm fine. Really, I am. No sex, no blood." By that time, the yellow caution signs on hospital room doors had gone because we all knew what to do to protect ourselves.

Tom lay back down, worried, relieved.

"It's okay. It really is. I don't want to be anywhere else," I said.

He was released two days later and called me. "I have to talk to you. I've looked in the mirror and know I'm not going to make it. I need you to tell me everything I need to do."

I didn't want to have that conversation. I wanted to pretend, but that would have left him alone in the very worst part of dying—the part where you admit it's happening. I went to his apartment, and we sat with pencil and paper, mapping out what to say to his lawyer and how to protect his partner, Willy, to make sure his rights were secured, including inheriting ownership of Tom's apartment. Tom stipulated that he did not want interventions, that he wanted to die at home. We got the necessary paperwork done in the next month, and after that, I sat with him as he declined. One September afternoon, Willy called and asked if I wanted to come to the apartment, that Tom was dying. Willy had family with him so I said, "No. You be with him, and whisper my name at the end." I didn't have the strength to watch Tom die.

Tom's obituary in the *New York Times* was among the

first to bravely report that he died of acquired immune deficiency syndrome. When I spoke at his memorial, I talked about how we danced together, Tom chasing from behind, like a relentless wind giving me wings.

Martin

—

March 1988

Six months after Tom died, I took my turn at Martin's apartment, part of the rotation of caregiving friends who regularly showed up. My day was Wednesday, and when I arrived, he was asleep, looking thinner than the week before, his still-handsome face shrinking away from his skull. His right arm reached across the bed; the sheet balled into a knot that he held the same way he used to hold my hand when we shared a bed in London.

Now, like then, there was no clutter, and everything was in its proper place. There were fresh flowers—lupine, delphinium, and lilies in a porcelain pitcher. The west-facing windows of his Upper West Side apartment caught the afternoon sun, depositing it in bright squares on the wooden floor.

"Want me to wake him up?" asked Angelique, the day nurse. "I know he's looking forward to your visit. He told me this morning, 'It's Wednesday. Christine comes on Wednesdays.'" She smiled and added, "Usually it's men who are here. Keith wanted me to thank you again for coming."

"Tell him not to worry; I will always come.'" Lately, Keith disappeared when I took my shift. When Martin first got sick, I tried to talk to him, but Keith only gritted his teeth. "Has he been asleep long?"

"Nah, this is just one of his catnaps. You know, the AIDS." She waved her hands, indicating the unending, quixotic nature of the disease. "I'll take a little break then, if you don't mind."

"No, of course, you go right ahead. Have a cup of tea or something; I'm fine."

"I know you are. Like I said, you're the only girl. Nice to have girl company. How're you feeling?"

"Big."

She laughed. "Oh yeah. Can you tie your shoes?"

"Barely." My skin was taut, stretched across the bundle of my belly. My baby girl was due in six weeks. She pumped inside me while the oxygen machine pumped into Martin, green tubes tethering him to a silver canister. "Martin . . ." I whispered.

"Hi." He struggled to open his eyes.

"Sleeping in the middle of the day? You're getting old. Before you know it, you're going to be bald."

"Never. I still have a full head of hair." He sat up against the pillows, ran his hands down his front, straightening his freshly laundered denim shirt, and I knew that before he'd fallen asleep, he'd gotten dressed for me.

"You look like you swallowed a basketball."

I lumbered onto the bed, and Martin shifted, making room. We spent our time sharing the bed and my baby. I offered her like a prayer, lifting my shirt. "Jesus, it's so hard. Oh my God!" He pressed, and she kicked back. A small triangle, either an elbow or a heel, poked out, and he teased her, pushing against her assertive limb. "Listen, little girl. This is your uncle. I want her to know my voice," he said, looking up at me. Then he leaned back. The blueness of his eyes held the sun. "Amazing."

I cuddled into what was our sweet spot: him propped up on pillows against the headboard; me between his long, out-stretched legs, his arms wrapped around my daughter and me. I leaned back against his chest, felt his weight, his beard against my neck; he exhaled, and I picked up the rhythm of who we once were in the tiny sliver of intimacy that was us. I felt him relax against me, his fingers entwined with mine, the warmth of us lulling him back to sleep.

He napped and I rested, time meandering the way it can when all is cozy and safe. At some point, he started cough-ing, so Angelique came in. "Gotta beat his back."

"I'll do it."

Angelique hesitated.

"Christine can do it." Martin said.

"Okay. I just thought—"

"There isn't anything she hasn't seen," he said, and An-gelique looked at me, wondering.

I hit his back to clear his lungs, then he grabbed my wrist. "Was it enough?" His face was haunted.

"Enough?" The word tore through me. Was he speaking of life or of us? As if it mattered.

"Of course, it was enough." Death had made me a liar. "I'll see you next Wednesday, unless you want me to come sooner. I'll come anytime." I put his hands on my belly so he could feel how hard and indomitable life was, and I lied again. "It was. Enough."

I left the apartment dizzy and shaking. When the ele-vator door opened, I waved my hands to the expectant faces inside. "Sorry, I forgot something," and turned as if to go down the hall, but instead, I threw open the door to the stairwell and grabbed the handle to the trash chute, opening it. I heaved, throwing up lunch, breakfast, and everything I'd ever eaten in my entire life. And when I was completely emptied out, I sobbed, my face in the trash chute, which would have been funny if it weren't so tragic.

How dare he ask, "Was it enough?" I'd wanted to grab him by the collar. *I loved you. I've always loved you. It would never be enough. But it was what we had, and we'd made the most of it.* Long ago, when we'd been asked, "Are you lovers?" we said we didn't know, but we agreed that whatever was between us, it was *something*. I wanted to say now that I believed we'd shared a time and a place that had shaped some crucial core of being, and that that experience had always remained a flow within us, not in a river of memories, but in a wellspring: I was the person who gave him—always and forever—total, unconditional love, and he was the person who gave me a vision of myself that aligned with my deepest hopes for my life.

So no, it wasn't enough, and if he was asking about life—if his life had been enough—the answer was the same: *Not even close*, even though he'd been everything he could have been with the time he was given.

I didn't hear from him over the next couple of days and called the following Wednesday, before I headed to his apartment. That was the protocol: Call ahead of arriving to check in.

"Hi. It's Christine."

"Oh, hi. It's Vince." I knew his name but hadn't met him. A lighting designer.

"Hi. I come on Wednesdays, so I'm just checking in."

"Yeah, I know your name. Sorry I haven't met you. Just a minute." It was very quiet and then he came back. "I'm really sorry. I'm really sorry to tell you this, but Martin died."

"Wha—When?"

"Sunday. Everything happened so quickly."

"Wh—Um . . . is Keith there?"

"I went to get him, but he won't talk. You know Keith. I'm so sorry. I'm so sorry no one called you and you're hearing it like this."

"I was there last Wednesday."

"I know—you did Wednesdays. He started spiraling down on Thursday, then he died early Sunday morning, actually in the middle of the night. And he was cremated right away, so as soon as we got him back, we took his ashes out to the house in the Hamptons and came back last night. I'm so sorry no one called. I know, today is Wednesday, and you did Wednesdays. I'm sorry . . . I haven't met you."

"I'm sorry I haven't met you either. Tell Keith I'm sending my love."

"Thank you. You know, thank you for all you did."

"Sure." I hung up and sank to the floor, my knees giving way, then I crawled to the bedroom and into my bed, where I rolled into a ball and cried until there was nothing, absolutely nothing left. Then I looked for the *New York Times*, which I hadn't read that morning, and found his obit, the cause of death reported as lung cancer, the same cause we'd listed for Laughlin. Martin's death was reported by "his longtime companion"—clearly, a choice that Martin had made before he died. By 1988, there had been some progress in the march to legitimacy.

I lived in bed for three days, as if I'd been thrown from

the world, Martin's death opening some final wound, an impossible hole in my heart. I tried to take comfort in the fact that he let go after I'd been there, but the loss of him marked an ending, chilling me with its finality. Martin took with him a way of being in the world—something he shared with me and encouraged me to create for myself—that sent me to unknown places, through portals that led me nowhere or sometimes on the most wonderous, fulfilling adventure, and all of it shaped a wholly authentic presence of a life *that was mine.*

I kept coming back to the passion he and I attached ourselves to—the love of a good play, a human story. I'd seen magic. For a while, I'd lived it, and when it was gone, I kept looking for it, thinking the world had gone bad, when really, it was only that the world had become more complicated, which happens when you're no longer twenty and you learn that artists are always starting over, absorbing the scope of new realities, and translating them anew.

By some other grace, another heart—my daughter's—beat beneath mine, so on the fourth day, I walked to my bookshelf, where I found the book Martin had loaned me months earlier. It was by Jonathan Miller, whom Martin revered and who had directed the production of *Long Day's Journey.* I remembered that I still had it when taking one of my Wednesday shifts but decided not to return it. Now I took it from the nonfiction shelf and moved it to where it didn't belong—to the shelf of plays, where the *S*'s met the *W*'s: Shakespeare, Shaw, Shepard, Simon, Stoppard, Wilde, Williams, Wilson; and I placed Martin's book there so all that I had of him could live in the company of men we admired and who'd given us some of our most significant portrayals of humanity.

I'd never set a timeline, saying by thirty I'd have accomplished X, and by thirty-five I'd have added Y and Z. It was more that I'd chased what inspired me, recalibrating at different pivot points, each time trying to find that sweet spot where life had meaning. I felt the ghosts of Martin and Tom, Laughlin and Perry camped in my soul, waiting for me to find my next chance, and pressuring me with a conjuring—a shadow standing in the wings, someone I recognized but didn't yet know, someone to tell about how we made our lives in New York City when we thought nothing could stop us, when the world was spun like cotton candy, all that sugar and air making us high and sustaining us—not to mention the view from the top when we got there. Because we did get there, even if only for a short stay.

Epilogue

The theater district streets around Times Square had always buzzed with the hum of what went on from behind theater walls—the honeycomb of actors, dancers, musicians, and crew, warming up, setting up, doing make-up—while outside on the sidewalk, near the larger-than-life pictures on billboards, were the wannabes, hanging about and praying for a chance at being who they knew they could be. By the early 1990s, though, such vitality and hope had fizzled, the energy of the streets now supervised by ghosts, Jimmy Kirkwood and Alvin Ailey having joined the parade in 1989, AIDS growing worse, the list of dead mounting, people I worked with in different shows or commercials, as well as agents, casting directors, and friends of friends, all gone; their spirits arriving in droves to linger over Broadway with their unfinishedness and defeat. All of them died stigma deaths, like those of suicides or overdoses—from circumstances that many people judged as *the victim's own fault*—social condemnations that deny family and friends permission to experience the madness of grief or the comfort of full burial rituals. Society refuses to acknowledge such deaths as tragedies in the same way it turns out to offer sympathy and condolences when a son dies in a car accident or from an acceptable cancer. The souls I knew had no rest, so Broadway fluttered with a peculiar texture of silence and memory, of things alive, but dead.

A friend with connections suggested I become part of a legit theater company being led by an important new up-and-coming director.

"No, thanks."

"But if you leave—" she said.

If I *leave?* The world I belonged to no longer existed. Everyone was dead, even though I could hear their voices ringing in my ears. I *should* move, go to where no one knows me, and in the silent strangeness of a new place, let the past speak.

I had Bill and a little girl, who was soon joined by a brother—two curious little creatures to hold my hands when I thought it was me holding theirs. I went back to school, my children and I doing homework at the dining room table. I studied and practiced the way I always had when trying to make something beautiful out of what was senseless or empty, because that's the only way I ever got anywhere near to what I dreamed my life could be: "Use what you have," to which I added, "and what you know."

Martin and Tom live forever in the quiet collapse of time and space when theater lights go down and "Places" is called. I see Laughlin and Perry in the couple living down the street from me, two men with two daughters who have turned their basement into a second-grade classroom for their girls and several others in the neighborhood, creating a safe school pod during the COVID-19 pandemic. "Society has changed," I whisper to an immaculate sky. But let no one forget all those men who paid for that good news with their lives.

Early on, my brother John said, "Why do you want to write about *that?*"

Because sometimes a story is all that's left.

I scavenged for miracles in the patched syllables of words and started to work them the way I'd once worked my body. I knew the trick to balancing in arabesque: that balance is not something you do and hold by freezing in a position. Balance is having the faith to hover, to be suspended in that spot where two equal forces meet to play tug-of-war, each pulling with all its strength in an opposite direction.

I stand now, once again with my feet pressed to a singular, tiny mark in the universe, listening for the tinkling of response, someone saying: *Yes, I feel it, too. I know. I know.*

Acknowledgments

Writing became my closest companion during the silence and secrecy surrounding my brother's AIDS diagnosis. Finding that connection to words led me to choices that propelled me toward a life I dreamed of having. Along the way, I had the help, love, and support of those I mention here. Yet, even as I name them, I'm reminded of many more who also gave me confidence and hope. To all, I am thankful.

My sincere gratitude to Lori Milken, publisher at Delphinium Books, and especially to Joe Olshan, my editor, who called me on a cold November day to say I had written an important story about a time and a place that should not be forgotten. Thank you to both Lori and Joe, who took a chance on me. And thank you also, to the entire team at Delphinium who worked hard to prepare my book for publication. Colin Dockrill, in particular, skillfully transformed a few of my words into a beautiful book cover.

My agent, Kristin van Ogtrop, at InkWell Management is a force. With Kristin at my back, I felt that nothing could stop me.

I had the good fortune to work with Paula Derrow, who I can best describe as a writer's compass. Paula has keen judgment, always seeing the details within the whole. She knows the best way out of every entangled thicket of words.

Completing this memoir often placed me in narrow spaces of aloneness. Throughout the entire process of writing and revising, I had the valuable support of readers in my family, who offered their candid and discerning feedback, while championing my voice and buoying my resolve to keep writing. They are Suzanne, Kate, Bill, cousins Karen and Kate Goetz, and especially my daughter, Madeline, who read every draft.

Over the years of turning snippets of memory into a book, I had the willing ears and generous hearts of confidants, Marilee Wyman and Diane Sutherland. More recently, other friends—Tom Allen, Sally Brim, Karen Perlman, Jed Krasdella, and Caroline Brecker—also provided significant insights that helped lead to the completion of my manuscript.

At two precarious junctures early on, my dear friends, Val van Ogtrop and Linda Delgado, listened to my ideas, and then picked up their phones to help open doors to my future.

Work on this memoir began at Sarah Lawrence College under the wings of Vijay Seshadri, Carolyn Ferrell, Jo Ann Beard, and Myra Goldberg, some of the best teachers in the world. To Cait Kelly, photographer, and Robbie Minjarez, stylist, thank you for your warmth and the confidence you gave me about standing in front of the camera after so many years of avoiding just that.

Finally, to Bill, Madeline, and McClatchy, thank you for your patience, abiding faith, and the loving sanctuary of our family.

Author Bio

Christine Barker was raised in a military family and spent her childhood moving across Europe and the United States. By the time she started high school, her father had retired from the US Navy and the family returned to Santa Fe, New Mexico, a place they have called home since the 1880s. She devoted herself to the study of dance and at twenty made the brave decision to move to New York City to pursue a career in dance and theater. She appeared in the productions of *Promises, Promises, Seesaw,* and *No, No Nanette* before being cast in the London production of the Tony-award-winning *A Chorus Line,* which opened at the Royal Drury Lane Theater in 1976. She eventually joined the Broadway cast in New York City. Her theatrical life was shaped by Alvin Ailey, Tommy Tune, and finally Michael Bennett. She was working on Broadway when the AIDS epidemic hit and witnessed the tragedy unfold in the theater wings, fashion houses, and finally in the hospitals of New York City. In addition to her theater credits, Christine has appeared in numerous national television commercials. She holds an MFA in Writing from Sarah Lawrence College.